LEVIATHAN KINGS OF TERROR,

a true crime memoir

by

Paul E. Treadwell

Paul E. Treadwell

Copyright 2014

All rights reserved, including the right of reproduction, domestic, and foreign. No part of this book may be duplication, in whole, or segments, or transmitted in any form, or by any means, electronic, mechanical, recording, video or audio, photocopies, photographs, or by any information storage and retrieval system. No reproduction at all allowed under this copyright without permission in writing from the author and publisher.

Scriptures are from: "Holy Bible," "King James Version."

Permissions obtained to base the book on family events.

Child abuse statistics are from: www.info@childhelp.org
Graph of stats . . .

Schizophrenia information from: www.schizophrenia.com

Petmegoose Press edition 2014

Designed by Paul E. Treadwell

Manufactured in USA

Paperback ISBN: 9780972161428

(eBook ISBN: 9780972161411)

Library of Congress Control Number: 2014906430

© Copyright 2014 - Paul E. Treadwell - All Rights Reserved

Paul E. Treadwell

Table of Contents

Disclaimer	Page……..9
Dedication	Page……..11
Acknowledgments	Page……..13
Preface: by Kayte Vincent	Page……..15
Author's Introduction	Page……..17
I Am Born	Page……..19
She Danced with the Devil	Page……..29
Bitter Oxymoron	Page……..33
I'll Kill You If You Hit Her Again	Page……..41
What Is Sex? What Is Chicken SH**?	Page……..49
Chocolate Gravy and Father Shaman	Page……..57
Recompense, Blood, Flesh and Bone Flew	Page……..65
Paint It Red	Page……..71
The Hat Pin Lady	Page……..89
Forlorn, Where Did Lilly Go	Page……..93
The Burning Mule	Page……..101
Wolf in the Camp	Page……..109
There's a Monster in the Room	Page……..113
High Dollar Woman	Page……..125
Push Ginger into the Lake	Page……..131

Momma's Blue Party Dress	Page........141
What's an Orphan-Jug?	Page........147
Gone to Chicken Heaven	Page........155
Hog Wild	Page........159
Virginia, Oh Sheese	Page........161
He Fell Asleep	Page........165
Crazy White Trash	Page........169
Embarrassed	Page........173
The Snake Pit	Page........177
What's This?	Page........183
Don't Repeat This	Page........187
Cold Black Hearted Ol' Witch	Page........191
The Matchmaker	Page........197
Just Don't Look	Page........203
I Am Your Mother	Page........207
A Demon Named Trouble	Page........209
Denial	Page........217
Guardian Angel	Page........219
His Bag of Tricks	Page........223
Chicken Thief	Page........233
The Devil's Booger Men	Page........237
I'm Calling the Sheriff	Page........243
These Are My Kids	Page........253
Alone With Strangers	Page........257

Don't Be Rude Today	Page……..269
He Wouldn't Be Back	Page……..275
Kiss Me	Page……..277
Commit to Memory	Page……..283
No Charity for Hobos	Page……..285
Jake Stay Sober	Page……..293
Portals of Heaven	Page……..297
Epilogue	Page……..309
Afterward: by Diana Stevens	Page……..319

Paul E. Treadwell

Disclaimer

This is a true crime story. Characters' physical appearances are changed, along with their names to protect the innocent. The author has taken a few artistic liberties with the time-line for flow and development. Most of the actual people described in this book are now deceased. The characters have eccentricities best describing their personalities. Every possible effort has been taken to protect individual privacy. It is not the story that is important. The purpose is to educate, and encourage breaking the silence about abuse. This book is the penned version of the author's childhood memories. The publisher and author assume no responsibility for damages incurred by use of information found in this publication. It is simply a personal account of the author's early childhood. What is important is the message to never be silent about abuse.

Paul E. Treadwell

Dedication

This book is dedicated to Jane.

Paul E. Treadwell

Acknowledgments

Thank you: Jane, for sharing part of your story.

Thank you: Susan Malone, for help with developments.

Thank you: Diana Stevens, for writing the "Afterward."

Thank you: Kayte Vincent, for writing the "Preface."

Thank you: Chris Diddle, for the cover art illustration.

Thanks to . . . Child Help Organization for statistics from their website info@childhelp.org

Thanks to . . . www.schizophrenia.com

Paul E. Treadwell

Preface: by Kayte Vincent

To reclaim life requires acceptance of past experiences, rather than denial of painful memories. It demands the Hope of Faith in a future that is and should be, guided by a Power far greater than humanity. This book is exhilarating and provides a creative prose in subject matter that portrays love and respect for others in a rural family characterized through poverty, hard work, and severe physical and mental illnesses. The blessings revealed as one absorbs this reading, show these family members though poor, possessed something that the world's fortune cannot purchase: A Family of Love and Support for Their Children.

The beauty of this story is manifested in the author and main character coming to terms with his victimized past of physical, emotional, and sexual abuse. He energizes his life by circumventing the failure of society to protect him, and those, innocent of potential and on going maltreatment.

This nonfiction true crime memoir has candidly and honestly, confronted communities who have been guilty or unfortunately unknowledgeable of bigotry. Social prejudices and injustice are noteworthy throughout this reading, citing hardships for the mentally challenged, those in slavery, and those crucified with labels. There are various chapters, which present those perpetrating and discriminating within social status as well as bearing sarcastic and carnal attitudes, forcing no choices for those limited in resources and political power, and seeking to teach generations in a familial undertone, which undoubtedly projects anger and abuse to others.

Society has tonal qualities displaying guilt from past generation failures, but the nature of this memoir is to confront and apprise the present. That these prejudice must not, be repeated in families who are responsible as protectors and supporters of children and youth.

After reading this story, my heart rendered a recommitment to protect those who cannot protect themselves, young, old, able or disabled.

May you as a reader, become convicted to teach and become responsible for humanities . . . There are no shortcuts in giving your best to others.

Preface: by Kayte Vincent (pseudonym) Professional and Educational Background:

Kayte Vincent graduated from the University of Central Arkansas with a Bachelor of Science in Education. She has a Master's of Science in Home Economics/Child and Family from Southern Illinois University, Carbondale, Illinois. Her thirty years of career have been in related fields of family preservation, child maltreatment assessment, safety/health protection of children, and permanency plans for children's stability and human welfare. She also has a Master's Degree in Special Education. Kayte has worked intensively with the developmentally disabled.

LEVIATHAN KINGS OF TERROR, a memoir

Author's Introduction

My family came from a land of extremes. The rural Ozarks lagged behind times by more than twenty years during the 1950's. Strength in body, mind, and pocketbook commanded respect. Noble character, or loathsome, the majority had one thing in common--the extreme poverty. Only the strong survived.

Snuffed dreams and abandoned lands for the promise of a future in another state. Her young people spilled out from the hills to make their abodes in more prosperous towns with hope of a gentler face for survival. Loafer's Glory was my home. My parents met here at the breeding grounds. They too would journey afar in hope of the promise of an easier life, before my fifth birthday.

My mother and father should never have married. Nevertheless, in 1953 they wed. The year Momma, Ora Bip, the defiant daughter of the local bootlegger turned thirteen. It was a touch of the red, Indian Paint Brush, Cherokee, that gave her exotic beauty. Graceful, feminine, and mature for her years, Momma turned lots of heads. She was a child bride. The practice was common in the hill culture.

Married one year after Daddy, Enoch Hotman's head, split open with an axe during a logging accident. The ill fortune left him progressively disabled. He suffered from brain damage at age twenty-two, and later succumbed to schizophrenia.

Enoch's friendship with a malevolent Merl Judas, our criminal neighbor would be his ruin. The Judas was our family's torment. Merl brought destruction, misfortune, and a trail of sorrow into the lives of everyone his life touched. A godless atheist, his brand of evil and morally objectionable behavior was a malignant influence. His soul ruled by powerful malign spirits. He was the local dark prince.

Colors of the tumultuous culture, and the lustrous, callous, rocky lands helped to sculpt my parents and local relatives' characters. The majority were flawed, superstitious, impoverished and illiterate. They were some harsh, but good peoples. Hardworking timber miners, farmers, fruit tramps, and migrant workers. They were God-fearing, backsliding Hard Shell Baptist, Pentecostal hillbillies.

These beginnings provided the witch's brew for my impoverished, turbulent, miserable, and sometimes phenomenal--joy filled childhood. These people, with their striking personalities, and the culture, forged my youthful attributes.

The hardships and happiness they experienced prejudiced how their lives penetrated mine. For better or worse, they touched my soul with a part of themselves. I am the product of the hill culture, and the influence of its sinners and saints. This true story is about more than one little boy's will to survive. This is a universal tale about resiliency of the human spirit. When faced with insurmountable circumstances one can find hope, an inner strength--the courage to overcome.

I Am Born

Kicking my way out of the womb, I am born. Presented to my parents, I was, with the exception of dirty-blond hair, a picture of Cherokee heritage. From the beginning, I am a distasteful sight for some. I do not look like a Hotman.

Petite and pretty, fifteen-year-old Momma said the delivery was hard. Her water broke days before I finally popped out of her oven. She said I damn near killed her, as the pain felt like she squatted to pee and fell on a sharp burning stump that rammed up inside her forbidden zone. The agony was a dry birth. Relieved when the labor was over, Momma said she laughed when the local country doctor placed me on her abdomen.

Temporally, she forgot the pain that had been intense only moments before. She did not hold a grudge but forgave me for all the travail I caused. She vowed to never, have sex again after that. She would not be true to her promise.

Family members gathered around her bed. Grandmother Anne politely asked them all to leave the room as she stroked Momma's forehead with a cool wet rag. They left, congregating in other parts of the house. Momma's dark-hair laced about her feminine brown form to her hips as she lay on the bed, and tolerated Anne's stares.

Plain dressed in an ankle length black skirt and white blouse, graying, religious holiness Anne glared suspiciously. She gathered Momma's raven wavy-locks, gently bunching them into her fist. She positioned Momma's long dark-glory across the pillows, and lifted me out of her arms.

Scrutinizing my infant form while searching for Hotman traits, Anne sighed. She lay me down next to Momma. She says, "Well, girl, you've gone and done it. Yah got you a high-yellow-brown-eyed Judas chicken there. You should be ashamed. You should repent."

Momma said she turned to face the wall. Biting her tongue to hold back vulgarities as rage bubbled in her guts. She knew Daddy's siblings were standing outside. "This old religious hag and I are going to have it out one day," she softly mumbled. Realizing now was not the time. She held her peace.

Agonizing, calling for Daddy, she moaned, and said, "Enoch, ask them to come back tomorrow." Her cold dark-brown dagger eyes glared back at Anne, "I'm not feeling well," she said through clinched teeth. Her constitution was clear. She did not want Anne there. Promptly, Grandmother Anne left the room.

The connecting room, surrounded by robust well-wishers a potbelly wood stove glowed-red. Fire inside the heater crackled and roared. North winds howled outside. Momma yanked the covers up over our heads, seething, "I'll be glad when the old witch is dead," she said.

She breast-fed me, disappointed she sighed, and whispered, "Little Saul, I wish you were Merl's child. Why, couldn't you be a girl? I never get what I want. God always hands me the short end of the stick, but I'll try to love you." She exhaled again.

One-by-one family and visiting neighbors marched into the room. They gave their reserved approval, making the effort to be polite. Momma knew they all suspected I belonged to a Merl Judas. That was the reason they were there, just to see what kind of living creature, pushed its way out of her bowels. They were curious to know if I was a Judas.

Merl was a neighbor, Daddy's lumberjack co-worker. They were fast friends since grade school. Momma said she was infatuated with Merl when she gave birth to me. He resembled Elvis Presley. No way, would she defile his young wife Lilly's trust. Lilly was her best friend. I was not Merl's, she knew. She was glad when the whispering, and suspicious relatives were gone.

Other rumors had it that I belonged to Grandfather Pops. I inherited a smaller version of his large irregular shaped nose. Angry, Momma questioned how-could-they accuse her father of such immorality! Her fifteen-year-old young girl's heart was broken. She wanted me, but also wished I had never been born. She knew the feelings were the same with other family members, but their reasons were different.

Momma said she married to escape home. Fanny, Momma's drab middle-aged, third-cousin considered herself a matchmaker. She told Momma the Hotman clan had means. She said there was Loafer's Glory gold on Hotman land. Daddy's family did not have money. Fanny was wrong. At the time, Momma believed she told the truth.

Impetuous Momma set her sights to marry Daddy. They did, within a few months. Two years later, I came into the world complicating Momma's life. She was only a child assuming adult responsibility.

Momma said she never loved him. She hoped that would come later. The Hotman people do not love her. She sensed they felt she was beneath them. She hoped to win them over.

Maybe, she considered, that was why her love never grew. She wished on a star that never fell. No young girl wishes coming true in her less than holy-matrimony. Compromise, yes, Daddy worshiped her, giving reason to stay.

Loveless marriage for her or not, she could not go home to Pops. Delena, Daddy's harsh eldest sister said Pops sold Momma for fifty dollars, under the old custom. Momma said it was a loan. Delena said the exchange of cash for a bride was a sign Daddy would provide for her.

The deed, done, was now history. Whatever the reason for money being involved, did not matter any longer. Her youthful plan had worked and she was stuck. To leave him was out of the question, especially, after being his wife for the past two years.

Her maidenhead was broken. No respectable bachelor would have her now. She could not dishonor her father or admit to herself, her ill-conceived plan had brought her more misery. The baby, I was an undesirable gift of nature.

Her life was better married to a man she did not love. Divorce could send her to Hell. She would endure. She would simply stay. Her choices were limited because she had no work skills. Hardly able to read or write. Trapped inside a prison of her, own making. Going home to Moms and Pops was not an option. Her mind was firm. She would not resume being her mother Iris Bip's domestic servant and caregiver.

Moms Iris had the shaking and slobbering disease. They called it Palsy. She needed a-lot-of help. Backwoods ignorance prevailed concerning Grandma Iris' disability. The community shunned her as a leper. Suggesting her disability was a curse because of some gross deed, iniquity of the ancestors. She suffered God's wrath because of generations past. If not for Iris' religious sister-in-law Diana's help, none of her babies would have survived--seven of thirteen did.

Pops' moonshine alcoholism added to Moms' strenuous efforts. Raising her clutch of young, would prove impossible without a miracle. Diana was the miracle.

Iris could read, and write a bit. She was an intelligent, beautiful woman with bright-green eyes, and raven waist length black-hair in two long braids. Moms' limitations were unsparing. Struggling at home to overcome, by age twelve Iris finally learned to walk with a cane, one in each hand. Before that, she could not walk at all. She was fifteen, and Pops thirty-five-years-old when they wed, against the reluctant stance of her parents.

Some twenty-years-earlier before I was born. The year was 1934, one look and Grandpa Daniel fell head-over-heels for her. Momma was their second child. I was Momma's first born, and their first grandchild.

Pops Bip was a homely little man by most standards, a moonshine runner, and a drunkard. Grandma's parents held concerns from the beginning, as did most of the community. Reality was, despite everyone's misgivings Daniel and Iris were in love.

Moms worked hard to overcome. She wanted a normal life, to marry, have children, and a home of her own. Ill advised or not, Daniel Bip (Pops) made her dreams a reality.

Black-Dutch-Cherokee Pops was beaten near to death in '45. A local chapter of the Ku Klux Klan did the deed. The ambush left him permanently disable with use of only one lung. Moms, was too frail to protect him. The KKK said he would neither work nor provide for his children, and black African blood was in that wood stack. Vigilante justice ruled.

Momma witnessed the beating. She was five-years-old. She hunkered in a corner of the make due smokehouse home. The hooded criminals burnt a cross in their front yard, and dragged Pops out of his bed. She thought that those men were actually demons, intent on killing them all.

Rumors were that my parents' union would produce halfwits, possibly inheriting Grandma Bip's dreaded slobbering-disease. Racist, degrading words were harsh and cruel, meant to belittle Momma's family. Some said her babies would pop-out looking like, kinky head throwbacks from the days of slavery. If that did not happen, their offspring would not be right in the head, crazy like Enoch.

Woes spoken of Daddy were not any kinder. Anne gored by the milk cow, during the eighth month of gestation. Superstitions marked Daddy before birth. Some called it the cow-horn-curse. Gossipmongers whispered his mind would never be right. Daddy treated less than normal all of his youth.

After my birth, Daddy got religion. He was then, labeled the village idiot preacher--a poor backsliding Baptist. At first, the religion made him a bit more acceptable, respectable with some pious Loafer's Glory folks.

Grandmother Anne took great pride knowing her youngest offspring was preaching the Gospel too. She became a Pentecostal evangelist/pastor shortly after her husband Isaiah died in '33. Anne prayed daily for the anointing on Daddy's ministry.

Anne's heart-dropsy worsened a year before I was born. The Hotman children insisted she see the local doctor, and take a break from preaching. Doc. Anderson prescribed a pill to clear the fluid from around her heart. This went against everything she believed.

Momma said a guilty Christian complex had a hold on Anne for two years, before she told her country pastor about the pills. He pressed her to throw them away and trust the Lord alone. She did. The illness put her on her deathbed within a short few months.

Daddy said despite all her flaws, Grandma Hotman was a praying woman, with a good heart. Her religion was most important.

Life was extremely impoverished and uncharitable after her wife-beating, drunkard husband, Grandpa Isaiah died of rabbit fever. Before his death, he changed his ways. Quit the corn squeeze and accepted the Lord in '29. Their last years together were peaceable. Anne hoped he made it to heaven.

Alone, she raised nine children during the years after the stock market crash. They called it "The Great Depression." Depending on the Lord to provide, she grew closer to Him. She felt called of God to preach, a year after Isaiah passed.

No good local Baptist congregation would accept a woman preacher. Women were to stay silent in the church, and not hold positions of leadership. Grandma Anne was determined. She would find another way to fulfill her spiritual assignment.

The summer of 1910, Pentecostal missionaries from California headed east. By 1914, they founded the Assembly of God Church headquarters located in Hot Springs, Arkansas. A. O. G. missionaries evangelized across America. It was 1920, when they journeyed north from Hot Springs, reaching their destination, Raccoon Springs by way of the Galloping Goose train. They shared their message, a new religious order and ways of worship.

During these gatherings, Anne and Isaiah heard of William J. Seymour's Holy Ghost worship services. She was intrigued when they shared, teaching about the outpouring of the Holy Spirit, and the unknown tongues revelation. They taught on Gifts of the Spirit, including supernatural healing. Anne wanted these experiences to be a reality in her own life. She would not stop seeking until she received the baptism of the Holy Ghost with the evidence of speaking in the unknown tongue.

Women, preachers were acceptable in the Pentecostal movement. Grandpa Isaiah was a firm Baptist. He did not approve of the Holy-Rollers. Anne had held back all those years, and secretly believed Pentecostal doctrine. Now, he was gone, she was free to worship as she pleased. Grandma knew for certain, her calling was real. The new Pentecostal denominations would accept her ministry.

Anne raised her brood with the Lord's help. Tending to the children, their one-hundred acre farm, livestock, and crops by day, she preached her revivals in the evenings. Sundays, she was a pastor, and ministered to the congregation of their small, local, rural Pentecostal church.

Often passers-by could hear her haunting prayers as she stole away down by the pond near the homestead hollow. This was her natural sanctuary, a serene place of God's beauty where she had time alone with the Lord. It was here that she found inspiration to deliver her fiery sermons.

Daddy said her gospel preaching, unknown tongue prayer language, and the Hellfire Brimstone sermons against sin were harsh. Strange were the antics of the Pentecostal movement and their church, for nonbelievers. Some called it the devil's house of screaming demons.

Grandma willingly endured the persecutions, snide remarks, and public mocking of this new religion rolling across America. Known as the Holy Roller Preacher Woman, some said she lost her ever-livin' mind.

She forgave them, and loved her enemies anyway. It was the true Christian way. She said those folks were just ignorant infidels. "God, have mercies upon their souls," she prayed.

Anne's heart of gold, she was willing to help all in need with what little she had to share. She was full of the love of God for others around her. Though stern in her holiness beliefs, she would not tolerate sin. Grandmother wanted all her family to walk the talk of a holiness Christian life. They resisted.

Daddy said her religion was hard for him to swallow. He was a rebellious child. He surrendered to the calling as a Baptist. It was an easier walk.

Eighteen-months-old, I was there when Anne lay dying. Gathered around her bed were the daughters she loved. She spoke softly to each one of them. They were all present but Lou, number six. Anne asked when Lou would arrive.

Tina, the second to eldest, large boned, fat, and married to big Roscoe, moved closer and kissed Anne on the cheek. She wept while holding her ma's hand and nodded.

Daddy's sister, pretty, sophisticated, tall and blond Lou, lived in South Bend, Indiana. She made a home with her arrogant, alcoholic husband, drywall contractor Martin. Everyone said he was a show off. They called Lou a high dollar woman.

They were rich. Lou would not be making the trip home. She held bitterness against Ma. Anne refused to give her blessing to their union. They ran off, eloped five years earlier.

Beautiful, saintly, violet-blue-eyed Leve, number three in Anne's clutch, rode the bus some six-hundred miles from Amarillo, Texas the day before. Her husky husband, Jake, had a dream, early the same week. It was heaven's message for Leve's sake, forewarning of this day. She bellowed ceaselessly, as her bond was strongest. The thought of losing Ma was gut wrenching for Leve.

Sneaky, dark-hair Sonny, the youngest of the girls in her mid-twenties had the look of bewilderment, and great fear on her pretty face. Silent tears dripped off her cheeks, splashing downward onto the worn linoleum.

Daddy was the baby boy, Anne's ninth offspring. Born in 1932 his father Isaiah died when he was nine-months-old. Anne asked them all to look out for Daddy. She said Enoch was the only reason she would want to delay her flight for a heavenly home.

Often, she spoke of him as poor Enoch. His mind is not right. Who would love him when she was gone? She worried most over her baby, Enoch.

At twenty-four-years-old, Daddy was a peculiar, shy man. He was tall, and strong. His sunburned ruddy complexion spoke of the outdoorsman's life he led. Soft, fine textured strawberry-blond hair crowned his head. He fidgeted, and exaggerated facial expressions while talking with his hands. His deepest thoughts read on his face without him speaking a word. The look of insecurity and a little confusion shone in his steely blue yearning eyes.

Great resentment toward his older siblings secretly abode inside his heart. However, he would never confront them about the past. His brothers and sisters, ignorantly, were cruel during his childhood. He could not forget.

Most often, the least of conflict stirred Daddy's anger to excess. His every emotion was to the extreme. His moods swung up, and down. A virtuous angel, all was calm. Then, without warning, he snapped. Wild and crazy, chases away the unsettled peace, and all goes to blazes. For those around him, he was an emotional rollercoaster. Daddy was a hothead.

Momma held me tight against her breast while standing in the open doorway. Anne motioned for Momma to let her hold me. Daddy's scowling sisters passed me from one to the other around the bed. They lay me next to Grandmother Anne. I beheld her face, wrinkled, and aged beyond her sixty-two-years.

Nearing the end, her worn-out body--beyond repair, from the hard life, she lived. She placed her leathery hand on my head. She held me in her arms, and prayed softly.

Without warning, under a surge of excited energy, she shouted the unknown tongue. I was terrified. Not knowing to crawl away or stay, I simply sat up and squalled. This was my first memory, Anne praying in the Holy Ghost. I continued to cry as those around me wept bitterly.

Momma was not sobbing. She seethed contempt.

Slim, blond Delena, Anne's stern eldest, cursed, "Get the damned kid off Ma."

I did not fully understand what was happening. The inability to comprehend death, and Aunt Delena's gruffness, confused my young mind. Sad, wonderful, peaceful, and I was afraid.

Seemingly, every emotion flooded my insides at the same time. Anne's, unexpected, loud, and strange sounding language had startled me far more than Delena's, cursing demand. I could feel a separate kind of peace. Even in her suffering, a perfect peace and a deep love seemed to flow out from Grandma's touch.

Anger flowed from Momma's dagger-eyes without her saying a word. She scooped me off the bed as Grandma continued her piercing prayer. Momma pulled me away, as Anne reached for me. I flung my arms toward her, as Momma swished me out of the room. We could hear her praying still, when Momma carried me outside to console my frantic bawling.

Grandma Anne died shouting the unknown tongue--praying in the Holy Ghost. Then came silence.

Mournful yowls, like the sound of wounded animals broke the hush and cascaded from inside. My aunts and father wept over the loss of their beloved mother. Momma mumbled profanities.

Daddy stepped onto the front porch. Grief stricken, his face wrenched. Trying to hold back the tears, he groaned, "Ora, Ma is gone," he said.

Momma did not care on this day if her anger stirred his wrath. The Hotman harshness caused her to hate. "Well," she said, unconcerned.

Momma held a grudge. Weeks earlier, Anne offered a truce, asked forgiveness, but Momma's heart was hard against her.

I could feel a tangible tension between my parents and the coldness in Momma. Daddy was tearfully silent. Great sadness seeped over the brim of his soul as he strolled inside, head-down.

Momma refused to speak a kind word. She was devoid of compassion, unable to attempt uttering a phrase that might console him. Flipping her hair back and adjusting me on her hip, she whispered under her breath when he was no longer in sight. Out of ear shot, "Good-riddance! The old battle axe is dead," she frothed.

Her heart of flesh was now stone, hardness formed by the coalescence of cruelty. The degrading vocalizations, and nasty deeds against her, emptied out any form of kindness she may have had for her Hotman in-laws, and her husband.

She felt dejected as a second-class citizen, not worthy to be Enoch's wife. There was little chance of her being a respectable member of the Hotman clan. She was his little darkie harlot, as some referred to her. She would never fit in.

Indignantly, she reached into her purse on the edge of the porch and frantically fumbled for something. She grasped a pack of ready-made smokes, then a fluid lighter. She shook down the pack, slowly drawing out a white cigarette with a brown filter. She lit up a Winston. Tossing the pack and lighter on the porch beside her purse, she leaned to one side and repositioned me on her hip.

Wreaths of smoke laced over our heads as she puffed and exhaled while bouncing me. My death-grip arms and locked fingers flung around her neck. I continued to shriek, clinging ever so tight.

She Danced with the Devil

Anne bequeathed the old homestead to Daddy and Momma. We lived there a few weeks before her passing. Momma resentfully helped testy Delena, twenty-years, Daddy's senior. They cared for Anne during her last days.

Delena favored the glamorous Joan Crawford. Her husband Shawn was a dark complexioned, likeable fellow. He was a genetic combination, blood of Hawaiian and European ancestry, birthed on the island Oahu. Shawn fluently spoke three different languages, having an upmost distinctive French accent. His extensive skills of languages were Polynesian, French, and English. Not so accomplished, he spoke a little Japanese. Local racist referred to him as Delena's "darkie buck."

Momma and Daddy loved kind and polite Shawn. They were deceived as was everyone by his generous personality. He had a secret. Delena would soon be the first to find him, out.

Anne was gone. Momma was happy to have the home free and clear. It was hers now. She set in to fix it up.

Daddy's sixth-grade education did not afford many high paying career opportunities, other than manual labor. He worked hard to provide for us those early years. As his forefathers, he toiled by the sweat of his brow harvesting timber.

Uncle Chad Hotman was the handsome domineering eldest brother. He owned several sawmills. There was Daddy's day job. His labors are from dawn-to-dusk, tending our fields, and livestock, when he was not cutting timber or hauling logs.

Though wages were poor, at Momma's insistence, he bought her many nice things to furnish our home. He purchased a television. Then he bought the new '57 Chevy Bel Air. The shinny new car was two-tone having white top and blue fins. The local banker helped Daddy buy the items. New furniture and quite fine clothes for Momma gave her smiles.

The old homestead shack had no indoor plumbing. Most no one in Loafer's Glory had indoor toilets. We used the outhouse. Running water or not, we were comfortable, and Momma was contented for a time. We were living high-on-the-hog, compared too many families. To Momma's relief we were more secure and prosperous than all her young years before.

Shortly after Anne passed, the Hotman family canonized her. They referred to Anne as a saint. Inspired by her testimony, Daddy was preaching more intently. He registered, and obtained ordination license through the Free Will Baptist Church organization. Hoping this would appease the memory of his mother.

I felt safe, and loved by both my parents as they were getting along most of those months. Maybe it was the religion. Momma said she gave her heart to Jesus when she courted Daddy. She added, "It didn't last long."

Her backsliding indeed came early on in the marriage. Bitterness ate at her soul toward Anne, and other Hotman relatives. Repenting, she tried, and walked in her salvation for a fleeting moment when her scorn for Anne subsided a bit, after the funeral. Her ill will would return.

I was too young to understand the demon thoughts that tormented both my parents' minds. The dynamic complexity of my dysfunctional extended family was a hot bed of conflicting negative emotions.

Momma supported Daddy's ministry for a while. Her reserved validation of his godly works did not last long either. Weeks before Grandma died, Momma said she too had the Holy Ghost, gifts of discernment and prophecy, just like Anne. She claimed to have heard the voice of God, telling her that Anne was two barks away from being the devil's disciple.

Momma's words were sarcastic expressions of her own pain. Momma, deeply hurt by the sharp tongues caused her to first fear, then loath her in-laws. She tried desperately to rid herself of the dreadful grudges.

To forgive and forget completely was impossible. Bitterness rooted inside her heart. She suppressed her true feelings, as her animosity was partially curbed and silent. However, the tree of her resentment grew. The bid to hide her hostilities slipping more frequently as the next two years passed.

Nineteen-fifty-eight came with blessings and a curse, when Daddy, elected by the local congregation, takes the position as pastor of Red Wood Baptist. Their different Christian beliefs and traditions caused conflict. Momma was Pentecostal, and he a Baptist. Differences in church doctrine, this speared heated religious disagreements. Neither of them won.

Reconciling in her mind for an-uneasy-peace, Momma's attitude became tolerable toward most everything Daddy stood for the first few months while he pastors the small country church. Even so, she was reserved in her commitment to his religious vocation.

She was not zealous, but reluctant over her public position as a Baptist preacher's wife.

She said her role of the minister's spouse felt more and more like a charade. She was only going through the motions, and doing so, poorly. She said Daddy was a hypocrite.

Nineteen-fifty-nine and Momma openly back sliding. Her talents and helpful spiritual songs in the church abided dormant. No longer did she participate when he gave his sermons. Often she refused to attend, but rather stayed home. She displayed open vocal anger, and full-blown rebellion against Daddy and the worship.

Her suppression of nasty sourness went and came with the seasonal breezes. She spat filthy words, polluting the atmosphere of our home. Neither Daddy nor his siblings could do any good in Momma's sight. She was miserable.

She slipped away from her faith. Every passing day, fewer religious convictions restrained her. She was giving place to the enemy of her soul. She gave the devil permission for a play day. It was only a matter of time before he took the opportunity to rob, kill, and destroy, while providing Momma the thrill of an all-consuming party. Momma was a covenant breaker, into the throws of sin's short season of pleasure. She danced with the devil.

Bitter Oxymoron

Migrant work was a way of life for many choosing to make Loafer's Glory, home. The Judas family's caravan made their yearly road trip to harvest oranges down in the Florida groves. Merl met sixteen-year-old Lilly when he and his family journeyed south in '52.

Lilly was a plain girl with short, mousey-brown hair, curled in ringlets. Kind hearted and quite intelligent, her eyes were windows of warmth, large and dark brown. She tugged on her earlobe when thinking intently, and when pressured to speak. She compensated shyness with forced smiles. Sometimes her thin lips twitched before she spoke. Like, she was changing her mind before she got the first words out. Lilly fell desperately in love with Merl.

Harvest over, and after a short courtship, Merl and Lilly married. Returning to Loafer's Glory, they built a home up the road from our house before I was born. Merl's shack set right next door to his ma's, Bertha Judas.

Bertha claimed to be the local witch. Her appearance resembled one. She claimed to have mystical powers. Her herbal remedies could cure the ailing soul. Some believed her. Others laughed at her boast.

Her youngest daughter, thirteen-year-old Della, lived there too. The spring of '53, Della returned from Florida with her little bundle of joy, baby Rafter. She was not married, and had no male suitor anyone knew of.

Hoping to lure a husband for the fat unkempt Della, Bertha placed an ad in the "Missouri Star" newspaper. The effort was not successful. No eager potential husband responded.

Lilly and Momma became fast friends at their first meeting. Being hitched never stopped Merl's opportunistic trifling around. He was after Momma from the day he lay eyes on her, when she was twelve-years-old. About the same time, she met Daddy. Merl said it was love at first sight. Momma hid her secret desires from Lilly. She resisted Merl's advances, concealing her own passions.

Daddy's popularity as a Pastor/Evangelist around other communities grew leaps and bounds by '58. Churches from all over the hills were requesting he hold revivals for their congregations, and communities. He obliged during the temperate seasons. Many a spring, summertime, and autumn brush-arbor services he led. Hundreds repented, experienced salvation, and he baptized them, as the revivals continued. Each meeting lasted near a month.

Despite his religious vigor, they continued to have their squabbles, inflamed by Merl's flirtations. Spats, emotional outbursts erupted, placing them in embarrassing predicaments.

Invariably they kissed and made up after every confrontation. Engagement in the ongoing different--religious disagreements ran their cycles, at least one a week. Daddy said the hounds of Hell were out to stop him from bringing the message of life to a dying world. He said the anti-Christ devil spirit was stronger in his own home than in the world.

Despite the heated household conflicts, at the beginning of his new ministry, Daddy trudged forward. He refused to be discouraged. After their domestic hostilities, he used them as a source of inspiration. He gleaned truths from their squabbles, attempting to draw something positive from the outcomes. He prepared sermons based on the conflicts between God, humanity, and the devil. Then he would preach, expressing his soul, exposing the weaknesses of the flesh. Momma always took it personally. She told him to stop airing their dirty laundry.

Momma sang fewer hymns as they moved onto other Gospel revivals. By spring of '59, Momma had all but quit taking part in the services.

Momma liberated, when Anne was gone. She was with the Judas people during the day while Daddy was working. Anne had warned her to stay away from their clan, if her marriage was important. Now, she was free to do, as she pleased, no accusing ol' mother-in-law to flog her. Ignoring Anne's words of wisdom, Momma said Lilly was her best friend and nothing would keep them apart.

Momma said it was not Lilly causing Grandma Anne's concern. Momma said she deluded herself, twisting Anne's advice, knowing she should have listened and stayed away. Daddy also ignored Anne's warnings.

My family and the Judas people became very close over the next three years, after Anne passed away. I was four when reality of the situation struck. Great furious storms of life and stronger attacks of the devil roared about us. Changes came as sure as the seasons. We would never be the same again. We had a Judas in our midst. He was Merl Judas.

Daddy said it was Merl flirting with gullible women. He ruined many a good girl, and destroyed numerous marriages. He had known Merl since they were in grade school. Despite Merl's godless ways, Daddy could not help but like him. Merl had away about his personality--a likable fellow if he wanted a person's trust. Daddy knew both sides of Merl's character. One he despised. The other he cherished as a best friend. He trusted Momma more than Merl. He cautioned Momma to watch herself, and not to be enticed by Merl's charms.

Anne gone near three years, Momma's secret fantasies budded and bloomed. Anne's prophecies of doom for their marriage were beginning to come-to-pass.

Merl started frequently missing work, leaving Dad with no helper. Secretly, he would steal away to meet Momma at our home while Daddy labored in the forest. Daddy found out, and drove to cousin Poojam's store where the young folk's hangout. Purposely, he sought out Merl with the intent of publically humiliating him. To Merl's shame, Daddy confronted him, shouting about the sneaking around, and his constant passes thrown toward Momma.

When Merl denied it all, Daddy did not believe him. He was outraged at the local gossip. He pounced on Merl like a wild tiger. Enoch beat him with his fist, one blow after another to the face and gut, warning him to back off his pursuit of Momma.

Pops passed by during the heated fight, and whipped into the parking lot. If not for Grandpa Daniel's words to the wise, "That man isn't worth going to prison, Enoch. Let him go before you kill him," he shouted.

Daddy released the headlock out of respect for Pops. Bloody, Merl cried off like a sissy, hiding behind the store. Changing his mind, Daddy gave chase. Merl found refuge, locked inside the stinking, women outdoor toilet. The gathering crowd watching the rumble, laughed hysterically.

Pops shouted, "Enoch, Let it be."

Daddy restrained himself again out of respect for Pops. He wanted to push the outhouse over with Merl inside. Panting to catch his breath he said, "There's where a sack-of-sh** belongs."

He leapt into the '57 Chevy and squalled tires as he sped toward home. Merl refused to come out until he was certain Daddy was gone.

Daddy would have terminated Merl, if not for Pops. He lost all sense of reason during the adrenaline-fired rages. A preacher or not, everyone knew Enoch was not one to be messing with when he was angry.

Later, Daddy asked Momma if anything was going on between them. He explained that there were rumors floating around. She denied it all. Daddy did not know if he should apologize to Merl, or beat him again. His emotions were in extreme conflict, not knowing whom to believe.

Momma had nothing to do with ugly Fanny who was married to Merl's eldest brother, an Ely Judas. Ely did not inherit Merl's good looks or charm. He was a gangly, plain, hillbilly, simply a Gomer Pyle, with a generous good soul. Ely and Merl were as different as night and day. Fanny ruled the Ely Judas roost. Their home was up the way from Merl and Lilly's on Judas Hill.

Momma said Fanny had made her life a living Hell. Encouraging her to get involved with Enoch at such a young age, ruined her childhood. There was no Loafer's Glory gold on Hotman land, as the Judas clan had implied. There was in reality only fools' gold, bitterness and hard labor. She was a fool for listening to Fanny. Momma shunned her.

Momma has forbidden desires. Her daydreams, sexual fantasies for Merl were about to explode. Her youthful vanity was scrumming to his flatteries. The secret meetings with Merl made her feel powerful. Like she was doing something, she should not be doing, and getting away with it.

She was a teenager, yet a wife, and mother. Despite the fact that he was a married man and she was the pastor's wife. She made less than honorable choices, because of her youthful age. Willingly, she embraced a devil of temptation.

Lecherousness overpowered Momma's soul. She was losing her moral compass. She had resisted giving herself completely to Merl, thus far. The carnal passion of her body and soul warred against her spirit. If she succumbs to forbidden desire, the label adulteress, as a bull's eye burned, branded onto her forehead for all to judge. Betraying her best friend Lilly was not an option. She chose not to give in for the time being.

Reacting to her mind's-wondering-lust, her body and emotions protested against conviction and moral reason. If she did not suppress, there would be worse blood letting than already spilled during Merl's beating. Daddy was not ignorant. She knew he sensed her desires for Merl.

Swayed easily, Daddy said he fought to ignore the signs. He was suspicious, time-and-time again when she denied any romantic relationship with Merl. She insisted they had never lay together. Daddy could not read the pages of her heart. However, through the depths of his being he knew, something was up, Ora had changed.

Knowing, Merl was a whoremonger, Daddy feared more. Merl might force himself upon her. She was a married virtuous woman. He hoped. She would never give herself to another. She was the pastor's wife. His internal warning signals were making a loud clamor. He was ignoring his gut feelings that something was amiss. Blinded by his love for Momma, he refused to listen to his inner voice, and act upon the warnings appropriately. He gagged his intuition.

Delusional, he wanted to believe she loved him. He did not follow through and disconnect from Merl Judas. Rather, he apologized. Momma made him. He suppressed his desire to act, not knowing actually how to handle the situation.

Daddy was hoping she respected herself, and their union enough to honor his office in the church. Her reputation affected his ministry. He had to have faith. Trust her if for the ministry sake alone. He hoped. Blindly he hoped. Maybe, God would step in and fix their marriage problems.

Try as he did, Daddy was not able to completely, turn off his jealously. He became a tortured prisoner of doubt during the coming months. She continued insisting nothing was going on. Silently, he did not believe her. The jealous monster raised its ugly head more often.

Their fighting only stopped a bit when he made a concerted effort to control himself. All his life he had struggled with a bad temper. Eradicating the fire completely was not possible.

He was confused, suffering from a broken-heart. Not knowing and uncertain if Momma was true to him alone, or a lustful cheating wife. His mind replaying over-and-over, what might-be. This was their love-hate dance. The situation became his torment, his oxymoron. His jealousy was crueler than death, driving him closer to insanity.

Momma said Daddy robbed her of life's joy. She found more often than not, greater pleasure in Merl's presence than with him. She yelled the hurtful words during their frequent and spiteful rages.

Momma said Merl made her feel like, a special woman. There was nothing wrong, after all, Merl was Daddy's lumberjack partner, and his best bud. She had not rolled in the sack with him. When he was around, she had to be a genial host, to maintain cordial relations.

Momma's story was innocence. Insisting Lilly's friendship was the reason she visited them so often. This was her attempt to justify herself. Her guilty conscience spoke to hide, as she worked to conceal her deepest thoughts. She proclaimed the truth. She lay with Merl, but only in her fantasies, not for real. The secrets of her heart were obsessive wild lust, the desire to be with Merl Judas, and rid of Enoch Hotman.

Daddy's broken-heart sang its song of sorrow. His emotions delivered with a melody of suspicion, a raging vibrato's jealous confusion.

Nine months after Anne's death, a blood vessel burst in Delena's husband Shawn's brain. After World War II, fruit tramp Delena met Shawn Zablan harvesting apples in Washington state and they married. Returning to Loafer's Glory in '54, they built a new home up the road from the old homestead. Shawn died in '58, two days after the cerebral hemorrhage.

This was the beginning of Delena's foreboding. Grief struck, and burdened with forbidden unwanted realities, a time of great losses for her.

After applying for his life insurance and trying to take claim of all his other assets, the ruse revealed. Shawn's, true character, he was a lying bigamist, with five living children in Hawaii whom he had abandoned years before. Shawn's estate went to his legal family. However, his lawful wife was gracious enough to give Delena the home he purchased in Loafer's Glory.

Now, mid-forties, widow Delena discovered, Shawn deceived her for over a decade. Overwhelming grief intensified. Her love for him turned into hurt from the betrayal. Knowing nothing, she had no idea his official family even existed. Then to hear the shocking news, Delena felt degraded. Bitterly, she proclaimed she had been his concubine all those years.

Despite his sin of adultery, there was no excommunication, from the Catholic Church for Shawn. A black-cloaked Catholic-priest-chaplain gave him last rights at the Little Rock Veterans Hospital.

Delena said she wanted to vomit as she remembered the scene months later. Her emotions were all mixed-up. Bitter, and heart broken, Shawn betrayed her trust as badly as had the rapist, Newton.

She was a seventeen-year-old virgin. Nineteen-twenty-nine, the year she thought she had found a new beau in Newton, the pastor's son. The reality--he charmed her for weeks, only to get alone in the woods. That warm summer night while walking her home after Sunday evening services was the telling of his true intent.

Taking a shortcut, off the main trail, he brutally attacked. He raped and beat her. She feared for her life and lay motionless after the deed done. She pretended to be-knocked-out from the blows to her head from a large rock. Newton left her for dead.

Thanks to her pa, the local chapter of the KKK found out. The next week Newton pleaded for his life as Isaiah and Klansmen retaliated with angry fists. Grandpa Isaiah threatened running him through with a pitchfork.

Worse than being physically beaten, Newton's recompense was public humiliation. He was threatened and forced to ask for her forgiveness before God, his parents, and the church congregation during Sunday morning service.

Watching him grovel gave Delena great satisfaction. The taste of revenge was sweet, especially, when she spat in his face while standing beside him at the altar.

Now, Shawn was as evil. This time there would be no justice. She was his fool. The treachery ripped her heart out by the roots. She would never trust another man. Securing a loan, she built a new restaurant next door to her home across the road from cousin Poojam's store. She never returned to backbreaking field labor.

Delena did not have time to grieve her losses for long, nor to have a pity party. Survival was necessity of the moment. She dove into her new career, shoving the pain inside an emotional lock box, sealing it shut.

Delena's burger joint became the center of activity. She catered to young people from miles around. Business boomed. Pinball machines and Juke Box brought a hefty profit every week. She made a good living flipping burgers, tossing fries, selling cigarettes, pop, and ice cream.

Soon, competitors' stores, other restaurant owners, and resentful, envious community members falsely accused her. They say she was serving moonshine by the dipper full out of a galvanized water bucket she chilled in the pop tank. Though these accusations were unfounded, her business suffered.

She learned to accept slander and gossip as a way of life. She said it was that way everywhere, in any town or village where two or more lived. One good thing said about a neighbor, ten more had a negative comment. All she wanted was to make a living. It was impossible to stop wagging tongues.

Most folks liked to hear the down-and-dirty enhanced stories, whether the tales were true or not. She determined no one would run her off. She refused to allow the gossip to ruin the business. She hunted down the unruly-tongued trouble makers, and threatened them with a slander suit. That helped for a while. After that, some labeled her an uppity-money-grubbing-Jezebel.

She really gave the neighbors something to chat about when she commenced courting Saul, a dark-haired handsome gambler, fifteen years younger.

Delena was a suffering, intimidating woman. She was frightening, brazen as she was forceful. She was controlling, and quite vocal with strong opinions. Her steely-blue bitter eyes cut to the bone.

I'll Kill You If You Hit Her Again

Three months after Anne passed away, little sister Jane came along. The same degrading suspicions rumored about her genetic origins. Insulting Momma, some said she belonged to Merl, too. Jane was especially dark, but her features were the same as our very pretty aunt Lou's, with her long legs. Except for the darker tones, she was a Hotman. Kinder customers happening by Delena's Cafe often told Momma, Jane was the prettiest baby girl in the country.

When Jane was born, Momma clothed her in store-bought satin, lace, and frilly little girl dresses. She now had her baby girl, and my wardrobe changed to boys pants. Jane got my feminine hand downs as Daddy insisted Momma stop pretending I was a baby girl. He said I would not be natural if she kept it up. From eighteen-months on, I was Momma's boy.

Ripe strawberry fields were numerous. Raccoon Springs, six miles from Loafer's Glory, declared the Strawberry Capitol of the World decades before. I was four when our family stopped at Delena's Restaurant for ice cream cones during 1959's strawberry harvest. I was proud to show off my new red sneakers, jeans, cowboy shirt, and hat. A cap pistol strapped to my leg, we strolled in. Merl and Lilly were there sipping on root beer floats as we took our regular corner booth.

Momma pulled a coin from her purse and poked the nickel into the Juke Box. She punched up a snappy rock 'n' roll tune. Disapproving, Daddy frowned, covering his mouth with his hand. He did not like that kind of music.

Grinning at Daddy, she said, "Darn I hit the wrong one. I meant to play Johnny Horton's new one." Shrugging shoulders, she sighed.

Pops Bip quit cooking off the corn squeeze. Walking away from liquor consumption in '57, he sold the moonshine still. Abruptly, all transport and sales of his intoxicating brew stopped. He got religion, and as quickly, he divorced Grandma Iris.

The same year, he met Gert. The woman was in her mid-forties, graying, short and plump, a country-lady. Her alabaster, soft skin, stark compared to Grandpa Daniel's leathery swarthy darker complexion. They courted down in the Bottoms while harvesting cotton near Grubbs, Arkansas. The same year, they hitched.

Gert was his God-sent-bride. She tended to the needs of Pops, and his many children. She kept a clean home, and cooked delicious, rounded meals. Invalid Iris moved back in with her mother Gladdis.

Momma was not pleased when Pops divorced Moms. She said he did her dirty. Though she was happy he abstained from the hooch, and her younger siblings were now well kempt.

Jimmy Driftwood was internationally famous for writing the country music hit, "The Battle of New Orleans," recorded by Johnny Horton. Jimmy, the teacher lived a few miles up the road. Thanks to Jimmy's friendship, Pops was becoming a local celebrity, in his own right as an accomplished fiddle player and composer of new tunes.

Members of the Rack 'n Sack Folklore Society, and Pops wanted fame too. Momma said, "Pops says, Jimmy sure can write a song. He told me, Rack 'n Sack gonna get government money. They want to build a folk center in Mountain View."

She continued, "Pops and a hundred of his musician friends plan to drive a caravan to Washington, D.C. one day. Driftwood said he'd work on getting the trip organized."

She sat down next to Merl, and said, "The plan is to perform for the President at the White House. Reasoning, those powerful politicians are bound to like their music."

She chuckled, and slapped her leg, "Hoot 'n Annie, on Capitol Hill. Pops thinks that will influence the politicians. Could be lots new jobs when vacationers come to visit these hills? I bet with Jimmy being so famous, Rack 'n Sack can get it done too," she said.

Daddy dropped his gaze, "Jimmy's songs are better than devil music," he mumbled.

Lilly motioned for Momma to stand. She moved to let them slide out of the booth. Merl took Lilly's hand and they boogied to the center of the restaurant. Momma giggled as she watched them dance. Lilly's poodle skirt swirled high, showing her thighs while they bopped to the music.

Prancing about in their semi-stylish rummage sale 1950's attire, complete with bobby socks, scuffed black and white saddle shoes, worn blue jeans, and torn penny loafers. Their apparent enjoyment of the moment was infectious, as other young couples joined them.

Merl asked, "Are yah ready?"

Lilly nodded, and leapt. He caught and flipped her over his back. Her white panties flashed before she landed on her feet again. Other couples tried the move, but they were not as successful at execution.

Momma strolled over to find another selection and fed the machine one more nickel. She tapped her foot to the beat and patted the Juke Box.

Daddy sat with Jane and me. He mumbled, "Baptist, do not dance."

I turned, grinning, watching the joyous young adults. Delena double dipped the cones from a large bucket in the freezer behind the counter and motioned for Momma. They brought us the ice cream, and Momma sat down facing us on the other side of the booth.

Delena's unhappy facial expression, declared someone was going to get it. She sashayed over to Merl as he vulgarly wiggled the Black-Bottom. Sneaking up on him, and swinging the broom, she heaved and let it go, smacking his rump with the straw broom-head.

Merl jumped a foot off the floor, doubled his fist, and whirled around menacingly. He was ready to sock her. Bristling, he sneered at Delena. Then his expression softened as he winked. His fist went limp. Shamelessly, showing his perpetual devilish smile, his large hand pushed back his black-hair.

"I won't have any of that stuff here. Now, knock it off," she said, shaking her finger in his face. "I'm not running a vile jute joint. Go jump in Big Creek to cool yourself off." She glared hatefully at Lilly. She scolded, "You should be ashamed of yourself, you're a mother," she said.

Merl smugly chuckled, as blushing Lilly laughed along with everyone watching them. "We won't do it again," he said. Panting, they pulled two cokes out of the cooler and dropped down in the booth beside us.

His charismatic personality and good looks were magnetic. When Elvis took America by storm, Merl pushed his brawny palm over his luxuriant glistening black-hair, every time the comparison spoken. He worked continually to improve his Elvis mannerisms. He acquired good ol' boy status even in far off counties. Women swooned over him.

It was obvious, Delena loathed him. She called him a no-count skirt chaser. I didn't know what that meant.

Merl's blue sensuous eyes pierced the soul, a hard fellow to dislike. His innocent, boyish demeanor, constant ease of humor, and calm base voice made him a pleasure to be round. I liked him.

He was a trifling, rebellious soul, the ultimate-level-headed manipulator. A few considered him kindhearted. That was folks not knowing his second nature. They held a wrong impression of his character, had not been taken advantage of by him. It was easy deception by his vivacious attitude, and slick tongue.

Others had not one good word to say of the man. Momma had nothing but admiration. He was becoming the object of her daily focus. Her praises of him were never ceasing.

Jane and I licked our strawberry ice cream, snickering when Momma did with Lilly and Merl. They were whispering, pointing, and poking fun at Delena. They were provoked to animated, uncontrollable laughter. Jane and I did not see the comedy. I reasoned. It had to be hilarious, an adult thing.

Delena's anger frightened me. When she scowled at us, I stopped giggling. Standing beside me on the seat, Jane pays her no mind. She went on bouncing to the beat of the music, imitating the other young folks still dancing.

Daddy, sullen, squirming in his seat, he sighed. He is frustrated again, when Momma and Merl ignored him when he made the effort to join in the conversations. They did not want him to stop the fun.

Joviality subsided when Momma and Merl focused on one another as though no one else was in the room. Lilly left out of the discussion too. Facing Daddy, she shrugged.

Flamethrower fire shot out of his eyes. Daddy nodded.

Delena shook her head. Contemptuously, she rolled her eyes. Making every effort to keep her mouth cinched while wiping down the tables. She sighed, her razor looks cut toward little sister.

Jane was bouncing around on the booth-seat again. Daddy nodded, and gently grasped Jane's small hand. He patted his leg. Jane stopped squirming, sat on his lap, and licked her cone.

Delena hated Merl. She had told me so. I did not know why. I did not understand the words, immoral whoremonger. She continually referred to him by the name. I did not understand the courtship dance. I did not understand Delena's reasoning for despising Merl. I was too young.

I loved Merl. He was like a second daddy for me. He never yelled at Momma, and he always came bearing gifts. Most of the time, it was candy for Jane and me. He brought laughter into our home.

Sometimes he tickled us in a teasing way, by rubbing his stiff whisker stubs on our tender faces and bellies when he had not shaved. He perpetually played games, and gave us lots of frisky attention. Momma glowed when he was there. I agreed with Momma. He was a great friend.

Opposite comparisons, Daddy was distant, not showing much affection with any of us. He was perpetually serious, sad, and angry. Kind to Jane and me, Daddy never spanked us. Momma paddled, or slapped our faces when we misbehaved. Our parents' behaviors were one passive, and the other aggressive, flipping back and forth between them.

Merl whipped his daughters very hard with a belt. His eldest child, April was a year older than I was. He paddled her often. In comparison, he was overly kind with us.

I never wanted Merl to belt me. When he cursed and yelled at his family, the shouting echoed across the hollow. We heard the troubles in the Merl Judas home as they broadcast, airing their dirty laundry. Our, Hotman house brawls were heard by all the neighbors, just as frequently.

Merl placed his hand on Momma's knee. I did not know he shouldn't be doing that. Momma chuckled, and I giggled. She held the look of pleasure while lustfully gazing into his face.

Daddy, fit-to-be-tied, as furious winds come before a great storm, he shot out of the booth. His neck-veins throbbing as he got into Merl's defensive face. He protested, "Keep your filthy hands off my wife," he said.

Merl says he meant nothing by the gesture. Daddy did not buy it. Neither did Lilly. The expression on her face, anguish, and embarrassment, overwhelmed, there was a choking tone in her voice as she slid out of the booth and grabbed Merl's arm. She glared at Momma but said nothing to her. Glancing down, and tugging on Merl's shirtsleeve, her lips trembled.

She said, "Let's go, Merl. We've gotta check on April and Dotty. Fanny has other things to do this afternoon, than to babysit."

Merl did not resist. Trying not to display the depth of intimidation he felt. He stood, and said, "Crazy, fools, get out of my face." He reached around Lilly standing between them and shoved Daddy.

Hotheaded, hands on her hips, Delena's distinct voice rang, "Get out! Don't ever bring your stinking butt back."

Jane and I were crying as Lilly and Merl swiftly headed for the door. Merl mumbled profanities. Using a vulgar hand gesture, he shot Delena the BIRD, as they exited the building.

Furious and stalled for a moment, Momma was red faced. She cursed Daddy and Delena. Customers shot out of their seats leaving cash by the register not waiting for change as the confrontation escalated. The young dancers fled too. The Juke Box continued its Rock 'n' Roll.

Grasping the broom handle, Delena strode closer to Momma who was now by the entrance. "You ol' harlot, Enoch should not have married you. You don't care about him, or your kids," she bellowed.

Momma shoved Delena to the side as she yanked us out of the booth. Delena swatted her butt when we exited, racing for the car. During our swift flee we dropped our cones on the gravel parking lot. Jane wailed harder as Momma tossed us in the backseat and screamed for Daddy,

"Get your crazy butt in the car, now. We're going home," she said.

They crawled inside and slammed the doors shut. Momma profaned her every breath. Daddy floored the gas-peddle. The back tires spun a great cloud of gravel-dust into the sultry spring air. They fought the entire mile drive home.

Raging, Momma fisted Daddy's face, and pulled his hair. Daddy backhanded her. Wild eyed, he spat, "Shut your mouth Jezebel, I'm gonna finish this when we get home. You won't be lusting for any of that Merl Judas stuff when I'm through with you."

When we arrived, Momma sprinted for the house. Daddy was hot on her heels. Jane screamed as we stared at them speeding across the yard.

I tried to comfort Jane through my own tears when we crawled out of the back seat and toddled inside. I hid Jane under her bed. There, she calmed some. I crept into the back bedroom where they were yelling. Thinking I could stop the fight.

I stepped between, face smeared with a grin from ear to ear, I say, "You kids kiss and make-up."

They paused a moment. Glancing down, there was amusement on their faces. The corners of their mouths turned up, ever so slightly. They laughed together. It was not long until they were cursing, and the argument over Merl continued.

I sighed.

Daddy protested, "This affair can't go on."

Momma snorted, "I'm not going on in an affair. Your old suspicious, paranoid mother, and domineering sisters started this crap."

I was not sure, but I thought that was where the rides and elephants were. "Let's go," I yelped.

They hesitated. "Go where, Son?" Momma asked.

"To the affair for the rides," I said. They might be bickering over whether or not to go. Obviously, Daddy did not want Merl to come along. Glancing down, bewilderment on their faces, they cackled.

Feeling better, at least they stopped to catch their breaths. I am still frustrated. I did not want the disturbance anymore. I winced, "Like Uncle Joe told me," I quipped.

Momma forced composure. She says, "No, Son that is a fair. An affair is a friendship where married couples kiss some other men or women, and sleep with them, sneaking around, not to let the husbands and wives know. They keep the relationships secret. Kissing people they like a lot when they are already hitched to someone else. These are the easiest explanations for you to understand."

I didn't understand exactly, but figured the two words sounded alike and I had misunderstood. For Momma and Daddy to kiss, that was okay, but not other men and women. That would be an affair. We definitely would not be going to the fair.

"Your crazy Daddy is accusing me of having an affair with Merl. Have you ever seen me kiss him?" she asked.

"No Momma. Never," I say.

Backhanding her, Daddy roared, "Don't drag the kids into this. Don't call me crazy, in front of my children."

Placing a hand over the cheek, Momma wept. She growled, "You bastard, I'll kill yah, if you hit me, again."

Feeling, I had stopped the fighting fleeted. My Hotman temper exploded. I could be as hotheaded. Maybe I was more stubborn. I was trembling but bold as a lion cub. I flew into action. While pressing my full body weight against his leg to shove him away, I yelled, "I'll kill you, if you hit her again."

Rejected, Daddy shamefully stormed out of the house and drove away.

What Is Sex? What Is Chicken SH**?

The week after Delena's Cafe incident, Daddy held revival at the Redwood Baptist Church. He was their pastor for about two years. Crowds overflowed the chapel. Elders built a brush arbor outside in the parking lot the day before the religious fever began. Services continued nightly.

The last week of gatherings, one evening Momma slipped out with Jane during the middle of the sermon. She left me alone. Returning thirty minutes later, she hoisted Jane off her hip onto the bench next to me. Under her breath, she mocked Daddy, as she seated herself. Contemptuously she fumed, "You're making a fool of yourself. You're no preacher," she said.

I could not figure what Daddy was doing wrong. His gestures and emotions exaggerated as he shouted, "Praise the Lord."

Why? What had Momma found offensive? The sermon he delivered the same as all his Hellfire and Brimstone lectures. The congregation echoed his vocalizations. They shout, "Praise the Lord."

I decided a show of support was necessary. Next service, I will go up on the platform and help him. I would prove Momma wrong. I would be just like Daddy.

The folks liked his preaching. So did I. When I go up, they will like me too. Why was Momma saying that? Daddy was great.

The strawberry harvest at an end, caravans of poor Caucasian, and Mexican migrant field laborers were preparing to move on. Many had attended the arbor meetings. Dozens came and knelt on the sawdust around the rough plank benches the night the revival was closing.

Halfway through the sermon, I skipped toward the podium, leaving clouds of sawdust and footprints behind at every step. I leapt onto the platform, and held to Daddy's leg.

The last alter-call came. Momma strolled up front. She fell to her knees to pray with other repenting sinners. Daddy's sister, Tina's husband, Roscoe was at the end of the line of wayward souls, rowed on their knees weeping before God.

He was a big man, mid-forties, tall and brawny, with eyes as blue as Leve's, a handsome man, but an alcoholic. He came to the altar to give his heart to the Lord for the first time ever. Momma moved over beside him.

Not long, I caught a glimpse of Roscoe shoving Momma. She fell to her side, sliding, and stirring up the sawdust. Abruptly stopped, she lay prostrate on the ground. Slowly rising, she glared at him, saying nothing as Roscoe jumped to his feet. He ran out of the arbor, cursing under his breath at every step. The people around Momma stared in bewilderment.

Perhaps, I just witnessed a demon manifest. Yap, those boogers make people hurt each other. Demons sometimes appeared that way when the power of Holy Ghost is strong. Most act up worse. A majority slither around on the sawdust like snakes before coming out of repenting sinners. When that had happened in the past, I hid behind Momma's skirt-tail.

Some antics were hilarious, and other amusements were unadulterated boredom. Evil, loud screaming demons, trying to terrify were most frightening. Calling boogers by their names, or commanding them to come out, got the devil stirred up. They do not want discovered, especially by an anointed man of God. Howling, cursing devils resist the eviction. The laughing saints got everyone joining in. The blind walkers with eyes closed running the backs of the church pews, were a sight, to behold. Shouting-Baptist-Holy-Ghost dancers were the fascinating ones.

I tried running the pews and fell during the last revival. My legs were not long enough, but I was not under the anointing. Delena said those feats were impossible without the anointing.

We stood on the podium platform. I continued mimicking Daddy's gestures as he preached the fiery sermon. Waving hands, I shook my fist, and pointed my index finger. Puckering lips, a serious intense expression, then I jiggled my head. Daddy was a shouting Baptist. With practice, I would be as great, a Shouting Baptist Preacher too, when I am bigger.

The commotion of sour faced, wrinkled-brow folks whispering after witnessing the peculiar scene. Unfazed, Daddy and I went on preaching. We delivered a sermon with great power. The double anointing got hounds of Hell stirred up. Daddy and I must have run the demon out of the arbor. The devil named Trouble, the one holding on Uncle Roscoe. He did not get free. He was not, delivered. The demon caused him to flee.

Momma brushing away the sawdust that clung to her simple dark-blue skirt as she stomped to her seat, caught my eye. Something was terribly wrong. Her demeanor was embarrassed, and angry. What happened? I was not sure. Did I miss something? Maybe, it wasn't a demon.

My attentions turned toward Daddy. I looked up.

He says, "Praise the Lord. Repent."

I say, "Praise the Lord! Repent!"

Agitated, congregational sheep began strolling out. Daddy stopped his loud gospel utterance, and marched me down the steps to sit by Momma. Then, he resumed closing the service.

He had not seen the incident. He must have suspected I was causing the distraction. Uncle Roscoe was no longer on my favorite list. He had a demon. He hurt Momma. Because of him, I could no longer help Daddy preach.

After the service, Daddy told Momma to keep a watch on me, and not to allow me up front again. "Do you understand, Son?" he asked, while driving us home.

I felt shamed, because he implied I made the people leave. Roscoe was the bad guy. He shoved Momma. My lower lip fell. Sitting next to me on the backseat, I reached for the comfort of Jane's hand. A tear oozed up as I say, "Yes, Daddy."

Jane whispered in the dark, "Saul in trouble."

Roscoe never came back to Daddy's church. The next week he visited with Dad at home. I was hiding behind the big Red Oak, near the yard's edge, listening. Daddy met him on the driveway. Roscoe would not kill his '49 Ford pickup engine, as the battery was low. He spoke through the downed drive-side window.

He says, "Enoch, you got yourself a really cheap one there. You did. You did indeed. Her behavior has no reflection on your character. I ran out of the revival because she grabbed me. We were there, in front of God and everybody. She rammed her hand down inside my pants at the altar. She was fondling my crotch."

He paused. Sadly, he nodded. "She has no shame, just no shame in that girl. I got me one too, the first time."

Daddy's eyes widened.

Roscoe says, "Women like her, leave a trail of sorrow everywhere they plant their feet. They have no heart, no scruples! I am, blessed that God saw fit to give me your sister Tina. Now, there's a good woman."

Red faced, embarrassment, and angry, Daddy kicked the truck tire. His fist beat against the carriage bed. He yelped, "The woman has disgraced me publically. She has brought a reproach upon the family, and our ministry. Damn her to Hell."

Roscoe growled, "Hey, watch it, I know this jalopy isn't much but it's all I have."

Heart pounding, as his temples throbbed. Attempting to calm himself, Daddy breathed deeply. He said, "Sorry, Roscoe. She makes crazy mad. I should never have married her." He sighed, and tenderly he added, "But, I love her."

Now, why did Momma put her hand in Roscoe's pants? She did not have to check his diaper. Grown men do not wear diapers. I could not figure out why the adults were constantly hateful with each other.

I determined it had to be the demon. I nodded, agreeing with myself. Scratching my ear, I picked my nose, and pulled out a booger. I wiped it on the oak bark. Turning, I trotted toward the front door to ask her.

Inside, Momma paused from doing kitchen chores. She squatted to my eye level, pushed back her long locks and firmly held my shoulders. Angrily, she asked, "Who told those lies?"

"Uncle Roscoe," I said, walleyed and pointing toward the driveway. I knew then, it was the demon. The devil was a father of lies, and Roscoe must be his baby boy.

She sighed, and denied all the accusations. "He's a devil," she said.

I had assumed right. Roscoe was a devil. Momma just confirmed it. Glancing through the window, she and I watched him drive away. Irked, Daddy marched toward the house.

Her hands shook as she patted me on the cheek, and her voice trembled. The hint of fear in her tone when she whimpered, "Now, you run along outside and play. It's not true."

I stood eavesdropping outside the open backdoor, I heard Daddy scathingly ask her about the incident. She denied all. I believed her. She said it did not happen.

I figured Roscoe must have felt the Spirit and did not want Him. It could have been the demon making him run away that night. Demons cannot stand the presence of the Holy Ghost.

Maybe it was an accident when he pushed Momma, while rejecting the Holy Ghost. I wasn't sure. I was certain if Momma had grabbed his forbidden zone, she would have a perfectly logical reason. She did not do that! She said she didn't. That is the way it was. Roscoe was a liar. Momma could do no wrong.

Daddy was raging about affairs the entire night. Why was he being so mean to Momma? Why did Roscoe knock her to the ground? She never kissed other men.

Momma said Roscoe was a troublemaker. I thought, why was Daddy constantly yelling at her about a fair? Why, didn't he believe her? Thinking of booths, the animal shows and rides, I question his sanity, if maybe he was crazy, as I drifted off to sleep. I would figure it out on another day.

Community accusations continued. By week's end, Daddy heard, someone had seen Momma and Merl in the parking lot on the backside of the church. They were making out on the backseat of his car. They were having sex while Daddy was preaching. Some said unattended, little Jane was running around outside all alone. Momma and Merl were too busy to notice.

What is sex? The next morning, Momma and Daddy got into another verbal argument. It lasted for days. Would they ever kiss and make up? I worshiped Momma. She was the prettiest Momma in the world. I did not understand why everyone, seemed to always be picking on her. Telling lies about her, and making false accusations. Daddy made me angry for yelling. I was beginning to hate the religious folks who said bad things about Momma, accusing her of the sex.

What was that? It was one of those games adults play. Bad or it would not have everybody in such an uproar.

Momma's alleged hand-in-the-pant episode became a real problem as the rumors spread throughout the surrounding small communities, seemingly overnight. I did not believe she was a wicked girl. She never kissed other men. I did not see her do that.

The accusations about the situation at the altar with Momma and Roscoe brought our family much shame. Repercussions from the tale carried by gossiping old women implying Momma was having sex with Merl on the church parking lot, brought even more grief.

Afterward, Daddy was too embarrassed and angry with her to be a pastor. Social standards and expectations of the religious community required he resign the church. He had to, to save face. He had gotten away with smoking, and a shot of moonshine now and then as a sinning Baptist. Adultery committed by the pastor's wife? This was the big sin, not tolerated.

He could not face his sheep again for humiliation overwhelmed him. He loved her deeply. Daddy protected Momma. Going before the board of deacons alone, he would not put her through their pious grilling. He resigned, refusing to explain or answer their questions during the inquisition.

When Roscoe pulled out of the driveway that day, Daddy forbid any contact with Merl. He forced us to discontinue all fellowship with the Judas family. He suspected, if Momma would do such in church, God only knew with whom, and what she did when we were not around.

Motivated by his jealous heart, conversations changed during the following weeks. Their arguments, fueled by Daddy's strong suspicions became more frequent, as he focused most intense on Merl. Winding up his rages, he said Merl was lazy. The Judas wouldn't work. He had fired him, the same day Roscoe made the accusation. That was the end of the matter as far as he was concerned.

I decided Daddy was a nut. He was crazy for not allowing our Judas neighbors fellowship. Momma did too. She said he was delusional for believing the lies. He acted wacko when he was drunk. Momma kept telling me, Daddy was insane.

I was sad. April Judas was my friend, and I missed her. Momma was right. I agreed. Daddy was crazy. Momma was temperamental. Her temper was as quick, and harsh.

Burning hate seared Daddy's insides, expressed through his outburst of anger, and wrinkled brow. He began hitting strong spirits, the Kick-A-Poo-Joy-Juice. At the mention of Merl's name the putrid rotten, stanch of jealousy washed over him. Any sane person fled his presence as he began to rant while intoxicated.

Drunk on moonshine, he talked to me about a thing called divorce. I did not like the sound of it. The pain was more than Daddy could bear. He cried a lot when he thought no one was watching. I sobbed too when he says, one day we all will live in separate houses.

I over heard many comments, the majority said Momma was a bad girl. Relatives and neighbors, spoke not so kindly of her. I didn't think she was bad, except when she cursed Daddy. That's, when she was as nuts.

They had been who they were as long as I could remember. Why, such a drastic measure now? The thought of a divorce, it did not make sense. However, now the fights became an everyday ritual. I figured eventually they would quit, and make up one more time. That was their previous pattern.

The week he gave up church, Daddy got drunk as Cooter Brown on Friday night. He was feeling his jolly-ol'-good moonshine spirits, and should not have been behind the wheel when he drove us to Delena's burger joint for a sandwich. Jane and Momma stayed at home. It was boys' night out.

When we arrived, I ran inside. Daddy staggered several paces behind. I crawled onto a swivel stool by the counter. Grinning, while waving a dollar bill in Delena's face, I said, "Daddy, and I want a burger. Put lots of pickles on mine."

Delena wrote down the order as Daddy wobbled through the doors. Slamming her receipt booklet on the counter and placing hands on hips, she sneered. "Enoch, I can't serve you drunk, you'll have to wait outside. I'll send little Saul with the burgers. You really need to go home and sleep it off," she barked. Smiling when finished, she winked at me, and fuzzed my dark short hair with her hand.

My mane had changed colors, going from dirty blond, to a darker-shade-brown with a slight red cast. Daddy said it was the color of his deceased uncle Jimmy's. He was Daddy's favorite uncle. He died of Tuberculosis when Daddy was ten-years-old.

Across my face dotted an inch wide band, freckles speckled over the bridge of my nose to the high cheekbones. Momma called them angel kisses.

"Stop," I grunted, while grinning, and slapped her hand away. Delena chuckled, when she turned and strolled into the kitchen. Daddy shrugged, threw his hands up, and swayed out the door.

When I got to the car, he glared over at me. Smirking drunken slurred speech, he says, "The whole world is a chicken sh**."

I pulled a burger out of the bag and laid it on an old Raccoon Springs newspaper beside him. I began wolfing down the other burger and sipped on a bottle of sweet coke. With my mouth full, I struggled to speak. "What's a chicken sh**?" I asked.

He chuckled. "Chad's a mean chicken poop. Your, Momma's a lying chicken poop. Merl is not! He is hog sh**! Delena is a bossy chicken poop," he says.

I swallowed the half-chewed mouthful. "I know Daddy. But what is a chicken poop?" I asked.

Laughing hysterically, he shouted out the parked car's window, "Chicken poop! Chicken poop! Chicken poop! The whole terrible world is a pile of sh**," he said.

I say, "Daddy, you're drunk. Take me home to Momma."

Laughing, he says, "I'm poop, and you're a little chicken poop."

I whined, "Daddy, take me home. You're crazy."

He says, "You really are a chicken poop brat. You love your Momma but you hate me. Everybody hates me. You think I'm crazy just like everyone tells you." Bowing his head over the steering wheel, he sighed.

"I love yah, Daddy," I mumbled, dropping a chomped morsel from my lips while reaching across the seat to pat him on the shoulder. I picked up the wad and poked it back inside my mouth.

Daddy raised his head. "Dookie! Dookie! That's, what it is, Son. The same stinking poops as in Jane's diaper. It comes from the chicken behind. The whole world is a chicken butt," he seethed.

Knowing the meaning of the word dookie, I threw my burger on the newspaper beside his. Shouting, I say, "I am no chicken dookie. Take it back! Take it back now!"

Daddy laughed, and started the car.

I say, "You might be a drunkard chicken dookie. I am not dookie! Take me home to Momma."

He drove us to the house, laughing uncontrollably, while I pouted. Lips distended, I watched out the car door window. Burning anger throbbing inside my guts, I said nothing.

Momma was right. Daddy was crazy, especially, when he was drunk.

Chocolate Gravy and Father Shaman

Springtime leaves were full-unfurled green. The hills sang with new life, sounds of nature, sights of fledgling birds, and baby critters. New beginnings and young growth brought the change of a season. Colors of hot pink, tones of blue, shades of yellow, purple, and white splashed a tapestry of happy hues. The bright glory of flowering foliage painted the promise of a good growing time, and hopes of an exceptional harvest.

Hot days of summer were drawing nearer. The dogwood and redbud's blossoms faded and dropped off branches. Nineteen fifty-nine's, berry harvest was bountiful. The plentiful strawberry crops foreshadowed what was to come.

This would be Momma's abundant reaping season too. She would harvest what she secretly and deliberately had sown. None of us but Momma knew exactly what her garden held. The good or rotten fruit from her fields was an abundant yield too surely, be discovered.

On a warm Friday morning, the week after learning the whole world was a chicken butt, Jane and I played with our toys in the living room. Home had no running water except for when we peed in the chamber pots at night. Momma drew pails of rain from the cistern near the back porch. She placed an enamel dishpan filled with fresh water on the wood cook stove. She organized, getting ready to bath us, and to wash dishes while preparing breakfast.

They sat having coffee across from each other at the kitchen table. In only green plaid boxer shorts, with a wash pan and a mirror in front of him, Daddy sharpened his razor on a wide leather strap. Carefully, he proceeded with his morning ritual shaving his face.

Momma stood. Her cleavage showing slightly through the fading nightgown he bought her on their wedding anniversary the year before. She strolled toward the wood cook stove behind Daddy.

He turned, watching her slim brown form float past him. Like a ballerina in silk lace, she carried herself with poise and grace. She was his Cherokee princess. Politely, she refilled his cup before hers then placed the pot back on the stove. She kissed him on top of the head as she returned to her seat. He smiled and went back to shaving.

Some minutes later, Momma raised herself from the table, staring right through him. She said nothing.

Glancing up from the mirror and stopping to sip his coffee, he asked, "What you got on your mind, Honey?"

Shaking her head while coming out of a deep trance like state of thought, she replied, "I'm taking the children with me to pick canning berries." She sat, sipping the steaming hot black coffee from the thin glass cup.

Enoch was looking up from the mirror again, glaring suspiciously at her. He says, "There are no more berries. You're using this as an excuse to meet him."

Her tender composure and smiling, delightful face changed to frustration as her brow wrinkled. She says, "Oh crap. Here we go again."

I often wondered how Daddy would feel if Momma accused him of kissing Merl. He probably wouldn't like it either. I motioned for Jane to pay attention.

Finished shaving he tossed the razor into the wash pan full of hot soapy water. Splash, foamy leaped over the edges. Water ran off the table onto the cracked and worn linoleum. He wiped the remaining cream off his smooth-shaven face with a clean hand towel while keeping his mouth shut in a tight line.

When he shot to his feet, with a crash the oak-chair he sat in, fell over backward. Red faced, as his blood pressure raced up. Jugglers bulged with every beat of his heart. Holding back his rage, he calmly asked, "Do you not have any shame?"

She tossed her hair back off her shoulders. "I hate you. You're crazy! This marriage is never going to work. I want a divorce," she says.

Pounding the table, he pleaded, "You've got to consider the children," he says.

"I do a-hell-of-a-lot more for these kids than you even think about. Saul will tell you the truth," she shrieked.

"I forbid you. I do not want you around Merl. I won't sign any divorce papers," he growled back at her, motioning for me to come to his side.

I crawled off the sofa and ran to him, bright eyed and grinning. "What, Daddy?" I asked.

His eyes cut down toward me, and then hatefully looked up at Momma. He questioned, "Have you seen your momma kissing Merl?"

"No Daddy. Never," I said, and raced to kiss Momma.

She scolded, and pushed me away. "Go in the living room and play with Jane," she barked.

Momma had never shoved me away before. Something was wrong. I darted toward the sofa, trying not to bawl, and sat with Jane who was playing with a small red-haired doll.

Sarcastically, contemptuously, rolling her eyes, Momma mumbled, "I don't want you around Merl," she mocked. Then she yelled, "Go pray to your God like your momma did. He'll tell you the truth. He'll tell you this marriage was made in Hell."

Furious, he blurted, "Ma was right. You don't love me. I should have killed Merl years ago."

"I tell you. I'm not bedding down with Merl. He is just my friend. That is much more than I can say for you. I am not a loose woman. I'm a lady," she shrieked while beginning to sob.

Daddy turned. His brow stern, as a silent tear rolled down his cheek. He checked on Jane and me yearningly, as though we could come to his rescue. His gaze shifted toward Momma.

"Saul and Jane don't need to hear this. Now, shut it up before I shut you up," he whispered.

Momma threw her coffee cup across the table. Daddy ducked. It shattered into several tiny pieces on the floor beside the wood-cooker. Jane crawled from the other end of the sofa and huddled close to me for reassurance.

Momma ran out the back door screaming, "You fool. You're nothing but a simple-minded fool, listening to gossip mongers."

Daddy peered out the open door. Momma was racing toward the barn, cursing every breath.

We watched them from our perch on the sofa. Jane and I were peeking through the space between Daddy's long legs while he stood in the open frame of the outside doorway. We could see Momma flash across the pasture.

He wiped the hot coffee off his right shoulder with the same towel he used to clean his face of shaving cream. He drew up the half bowl of chocolate gravy left over from breakfast. Playfully, he cracked a smile. He winked. Wearing his infamous sinister grin, out the door he bolted. He hurdled off the porch taking great strides toward Momma.

She was dashing wildly. The closer he got, the louder she cursed. Like an Olympic sprinter with his six-foot-three muscled frame and long legs he pursued her. Faster he flew. He intercepts her fifty feet from the house.

Giggling, Jane and I hurried to the back porch. Daddy had a thing about pouring gunk on Momma's head when they fought. We knew what was coming. It was not going to be pretty.

They fell on the green ground, Betsy's spot. Soft, tall pasture foliage cushioned their descent. Betsy, our milk cow chose the area as favorite grazing. The tender shoots of rye grass and fescue surrounded them as the cow chewed her cud nearby.

"You will stop seeing him. You will obey me, Ora," he says, followed by evil laughter.

They struggled, rolling over the dew-covered ground. Daddy held her penned beneath him and rubbed the warm gravy on her head. He laughed hysterically as she cursed, and they continued to tussle.

Betsy strolled over toward them. She stuck her snout on Momma's head, sniffed, and waved out her long wide tongue to lick.

Daddy slapped Betsy on the muzzle. "Git," he shouted.

She bawled and trotted off toward the hollow with her heavy teats swaying back and forth between her hind legs. He had hurt Betsy's feelings. The next day's milk would be bitter. Every time scolded, she would hide in the hollow. Gourds grew there. Maybe, Daddy would give the bitter, putrid milk to the hogs. I wasn't going to drink the rotten stuff again.

Howling, and wailing Momma continued to fight. She cursed him even louder as he painted the remaining brown sweet goo on her face. She stopped struggling from exhaustion. He kissed her passionately, and released her arms.

She responded by whacking him upsides the head with the empty glass bowl. He kissed her again. She surrendered to his affections, wrapping her arms around him in a gentle embrace. They lay there, and held each other for the longest time.

Momma and Dad were fighting frequently, again. Often, bloodletting came from their blows. Nevertheless, their quarrels ended the same way. Kissing and everything was fine until the next round. Most of the time Jane and I squalled. Not this time, they made up quickly. There was no blood!

I dumped chocolate gravy in Jane's hair weeks before. Momma paddled me. She forced a promise, never again. She let Jane dump gravy on my head the next day. I cried for half an hour. Daddy should not do Momma that way. I decided to throw gravy on his head when he was asleep, and tell Momma I got him back for her.

Returning to the house, Momma was grinning, but behind the smile was her hidden anger. Humiliated, she wiped the mess out of her locks. Afterward, she proceeded to do her morning chores, absolutely silent.

He pulled on his faded, sap-stained overalls. His soft and tattered, dingy and discolored, green-white cotton-shirt had seen its better days. He slipped on gray socks and heavy worn work boots. Momma lit a cigarette as she swept up the broken cup while he finished dressing.

Making steps toward the door, he says, "Stay away from Merl, I meant it, Ora."

Momma cackled, cutting her dagger eyes, nodding, "Yes, Massa Enoch," she says, bowing before him.

He raised her off the floor, and held her tight in his strong embrace. Jane and I dashed for them, leaping into their arms. He pecked us on the cheek, goodbye. It was off to work again, as he did every day. Rain or shine, he would provide.

Outside he galloped toward the dilapidated '47 pummeled green logging truck parked in the driveway. Crawling inside, he tossed the lard bucket holding his lunch onto the ripped seat. The banger had neither a muffler, nor drive side door. The smashed passenger-door hung in place with bailing wire.

Two weeks earlier, Daddy missed a curve on a steep logging road. When that day's cutting was finished, Momma's older brother, twenty-year-old, rebellious, short and stout Joe helped him load logs higher than the cab on the truck-bed. The laboring vehicle inched its way up the hill from the hollow. After hitting a bump, the laden truck's left-front tire slipped off the road's edge. Daddy ground the gears, and pulled the emergency, but the brake failed. Joe hurdled out the passenger side, yelling for him to jump too.

Daddy threw open the door and vaulted, just as the unmanageable vehicle began to careen down the mountainside through a section of new growth timber. The monstrous truck rolled backwards, struck a tree, and flipped more than three times as it bounced, heading for the hollow.

Hobbled below, eating their daily ration of oats were the danger excited mules. Blaze and Mabel bucked and brayed. Their stretched tethers snapped as they broke free trotting out of harms way up the hill on the other side of the hollow. The truck came to an abrupt crashing stop--upright. All six tires grounded on the snaking road below, from where it was just driven.

Joe sprained his ankles. He could hardly walk as he limped down the steep way and helped Daddy capture, and secure the mules. Okay, the beasts, not harmed, just a little shaken.

Uninjured, Daddy forced open the hood. The engine and battery were intact. The crumpled drive side door was half way up the slope leaning against a bush. He and Joe sat down inside the cab as Daddy hit the ignition. Boom, she fired up at the first turn of the key and they drove home.

With no helper the next day, it was Daddy and the old mules alone. Together, they reloaded the harvested logs dumped the day before.

Two weeks passed, Little Joe, now recovered, returned to work as Daddy's partner. He and Enoch teamed up after the falling out with Merl. This was the beginning of their life long friendship.

Daddy, willingly let Merl go for more than reasons than jealousy. Merl's work habits left him in a bind. Constantly not showing up for work, Merl was causing Daddy to lose badly needed cash.

Daddy was thankful for Joe's help. Joe worked ten times harder, and never missed one day until the accident. He earned his pay.

While absent from the forest and a real job, Merl sold his ma's recipes--moonshine and herbal concoctions. He labeled, and peddled "Doctor-Feel-Good," over in the next county.

He took the title of Father Shaman, claiming to be an Indian herbalist healer when vending the jolly spirits. He says that the spirits of Sitting Bull and Crazy Horse rested upon him. They were his spiritual guides and helpers. He was their chosen one, and blessed with supernatural talents. He claimed the ancestors' spirits favor, made his medical marvel remedies powerful stuff.

Those not so naive and knowing him best said the spirit of Sitting Bull-Crap squatted on him, squashing his small brain. He was the ultimate flimflam, manipulator. Merl possessed no remorse for taking advantage of the less fortunate, uninformed, or ignorant. He would try any swindle, to get out of physical labor.

Father Shaman, the healer, pretending to be a Pentecostal preacher, held a brush arbor revival over in the next county. The offerings were too meager. He would perfect the idea, and try it again at a future date. Merl Judas, the ultimate oxymoron, loved and hated at the same time.

Daddy heard, and planned to rib him good over the fake preacher sham, at a time when he was not so angry. For now, Merl was on his sh** list. Daddy said Merl was lazy, and he needed a dependable helper. Disassociating was not a great loss. Daddy insisted he was through with ol' lazy Merl, once-and-for-all. His fears of losing Mamma, and the turmoil caused by the green-eyed monster, Jealousy, made the decision for him. He was glad Merl and Lilly didn't come around every day.

The house windows rattled when he started the motor, and drove off. Gone, Momma pitched the broom onto the back porch, and seethed, "Slim chance, you jerk."

I found myself angry a lot when Daddy made the accusations that Momma was having an affair. I did not know exactly what the meaning. It had something to do with kissing, touching, and sharing a thing called sex. What is that? It must have been more exciting and intoxicating for the adults than the moonshine.

Sometimes, I could not tell if they were playing or if the fighting was for real. Home life was confusing, frightening, and a little insecure for Jane and me. Especially, now that I understood the words divorce, chicken poop, and hog sh**. Those were the kind of words . . . I did not like to hear. These were bad words.

Paul E. Treadwell

Recompense, Blood, Flesh and Bone Flew

She cleaned the table of dirty breakfast dishes. Washing them in an enamel pan. When finished, she dumped the foul water out the back door. She warmed bath water, while Jane and I stood on the kitchen table.

Momma checked all our parts high and low, between and in the dark places for ticks. She scrubbed us with lye soap and a rough washrag. Our daily ritual finished, she lifted Jane, and then me off the table and buffed us dry with a coarse towel.

Heating more water, she shampooed her long wavy hair. Momma vigorously bathed herself in the privacy of their bedroom. Meanwhile, Jane and I ran wildly, naked and giggling through every room inside our plank shack. The strong, sweet smell of perfume drifted through the air after Momma gave herself a liberal spraying. Her damp, black-hair neatly combed, she dressed us in fresh-smelling-line-dried garments.

"Last one in the car, be a stinkin' rotten egg," she chirped, and chuckled. Playfully she teased, tickling us when we raced outside. After loading us into the '57 Chevy, she started the engine and cranked up the static, fuzzy sounding, a.m. radio to a rock 'n' roll station. Momma began to sing, and backed out of the long drive to the main road.

Our hair swirled, dancing with the warm breeze rushing through the rolled down windows. Elvis Presley singing "Hound Dog," vibrated through our bodies as we sped up the highway. I squinted, and shook my head, disapproval, frowning. Daddy called this the devil's music.

"Where are we goin' Momma?" I ask.

"To Bonner field for canning berries," she says.

Momma did indeed, drive us to the strawberry patch, but berries were not what was on her mind. I knew there were no berries. Other local families had already taken the best and cleaned the vines, bare. We were there only the week before and found no fruit then. The berry harvest was over. Perhaps, we would go to another field.

"But Momma, the berries are all gone," I say. My words hang suspended, and seemed without a purpose. She did not answer.

She parked on the road next to the patch and left the radio on. Another Elvis Presley tune, "Heartbreak Hotel," was playing, when I see off in the distance, at the edge of the field stood a man.

I thought he was Merl Judas. Momma was a devoted Elvis fan. Merl resembled Elvis. The likeness was a big deal for her, and him.

Glowing as she opened the door and got out of the car. She says, "You kids wait here, and behave yourselves. I won't be long."

Like a wild and free mustang, she galloped two-beat strides across the spacious, fruitless, faded-green field. Her mane bouncing as she swiftly made her way toward Merl. Waiting, his arms unfurled, and she fell into his embrace.

Watching them share a long, passionate kiss, I thought that Daddy's suspicions were correct. She was kissing another man. I had to tell him.

As I curiously observed a sudden wave of nausea came over me. Fearful angry tears rolled down my cheeks, and I wailed hysterically. The word divorce pounded inside my head. My wailing upset Jane and she howled. In my anger, I lay on the car horn. We screamed so loud that Momma heard us over the annoying blast of the horn and the blaring music. She and Merl ran back to the car to see what the matter was.

Aggravated, her piercing brown eyes glared at me. I knew that look very well. Would she paddle me? No, she slapped my hands off the horn switch.

Realizing neither of us was hurt, she scolded our making such a fuss. Then she lightly knuckled my head and fuzzed my short hair as she smirked. We stopped crying.

Resentfully, I watched her hug Merl goodbye. This did not feel right. I'm not so sure I liked our Judas neighbor anymore. I did not want him kissing Momma.

Daddy was not crazy after all. Momma insisted he was delusional. I no longer believed her. She was a liar and a deceiver. I had witnessed it myself. Yes, I would tell Daddy.

She got into the car. I kept quiet, angry, thinking it was as everyone had said, as Daddy had said. I stood up in the seat and turned to look out the back glass as we drove away. Merl was waving. Momma was smiling. What was that word? Oh yes, I remembered, affair.

Entranced by the music as she drove, Momma flipped through the stations to find another song. She lit a cigarette, and exhaled.

Sick to my stomach I did not speak for most of the five-mile drive. When she pulled off the main highway onto the dirt road that led to our place, my face wadded like a dried prune. Furious, my silence broke with a gush of tears. I could no longer contain the avalanche of negative emotion wailing up inside of me. I announced, "I'm gonna tell, Daddy."

Enraged, she tossed her burning smoke out the window, saying nothing for a moment. Her cold, disapproving eyes cut through my soul.

Elvis', "Don't Be Cruel," played when she tried to convince me the scene I had just observed was not what I thought it was. She explained that she and Merl were only good friends, nothing more. The embrace and kiss were excitement from not seeing him for so long.

Reacting to the sound of her words like a threatened badger pup, "You shouldn't be kissing Merl. Not on the lips, Daddy told me so," I said.

She says, "Child, don't you get smart with me. I should slap your sniveling face, right now."

Questioning her, I asked, "Why are you lying to me? Daddy says only married folks kiss on the lips. You said so!"

Again, with a firm voice, she denied what I had seen and demanded I say nothing. Expressing her frustration, she tuned to a different station. Grimacing, she tossed her lengthy dark-locks over the seat back. Above the boom of the radio she bellowed, "We're not talking about this anymore. Keep your mouth shut. You'll only make problems worse between your pa and me."

I felt the overwhelming urge to vomit. Just as she was turning onto our long, gravel driveway, I whined, "Momma, stop, I'm gonna puke."

She nodded, frustrated. "Let me park in the regular spot. You can wait two minutes," she says.

I could not wait. Desperate with nausea, I opened the passenger door, intending only to hang my head outside so I wouldn't mess up the car. Soon as I pulled the handle, the door swung completely open and yanked me out of my seat. I found myself hanging with my head and chest suspended over the gravel roadway that whizzed by beneath me.

She screamed, panicked stricken. She cried with a loud voice, "Saul, don't open the door. Shut the door. Oh, Baby."

I heard her defeated whimpers. It was too late. "Momma, help me." I pleaded, while struggling to hang onto the door latch and fought to keep my feet and legs inside.

She hollered again, this time letting-go of the steering wheel as she grabs for me. I felt her hand touch the tail of my shirt just as my legs dragged out. She could not hold me.

I clung to the door handle with all my might and attempted to pull my feet up under my body. It was a futile effort.

The door swung back toward the car. Now my upper body was wedged between the moving automobile chassis and the half-open door. Unable to hold my legs up any longer, I let them fall. They bounced along the roadbed and I watched as rocks ripped into them, tearing off the flesh.

I heard the engine roar. The car lurched forward, going even faster, and gaining momentum at the passing of every second. My arms grew weak. My hands slipped and I tumbled to the ground. Landing flat on my back, my head prickled at the center of a cactus tree alongside the driveway. My frightened brown eyes opened just in time to see the rear tire spin over the top of my left ankle.

In her confusion and horror, Momma hit the gas instead of the brakes. The blood, skin, and flesh flew through the air behind the back tire. The fast-whirling motion of the wheel pulverized, and splashed away all the soft tissue while crushing bone. Road dirt and tiny pebbles were ground into the open wound. Momma very nearly crashed into the side of the house, stopping only two feet from impact.

Overwrought, screaming Jane had seen the shower of blood. I could hear her bellows. Jane always squealed at the sight of blood. Frightened eyes on her terror wrenched face, as little Jane watched through the back glass. She pulled and yanked at her dark-brown hair.

Momma frantically jumped out and bolted to my side, sobbing uncontrollably. "Oh, baby, I am so sorry," she says, with a crackling, crying voice.

Her hot tears splashed downward onto my face, into my eyes. Mingling with mine, her tears became my tears, as they bled together. My anger with her was gone, only empathy for her grieving heart surged through my young mind. I did not like to see Momma cry.

She asked, was I in pain. I told her, no. Miraculously, the leg was numb. I felt no pain. I was experiencing only warmth, and a sense of perfect peace all around me. My love for Momma intensified as she wept hysterically.

I wailed, for being unable to comfort her. My tears were not for physical pain's sake. Rather, I wept over her heart's ache.

Between shrieks, terror, and yowls of grief she sobbed and whimpered, "This is my fault, God's recompense!"

The accident was not her blunder, but guilt ate at her soul. Maybe it was her sin. Daddy's sermons always connected "recompense" to repercussions of a sin. Not understanding that word completely, I ignored it.

"No Momma, I'm to blame. I opened the door," I said, wanting to console her.

Moments before, her deep-tan pretty face, washed white from shock. Moaning, trembling, saying nothing, as she hoisted me into her slim arms, and raced for the car. Blood spewed profusely from my nearly severed ankle, leaving a trail of crimson across the yard and blotting her skirt.

I sat on the front seat as she wrapped taut my injured limb in Jane's new Easter coat, which happened to still be in the backseat. Jane had worn it to Easter Sunday church services weeks before. As I watched it being soaked with my blood, I knew she would never put it on again.

Jane and Momma continued to caterwaul. The radio played. We shrilled and howled. Having no telephone to call for help, she had to drive us. There was no other choice, but to let me bleed to death, or make attempt to get help. Shaken near out of her mind, she chose to drive.

Through her veil of tears, Momma could hardly see the byway. Her nerves were rattling violently behind the steering wheel. She inched the '57 toward a neighbor's, a-half-mile away.

Paul E. Treadwell

Paint It Red

Mary Jones, twenty years older, was Momma's best friend, second to Lilly. Now that we spent little time with the Judas family, she and Mary became closer.

Mary played the piano during church services. She had six stair-step children who often came to our house on visits. She babysat Jane and me on occasion, and we stayed overnight with her children from time to time. I had a crush on her eldest daughter, Sally Mae.

Momma didn't know about the crush. I was not sure myself why I felt this way at such young age. Pretty is pretty at any age. Thinking, I'm in-love with a high school senior, because she was as beautiful as Momma was.

This day, Mary's offspring were at the Baptizing Hole. The splendor and beauty of God's handiwork, an artesian spring half-a-mile down in the hollow behind their home was a sight of great beauty. Flowing, natural spring waters were icy-cold year round. Many church folks baptized there. Most of the Hotman clans submerged at the place, going back generations. Mary's children were gone. They were out for a cold swim. Her offspring were taking a refreshing dip in the Baptizing Hole leaving Mary alone.

Cutting the wheels too sharply, Momma, missed the turn into Mary's driveway. The Chevy jumped the ditch, sending us bouncing inside as the car came to an abrupt stop. Momma leaped out yelling, "Help me. Help me, Mary."

Her long-waves tossed from side to side as she galloped for the shanty. Pounding the door, she shouts, "Mary! Mary! Mary!" No answer, a pause, and she screamed again, pounding on the door, tears streaming down her cheeks. She bellows, "My baby is dying."

Adrenaline surging through her body, wide-eyed Mary bounded out of the house. White sticky bread dough was on her hands. Wearing a half-skirt apron around her waist, she gave chase, following Momma racing back to the car.

Pre-mature-graying-hair, Mary caught and grabbed Momma's arm. Mary said, "I'm here honey." They sprinted together toward Jane and me, as we sat waiting and watching.

Momma raised her face toward Heaven, anguishing, "I can't drive, Oh God, don't let my baby die," she wailed.

Wiping the kneaded dough off her hands onto the apron, great calm in her tone, Mary proclaimed, "He's not going to die."

Then she hoisted me out with her stocky arms and placed me on the front seat of her black '53 Plymouth. The smell of warm yeast drifted up to my nostrils as my bloody leg swiped against her soiled apron. On any other day, handsome Mary would allow me to sample one of her hot fresh buttered rolls. The scent was so strong. My stomach churned. On this day the aroma, and thought of eating one, repulsed me.

Smiling, Mary reassuring, whispered, "Don't be afraid, Honey. Your momma and I are going to get you to Doc Anderson. He will stop the bleeding. God is not going to let you die."

I nodded.

Momma was trailing behind us as she shuffled Jane the few feet from our back seat into Mary's Plymouth. We sat waiting, watching Mary dash inside the house for keys. Bellowing, Momma slithered into the front passenger side, and lifted me onto her lap.

She squeezed Jane's bloody Easter jacket taut around my ankle again. At that, a crimson stream flooded the floorboard beneath us, splashing onto her white cloth tennis shoes. My blood coated her hands.

Mary charged out of the house, and lunged into the driver's seat. She started the car. Spinning tires as she backed out of the driveway. We flew toward Raccoon Springs.

Mary's large blue eyes sparkled as sunlight reflected off the moisture, while she fought to hold back her tears. She grimaced, trying to cover her anxious feelings. She quoted scripture.

Mary says, (Ezekiel 16:6) "And when I passed by thee, and saw thee polluted in thine own blood, I said unto thee when thou wast in thy blood, Live; yea, I said unto thee when thou wast in thy blood, Live." She said it over, and over again, believing the stop blood scripture. Even Momma jumped in a time or two, as they spoke the holy words in unison. They continued praying, quoting Scripture, while the car zoomed around the winding curves over the steep hills.

Looking down, I beheld a lagoon of blood on the rubber mat beneath our feet rolling back and forth at every sharp curve. The scarlet liquid body-fluid was washing the dirty black rubber mat, a color red. My blood, but it could not clean white as snow. Only Jesus blood could do that for sinners, I thought. Like when Daddy preached his sermon, "His Blood Washing Dirty Sinners Clean."

I wondered would the mess down there come out. I am not Jesus. How would anyone ever get the stains out of our cars? Momma always insisted Jane and I help clean up our messes. I figured. It would be my job to clean this up too, when I got better. This all started with me not wanting to soil the carpet in our car. Now two automobiles were a ruined bloody mess.

Momma's bawling saddened me to tears again. She continued wailing, and held me closer. Jane cried too. Momma wept harder when Jane tried to comfort us by reaching over the back of the seat to kiss us through her own fright. Salty teardrops gyrated down Momma's face and permeated onto my shirt.

I say, "Don't cry Momma." I pleaded again, while wiping a wet sparkling speckle from her chin.

Calming some, she asked, "Oh baby is it hurting badly?"

I shook my head.

"Then why are you crying?" she asked

I say, "Because it hurts me to see you squalling."

We both grinned. She stroked my forehead and bellowed like a newborn calf when I began drifting off to sleep in her arms from the expenditure of blood. Her panic screams unnerved me. I awakened, and immediately fell asleep again. We drove the six miles from Loafer's Glory to Raccoon Springs. I am unconscious most of the trip.

Arriving, Momma roused me. She tells me to clamp my arms around her neck and hold tight then she would carried me inside. I was drunk. In and out, I tried to do as she requested so I would not fall--going unaware again, and then blackness. I awoke once more, as Momma hoisted me into her arms, and slid out of the car, then again came darkness.

She carried me inside the small hospital. Coming to, reeling and weak, I desperately tried to keep my arms around her neck when she lays me on the emergency room table. Jane and Mary remained in the waiting room. The nurse forced Momma to step out of the cold chamber and sit with them. I was not having any part of it.

"Don't leave me, Momma," I whimpered.

Momma jumped to her feet. She ran to the doors, and stepped inside again. Nervously, wrenching her hands together, she sobbed, "I'll be right outside, Honey," she said. An orderly slams the heavy wooden door in her face. Again, I could no longer see her.

Unexpectedly, the doctor slapped a nasty smelling rag over my nose and mouth. I could not breathe and threw it off, while fighting with the nurse's soft hands when she put it back, attempting to kill me again.

I never smelled anything so horrible in all my life. Jane's soiled diapers could not even begin to compare. I managed to get free again.

The nurse held down my arms while the aging doctor forced the rag over my face once more. He says nothing.

Slowly losing consciousness, fighting, determined to get away. I struggled. My muffled screams turned to whimpers as I tried to holler at the ancient graying, thinning-haired doctor.

"I hate you. Leave me alone." I mumbled the phrase again, thinking he was my executioner. They were monsters. I would never leave this horrid place alive.

Compassionately, the middle-aged nurse with luminous red hair under her cap says, "Don't struggle, sweeties, try to relax. We aren't going to hurt you."

Right, I didn't believe her. I squirmed even more to get away from her grasp, and the pungent odor. My fight was gone. The effort had been futile. Everything faded away--blackness, nothingness remained.

I awakened, smelling ether. Groggy, I heard Doc Anderson's concerned voice in the distance as Momma held me in her arms.

"Ms. Hotman, we stopped the bleeding. The bandages will need changed in a couple of days. Bring him back. His leg is broken in eleven places," he said.

Safety, comfort of Momma's arms, I dozed off again. I awakened at home, lying on the sofa, too weak, unable to sit up. Neighbors, friends and relatives gathered around, peering down. Their faces and bodies are misshapen. Like, in a carnival house of mirrors.

I am nauseous. The ankle was numb. I felt no pain except for when Momma yanked some of the cactus prickles out of my scalp with tweezers. I whined for her to stop. She did, and then she kissed me on the forehead. Her eyes were bloodshot and puffy from constant crying.

My vision cleared a bit. I was happy to see everyone, until my eyes caught a glimpse of someone off in the distant doorway connecting the kitchen. There she stood, the witch, Merl's mother Bertha. She claimed to be the local hexane, proud of her dark proclamations. She looked like one too. She was homely, skinny, seventy-years-old with wrinkled swarthy skin, and dingy-white-gray hair to her hips. Most of her rotten teeth were missing. Her black eyes seemed to cut right through to the soul with evil. Her smile was that of a jack-o-lantern. I closed my eyes, and turned my head.

When I opened them again, Bertha and Momma kept glancing at each other, as though they shared a secret. I knew their secret--Father Shaman--Merl.

Daddy told me Bertha's heart was dark with wickedness, and blasphemies against the Lord. She frightened me. I did not want her around. I was afraid she and Merl would take our momma away.

Jane and I had heard her cursing. Profaning her family many times, her harsh obscenities echoed across the hollows.

Merl was at her house a lot. His home was only a few yards from hers. Jane and I never crossed over into Bertha's yard on our past visits while at Merl's house. Many stories abounded about her being a mean witch. Often folks mispronounce the word, "witch." They state it with a "B," instead of "W."

I figured the words were interchangeable--B or W. Witch or bit**, but the defining name didn't matter to me. I was simply afraid of the woman. Had she cast the spell on me to make Momma hate us and love Merl? Those were my secret thoughts.

Numerous visitors came, so many I could not count them on all my fingers and toes. They came, expressing sincere concern. Their offerings of help were good tidings from the local gracious community, and neighbors. Our caring community was like having an extended family. I was glad to see most of them. However, too frightful to look upon, there was another woman. I did not know her. She was ugly as sin, with an extremely long crooked nose. I closed my eyes so not to see.

I wanted the Judas witch Bertha and the long nose woman to leave. They did not stay long. I was sighing relief when they were gone. Maybe, they would not come back.

Retarded Rafter, now six, came with his grandmother Bertha. Della's boy, the spawn of illegitimacy, he was conceived out of wedlock. It was said, she too be retarded. The Judas clan labeled her nuts; because, she said Merl had hurt her whoo-whoo since she was four-years-old. Rumor had it that Rafter was possibly Merl's son.

Rafter and crazy were a lot alike. Crazy was worse, especially when Daddy was drunk. Della didn't come to see me that afternoon. I was glad she stayed away. Fat and un-groomed with long-black-stringy-hair, she smelled strong, the odor of sour pee.

Delena said eighteen-year-old Della was nasty, nasty as could be, a grown woman and she still wet the bedding at night. Being around her gave me the he-bee-gee-bees. I was glad she did not come.

Rafter brought a small dartboard he found on the side of the road. I held the dirty piece of cardboard. For some reason I cherished his gift. I felt pity for Rafter. However, I could hardly stand to be in the same room with him. He too, had a pungent unsavory body odor.

I thanked him with a grin. He held my hand the entire time he was there after Bertha walked home. Little Rafter had no friends, or playmates. He never left my side, as I visited with him and others, best I could. The attention and gifts perked up my spirits. Before a long time past, once again, I descended into unconsciousness.

Evening shadows came upon us as the sun began to set. My fever rose to one-hundred-five degrees. Tall and brawny Chad after getting the news, went directly from his sawmill to chat with Doc Anderson. Doc insisted I needed to see a specialist.

Uncle Chad, drove to the homestead, and spoke with my parents. Told them to make sure my fever didn't rise. If it did, they were to get me to the hospital in Little Rock immediately. He knew they did not have any cash on hand. He was concerned that I would not get the proper and necessary care.

Blurry eyed, I awoke as Chad knelt over me. He smelled of tobacco smoke, soured wood, and sawdust. He always smelled that way. He ran his strong, but gentle hand over my hair. He sighed, and examined me as Momma and Daddy watched.

"You best get this boy to a hospital emergency room now, or you will bury him this time tomorrow. He's hot as Hell," he snorted.

Am I going to die like Grandmother Anne? Maybe, I needed to pray in her strange language. Would I go to heaven? No, I am not going to die. Mary said so. I will fight, I thought, as I succumb to the fever and drifted off to sleep again.

The family war veteran, Chad fought in Germany. He knew the face of death from battle wounds. He was familiar with the pungent odor of Adolf Hitler's Nazi concentration camps, rotting bodies, the stench of burning human flesh, and the many odors of war.

Feared, and despised for his harshness and blunt manner, his word always respected as law by everyone in the family. He was only thirteen-years-old when his pa, Isaiah died of rabbit fever. Chad became surrogate father for Daddy and his other siblings. His word ruled second only to Anne's, while she lived. Now, his wishes above all others were law. Intimidated by his harsh manner, Momma resented him immensely. She was not alone.

Tenderness buried under his strident image--gentleness most never saw. I felt it and observed his hidden weakness on many occasions. He and I did our best. We kept the secret. There was kindness beneath his scowl.

I came around about the time Chad hoisted me into his arms, and carried my limp body outside the house. Momma opened the door. He lays me on a blanket in the backseat of his car. Momma ran inside to gather wet towels, ice, and packed an overnight bag. We sped to the Little Rock Baptist Hospital, a hundred-mile trip from home.

Chad gave the medical center one-hundred dollars for admission. Momma hardly had money to buy a coke. He handed her a twenty-dollar bill, before leaving.

Daddy stayed behind. He made arrangements, someone to care for Jane. The next day he arrived, driving our blood stained Chevy. He brought Momma extra clothing, and cigarettes.

Making the trip with him was Aunt Delena, Uncle Chad, Uncle Joe, and good-hearted neighbor, Mary. My blood type was rare. None found, in the hospital blood bank. They came to be tested, hoping to be a match. I was dying from loss of blood, and a raging infection.

I awoke, strapped to a hospital bed. Momma and Daddy were arguing across the room about the affair with Merl. Momma stuck to her denial. She informed Daddy that he was a mad man, for believing lies and gossip.

She said she had not seen Merl in weeks other than to wave at Lilly when driving past their house. Hypnotized by his love for her. He wanted to believe. However, the serpent, a jealous demon had a strong hold on him. I knew she was a liar. Sulking, I drifted off to sleep again.

Moments later Daddy awakened me. Kissed my forehead, then he squeezed my shoulder with his large calloused hand. He says, "Son, be brave. I've gotta to go back for Jane, and take the other folks home. We want to stay longer, but can't."

I nodded, saying, "Okay Daddy. I'm brave! Momma is here. You go take care of Jane."

He had stretched his credit to the limit with the new automobile and furniture. He labored as many hours a day as possible or we could lose everything. He told me so. The good-bye saddened his heart, but I knew it was necessary.

I ask, "Who are the others?"

He says, "Aunt Delena, Uncle Chad, Uncle Joe, and Mary."

I ask, "Pa, may I see them?"

He says, "Son, Doc says you don't need a lot of excitement, until you get your strength back. They'll file by the door and wave as we head out."

Disappointed, I say, "Okay, Pa."

One-by-one, the well-wishers stuck their heads inside the room through the open doorway. Speaking briefly, then, they were gone. Uncle Joe didn't show. I wondered why, while falling into unconsciousness, again.

A little while later, I awakened to discover gnawing needles and snaking tubes stuck into my strap down arms. I could not move them.

Shivering, dazed, I thought these must be copperheads. Not thinking clearly, I look again. No! Perhaps, these are the doctor's torture-tools! Are needles actually red wasp stingers? Two glass bottles filled with red, hung on a rack at the foot of my bed.

I call out, "Momma."

A tall blond nurse came into the room. Towering over my small form, she grinned.

"Where's Momma?" I asked.

She explained Momma had gone to get something to eat with the rest of the family. She would be right back, but Uncle Joe was waiting outside the door to see me.

I asked, "Why is he here? Why didn't he go with the others?"

She says, "He was the only perfect match. He gave as much blood as possible, because you needed a lot."

She continued explaining, "None of the others could donate, and those with the same type had low counts. Only, your uncle Joe shared his gift of life."

Pausing for a moment to check the IV drip, and to adjust my pillow, she says, "He fainted after the blood draw. He was forced to lie down, rest, and drink orange juice before leaving."

I asked, "Is he okay?"

She said, "He is feeling better now. Your Momma is bringing him something to eat for the trip home. She should be here any minute. I'll let your uncle stick his head inside the doorway to say hello. But then you go back to sleep, young man."

I nodded, and she left the room. Outside in the hallway, I heard her whispering.

To my joy, stout, and short, Uncle Joe swung the door partially open. He pokes his head through the doorway, just as the nurse had promised.

Pointing to the bottles of blood, he says, "Peter Saul, that will make you strong like me. My blood is dripping into your body."

I nodded, and he waved. Shutting the door, he was gone.

Good, in a little while I'll be as powerful as Uncle Joe. As soon as, my veins suck up all his red strong juice. I thought, better stuff then Popeye's spinach.

I did not want him to go. Alone in a strange place surrounded by unfamiliar faces, I wanted Momma. Before I could call out her name again, I fell asleep.

I awoke, a stocky handsome man wearing a dark-blue pinstriped suit peering into my face, calling my name. "Saul, Peter Saul, can you wake up and talk to me?" he asked while tickling me tenderly in the ribs.

Mamma was standing beside him. Exhaustion creased her sullen expression. She held my hand in moody silence. I was reassured at her presence, as I stared into his large brown eyes.

The doctor had ruddy cheeks from being in the sun. His short dark-brown hair highlighted with sparkles of gray sprinkled throughout. He combed it neatly back.

I liked his big pearly white teeth when he smiled. His breath was as if mint candy, and he wore a light and spicy man's cologne.

I never knew a man could smell as sweet, as a woman, but in a strong way. When he cheerfully spoke about the upcoming operation, and the reasons for all the tubes and bottles attached to my arms, I was comforted. He calmed our fears.

Reaching over he ruffled my hair, then tapped my chin with his right index finger.

"You're a courageous, bright boy. I'm going to have my wife come visit you after surgery," he said.

We smiled at each other.

"She will probably bring you something special for your bravery," he said.

Thrilled, grinning, I asked, "A new set of toy soldiers?"

"Is that what you want?" he asked.

I nodded, and asked, "Will, you give back my arms?"

He asked, "Do you promise not to pull at the tubes and needles?"

I say, "Yes sir."

He says, "Good man." At that, he unleashes the binds.

I say, "Thank you."

He winks and says, "You're welcome." Then he ruffled my hair again.

He says, "Okay, Peter Saul. We will see you in a few hours. You are such a brave little man."

Momma kissed me on the forehead, and they left the room. I fell asleep dreaming the promise of new toys.

I awakened to find my arms and legs strapped again, this time to the operating table. My head restrained. The needles and tubes remained--infusing the veins of my arms. Momma was there at my side.

Doctor Nix, now dressed in green surgical scrubs, leaned over and told me, I have a staph infection. They were going to do everything possible to save the limb, but if they could not, they may have to amputate and give me an artificial leg below the knee with a wooden foot. The corruption was spreading rapidly.

Snarling, I peered up at him. "Save it," I shouted.

The surgical team and Momma chuckled. Doctor Nix and I were best buds. I am having full confidence he will not saw off my leg. His eyes were laughing along with the others and me. A giant smile emerged between his lips.

He said, "We'll do our best. But . . ."

I interrupted him, "A wooden foot?" I asked.

He nodded.

"Paint it red, and blue if it comes to the worse," I said.

"You got it." He said, as he lifted his gaze toward Momma.

I closed my eyes dreading even the remotest possibility of losing a leg. I had to be brave, not letting them see my anxiety. If I didn't, Momma would fall to pieces again. Her crying hurt me worse than any physical wounds.

He explained the procedure to Momma. I heard him say, because of my age and weakened state, they would not give me enough anesthesia to put me completely under. He said he would not even start the anesthesia unless I began to feel a lot of pain. I glanced up as he turned to me.

"You're going to be very brave. I just know it," he said.

Fierce faced, I ground teeth, growled and nodded. "Like the soldiers," I responded, reminding him to keep the promise of toys.

He grinned, letting me know he would honor the vow. Then the nurse tied a surgical mask over his face.

He said, "Let's begin."

Vibrations traveled upward the leg, as the knife scraped against broken bone. Remarkably, there was no pain. Finished cleaning the wounded area, he moved around the operating table and leaned over, near my face.

"Well, you're one courageous little man," he said, and continued, "We've got the first part done. But we aren't finished yet."

I nodded, as best I could with head restraints.

He explained they were going to slice skin from my right thigh and graft over the exposed left anklebone. One more time he asked if I was ready.

I nodded, "Okay," I said.

The surgical nurse secured a sheet as a curtain raised high over my chest so I couldn't watch the process. He raised his hand, and I could see above the sheet as she handed him the scalpel.

Feeling the first incision, excruciating pain as the knife cut into my thigh. I grunted once, and then no more pain. Again, the perfect peace I had experienced when the accident occurred.

Heavy crystal-colored tears streamed down Momma's face as she held my hand and stroked my arm. I smiled, as she wiped her salty wet cheeks. Her eyes were showing the exhaustion, with puffiness from the sorrow. She kissed me on the forehead and grinned. Warmth and peace blanketed me. I simply fell asleep.

I awakened on the ward, in the same room, and the same bed as before. The surgery was hours ago, and my eyes peep open to find Momma and Daddy smoking cigarettes. They were arguing again.

Momma wore her baby-blue party dress. Momma looked like she just stepped out of a music-band-box. Resembling pictures, I had seen of celebrated female country music singers on magazine covers. Momma reached over and turned on the radio beside my bed. The sound of soft country music filled the room.

Momma's dream was to be a famous country music star some day. She liked to listen to rock 'n' roll; she couldn't sing the devil's music. She was a country girl, and so was the sound of her voice. I liked her singing especially when she yodeled. That was my hope for her as well. I wanted to be the son of a famous country music star, but my motivations were selfish. That would increase the opportunities to have more and better toys.

Their voices raised as the argument escalate. I wanted them to shut up. Stop snipping at one another. Their barking reminded me of hounds fighting coyotes down in our hollow. Angrily, she cursed Daddy, and said he should leave.

Raging, profaning Merl, he crushed the fire off the cigarette butt into the ashtray beside my bed. He stormed out of the room. "Go to Hell with Merl," he howled.

Momma sighed, her head down she sat on the bed across the room. A few minutes later, Merl came inside. Momma perked up. He must have been hiding, waiting for Daddy to leave. They shut the door. I pretended to be sleeping.

Peeping eyes open slightly, to watch them, my insides are in knots as they embraced and passionately smooched. Sharing a cigarette, they whispered about how much they loved one another, and Momma's plans to divorce Daddy. Drawing the last drag and exhaling, Momma then crushed the fag into the ashtray that set between them on the other bed across the room. Grief overpowered me. I could not take anymore, and once again, I began to wail.

"Son, it's gonna to be okay," she said, racing with Merl to my bedside.

Stroking my head, Momma bawled with me. We were lamenting for different reasons. It was not okay. She was kissing another man, and going to divorce Daddy.

Merl glared down, then his expression changed, and he kindly patted me on the chest, grinning, "You're one tough soldier, Son," Merl said.

"I'm not your son. Don't call me that. Don't touch me," I shouted, picked up his large hand and tossed it off.

He scowled and took a seat on the other bed. Momma frowned.

"Don't be rude to Merl," she growled.

I turned my face to the wall, bellowing hysterically again. They were ignoring me. I looked to see if he was gone. I wanted him to leave. He didn't. When my squalling did not run him off, I simply stopped, and told them I wanted to go back to sleep. I lied. Sleep was not what I wanted.

I decided that afternoon. Momma was not to be trusted. One day she would leave Daddy, Jane, and me for Merl. They stepped outside, and when they were gone, I really did cry because of a broken heart, before drifting off to sleep.

Some minutes later, I awoke to the sound of Momma pulling a tissue from the box on the nightstand beside the bed. Merl was gone. She plucked up Daddy's crushed cigarette butt and placed it in the paper. She strolled to the other ashtray across the room, and pulled out another butt. One belonged to Daddy. Merl's the other one. She folded the paper around the two butts, and shoved it inside her purse. I wondered why she was doing this.

Later Momma says the cigarette butts were some sentimental mementos, a keepsake to remember the time she was torn between two lovers.

The antics presented, by my poor, uneducated and dysfunctional-family are noticed by hospital personnel. Momma left me alone for hours and was off somewhere in town with Merl as the days rolled by. Merl came to visit her at least twice a week.

Many times, they smacked and flirted in front of the nurses. Some of the staff rolled their eyes, knowing he was my mother's lover, and not my daddy.

Confined to a hospital bed for near two months, the days turned into weeks. Daddy never came. I missed Jane. I wanted to go home. I wanted my father.

Adding to the misery, a few medical personnel thought Merl was my father. "Yah Momma and Daddy really love you a lot. Your daddy looks like Elvis Presley," some said.

"He's not my daddy. He's our chicken-thief neighbor," I yelled.

Several of the nurses did not know how to react so they responded nothing, and exit. Others apologized quickly. A few got watery eyes. One shy, young orderly blushed, and asked why I called Merl a chicken-thief.

Rolling my large brown eyes, I fuzzed my hair, exhaling and then squinting, I explained, "Daddy says he caught Merl in the act. He was stealing Grandmother Anne's chickens. I call him a chicken-thief cause Daddy named him that, and hog dookie too," I snorted.

He chuckled, as he left the room. A bit later, hysterical laughter drifted down the hallway from the nurses' station. He had told them what I said. I smirked.

Two days after surgery, Doctor Nix's wife Tina did come by to visit. She was a high-class woman about thirty-years-old, diminutive and fat with frosted blond hair, the pageboy cut. She dressed in the finest of fashion, wearing a large diamond, ruby, and other rings with precious stones, one on every finger.

I never once saw a run in her nylons. Her makeup was not, over done. Those high-dollar high heels made her wiggle when she walked two inches taller. She brought candy, toy soldiers and little cars, small enough for me to play with while being confined to bed.

She read books aloud and smiled a lot. She struggled, hoping to win my friendship. I liked her at first, until she started asking me about coming to live with them. I am losing my momma, and this woman wanted to take her place before Momma was gone. It hurt too badly to think about.

Board to rudeness, I told her to take her stories home. We would make up one. That would be more fun, and I could help her if she was stuck. She did not read further. It was obvious she would have rather read to me when she packed up her books.

Her bribery was obvious. I was determined to let her know up front this was not going to work. Though it was a tempting opportunity, I thought about the possibilities with some hesitation, imagining many nice new toys.

I had to let her know where she stood with this developing relationship. She sat in the chair beside the bed. Leaning off the edge, getting within two inches of her face, I glared into her eyes. A creased brow, I say, "Mrs. Doctor, I already have a momma. I won't leave her, but we'll all come live with you."

She laughed hysterically. She says, "Peter, straighten up, you'll slip off the bed."

She stood, gently forcing, repositioning my head on the pillow. Suspicion quickly fled. I was not expecting that kind of response, figuring she would resist the idea of my clan moving in with them. Instead, she only laughed.

Mrs. Nix visited most every day. She consistently brought surprise gifts. One afternoon she pinned a bronze medal attached to a purple ribbon onto the chest of the open-back gown I wore. I smiled as she explained the token was for my bravery. She was working hard to develop a trusting relationship between us.

Eating up the attention, I decided, liking this high-dollar woman comes with benefits. Gladly, I accepted the mementos. We composed many make-believe tales. Incorporating toy soldiers and the cars, they played out the scenes on my pillow. I enjoyed her company, especially when Momma was away, somewhere in town with Merl Judas.

Mrs. Nix, could not win-over my heart, as the son she wanted. Her efforts were ineffective, not strong enough to redirect my loyalties from Momma to her. Even with all her kindness, gifts, wealth, and polish, my heart would always belong to Momma.

Dr. Nix and his wife realized the seriousness of our degrading, deteriorating family life. He knew about the impoverished environment where we lived. He pleaded with Momma many times, and then with Daddy the last day of hospitalization. Dr. Nix asked one last time, if they would give me to them. He would pay all the legal cost for adoption. I could hear them talking as they stood in the hallway, just outside my room.

"Your boy is special. He is a very intelligent child. My wife and I would like to have him as our own. I'm forty years old and we can't have children," he said.

Daddy said, "I know. Maybe, someday he will grow up to be a doctor or lawyer."

"Would you consider allowing us to adopt him?" asked Doctor Nix.

"Absolutely not, I have already given you my answer many times before," Momma says.

"If you change your minds, give me a call. My wife and I could give him a good life," he says, on a hope filled final note.

What is the word, adopt? Maybe this is the word meaning, parents selling their children. I did not like it. The sound of it stirred insecurity within me, and I trembled. Was he going to give them money for me? I was afraid and covered my face with a pillow.

The doctor said he could give me a good home. I had a home. I did not want to live with them. Adopt must mean, to take kids away from their parents. I did not want Momma to give me away, sold, or be taken forcefully from my own family. Are these the definitions of adopt?

I was confident Daddy would not. She might if she were to ever run off with Merl. I didn't trust her. She was a liar. Had Momma already sold me to these educated strangers?

Daddy snapped, "Is he ready to go home?"

A sigh of relief, Daddy would not allow it. He loved me. He was not leaving me with them. Momma sounded like she meant it when she told the doctor no. But I didn't trust her anymore. I thought, she might be lying again to cover up a secret plot to get rid of me.

Maybe she lied in front of Daddy so not to rouse his temper, and the deed was probably already done. They might steal me away during the night.

The doctor gave them instructions for my care. Two nurses lifted me off the bed. Down into a wheelchair, I sat. I am rolled out of the hospital. Then, nurses loaded me onto the front seat of the car. I was going home. Momma had not sold me. The Doctor would not be keeping me.

Determined, I had to fix my parents' marriage, immediately. Adopted, I did not want. Was I partially responsible for all the fighting? Was this part of Bertha's curse, or recompense? Recompense, the strange word Momma spoke when the cactus cradled my head.

At least, they did not get rid of me, or leave me in this dreadful place. I had a chance to maybe, make things better. I was going home.

I thought; when I get there, I will work on them, make their love for one another grow stronger. Determined, they would not divorce if I had any influence, and my way.

Paul E. Treadwell

LEVIATHAN KINGS OF TERROR, a memoir

The Hat Pin Lady

The car smelled of death where the blood-soaked carpet had soured. Momma was unable to remove all the stain after the accident. Daddy got behind the wheel and shut his door. Grinning, I held his arm tightly, and snuggled close.

Momma stuck her head through the passenger-window. "Jane is in Merl's car with John and Pete (Momma's younger brothers). I'm going to ride with them," she announced.

Daddy's fist pounded the steering wheel. "I'll be a coon's behind if you will. You go get Jane," Daddy yelped.

Defiantly, rolling her eye, she spat, "I will ride with whom I darn will please. I am locked-up here all this time with your son. I am tired and on the edge. Do not give me that tone. Don't need this crazy-crap now. Go climb a tree." She stormed across the parking lot and crawled into Merl's dark-green '53 Chevy where Jane was screaming.

"Well, Son, I guess that settled it," Daddy said, followed by an embarrassed chuckle.

I hugged him, and chirped, "Let's go home, Daddy."

We pulled out of the parking lot that hot afternoon in July for the two-hour drive. Momma, Jane, and the others followed behind us with Merl.

Months that followed, during the long recovery, my mother and father would eventually come to an uneasy truce. Before that could happen there was another unexpected event, they had to face. Momma conceived for a third time the spring of '59. Daddy suspected she carried Merl's baby. She started to show the week I came home from the hospital.

Daddy told her to get rid of the pregnancy. Malevolent forces were all around us. Fear and anger were concentrated inside the home. Wicked phantoms seemed to be pushing Momma to have an illegal abortion. He spoke of a black woman who lived in the back-alley slums of Little Rock. One of his older sisters used her years ago, when she got into trouble before marriage, not wanting Grandma Anne to know.

"The Hat Pin Lady, can fix this problem," he says.

She says, "It's your baby." Momma cried.

He says, "Even so, we don't need it now." He is convinced the baby bump is the illegitimate spawn of Merl Judas.

She says, "I won't kill our baby."

He says, "Why not, you, pert near killed, Saul. I guess it must be Merl's or you wouldn't be so intent on keeping the thing."

I lay on the living room sofa as Momma wept bitterly while changing the bandages on my wounded legs. The veins in Daddy's neck throbbed, as he continued to rage.

Whimpering, "Kiss and make up," I said. My words fell on deaf-ears. They continued their yelling.

During the healing days, I felt no severe physical ache. The itching in the wounds as they healed was extremely uncomfortable. I am, constantly scolded for rolling up tissue paper and running it under the bandages to scratch the never-ceasing itches. The enduring sting was a broken heart, because of Momma's infidelities.

Youthful lust, and her lies, avoiding the disclosure of their secrets, the stress for Momma must have been overpowering. As severe as the constant itching, hidden under my leg dressings.

Weeks passed, they eventually kissed and made-up. Momma persuaded Daddy. She and Merl had never tasted an affair. She promised not to speak with, or go around him. That was unless Daddy or one of his siblings was with them. Were these empty words the same as she vowed before the accident? No, this time she made the effort to keep her promise.

Fragile peace slowly invaded the house during the remainder of my recovery. The latter gestation months of Momma's pregnancy carried less stress for us all. No open animosity remained between them. All seemed forgiven, when she gave birth to brother, Bobby, November of '59.

Bobby looked exactly like Daddy. He certainly was not a Judas. He was definitely a true blood Hotman. Daddy was ashamed for accusing Momma of being unfaithful.

I chose not to tell Daddy. I knew she kissed Merl, and they had plans to run away together. She was a liar. I was not sure if she could be trusted ever again.

Time lets the truth slip. He holds no secrets for long. The truth, details about events, and how they fit together in this complicated puzzle is going to rattle an entire community.

Would they follow through on their plot to steal away together into the night, and be gone forever? For now, I would remain silent. I would not give Daddy any more ammunition. His angry mouth was like a machine gun, cutting anyone in half if caught in his line of fire. Momma's cursing during angry attacks if provoked could be as deadly. The shrapnel spray of words wounded those near to them, especially the believer. I wanted the peace to remain.

The dozens of stitches around the incisions removed as the graft took and mended the injury. The broken bones completely healed shortly after Bobby's birth. The house we lived in was the home of broken hearts. Would our hearts ever mend? Bobby brought a long awaited joy back into our lives.

I forgot how to walk. Momma eyed me one day, her determined gaze stealing my helplessness as she dragged me off the sofa. She was forcing me to take a step.

"Saul, the doctor says you should have been walking two months ago," Momma said.

I say, "I'm afraid, Momma."

She says, "Now Son, you can do this. Momma will help yah. Oops, I meant you."

Lilly's friendship inspired Momma to try, speaking properly. She taught her to watch her tongue, and get rid of some of the hick slang. Momma had only one month, of formal schooling. Lilly finished ninth grade down in Florida, the year she married Merl. When Lilly moved to Loafer's Glory, she helped Momma learn to read, and write a little better. Momma said she missed Lilly, desperately.

Momma placed my feet on the floor in front of the sofa where I had been lying. I was hysterical, sitting there resisting with all my strength not to budge one inch. Six months, not standing alone, I was hesitant to put weight on weakened legs.

Momma yanked me off the seat. She firmly held me upright. My feet dangled toward the floor. I bucked, clinging to her arms. Fearful she would let go. I could crumple, crashing to the hard floor. I didn't.

Ever so gently, she coached. I relented, releasing a trifle of weight onto my feet. Surprisingly, I was standing all by myself as she let go and stepped back. Legs were trembling as they supported a small frame. Our tears turned to laughter. Momma took hold of my hands. Squatting to eye level, she encouraged me to step forward.

Insecure, fearfully, I asked, "Do you promise to catch me if I start to fall?"

Grinning, a tear rolled down her cheek. "Yes, Saul, Momma is right here," she says.

I took a step, toward her. Both of us are bubbling joy when I took the second. She scooted backward. Tears of gladness flooded the room. Jane giggled and clapped from the end of the sofa. On the third stride, I fabricated a fall to let her intercept. She did. My trust escalated.

Momma and Daddy were getting along, and now I had a new baby brother to help look after. This motivated me to master the ambulatory skill of walking again, real fast. Within a month, Jane and I were frolicking naked through the house after our baths. I would trot to the barn early every morning to help Daddy milk Betsy before he went off harvesting the day's trees.

When we returned to the house with fresh milk, Momma had sweet chocolate gravy, cathead biscuits, homemade strawberry jam, eggs, and bacon waiting on the table for breakfast. The meal was the same every morning. Constant family rituals were back in place, without the brawling every day. We were family again.

Forlorn, Where Did Lilly Go

Returning to Loafer's Glory after the hospital stay, I developed a food allergy. Strawberries became forbidden fruit.

Merl and his family, for months were not in our lives. Not since, we returned home. When Merl dropped off Momma, Jane, and my young uncles that afternoon, he made himself scarce.

Momma and Daddy casually spoke to Lilly and Merl when happening to cross paths out in public. Other than that, they had no contact. Cooler weather set in, their big chill was about to thaw. Socializing with the Judas family was not in our best interest. Merl was Momma's forbidden fruit.

She did not seek him out, but I could feel her heart pine for him. I never really knew what motivated them to break off the affair, or if they actually did. I wanted to believe they severed the relationship and were not kissing each other in secret. I suspected perhaps because of guilt or godly conviction, she may have ended it. Maybe, fear of Daddy's rages, motivated the decision. I was not certain. It would take some time for her to regain my trust.

Momma said she felt trapped in an unhappy marriage with three small children but had no skills to provide for us if she left. Only she knew the true reason, for the attitude adjustments. Maybe they didn't break it off. Perhaps she just got better at hiding their rendezvous. I would never know. Momma was good at keeping secrets. She was great putting on the face of a content wife in a happy life, when it was a necessity.

October, of '59, Lilly gave birth to Merl's third child, Amos. That day, Momma was forlorn. She did not play her music or sing her songs and pick on the guitar in the evening. She hardly spoke and stared into the distance as if in a trance. Her belly was big with Bobby inside. This was Lilly's day of celebration. Momma wanted to be there.

I wondered if perhaps Momma cared less about comforting Lilly. Perhaps her true desire was to see Merl when she asked Daddy's permission. Maybe that was the reason for her sadness. He told her, no. Her blues for the next week were so deep the whales in the vast seas could not poop there.

I loved both my parents. If I uttered a word to Daddy, Leviathan would have raised his evil head, a malefic force of destruction, robbing the tranquility of our home again. I was intent on fixing their relationship. The kissing is no more! I had to forgive Momma. Reservations remained.

How could I make Momma not languish for Merl's embrace? When Bobby was born in November, her focus was on him. Her dreadful sadness seemed to ease a bit. I am glad.

Daddy wanted to evangelize again, in the surrounding communities and small churches. None wanted him because of the gossip about Momma's unfaithfulness. He was labeled, and considered by many, a public mockery, shunned. Making a hyena of himself while hopped-up on moonshine did not help his reputation. As a result, to this point he had altogether quit preaching.

Folks no longer had any confidence in him as a minister of the Gospel. Nevertheless, he was preparing sermons and preached again, his "Hellfire and Brimstone," messages. With a renewed vigor and assurance, he proclaimed the Gospel, shortly after Bobby's birth. His engagements were limited to our home. He presented new sermons on the attentive congregation consisting of Jane and me. He hoped a door would open soon. He wanted to pastor. He said that was his calling. He had to be prepared if that day came.

Momma and Daddy not fighting as often, and life is good. I hoped with him. Believing he would pastor someday. In his renewed faith, Daddy felt he had misjudged Merl and Momma. He wanted their forgiveness.

I thought it was because Bobby looked just like Daddy. Things were fine as they were. I smelled trouble coming. In an ill placed gesture of goodwill, Daddy asked Merl to come work with Uncle Joe, and himself again. Merl agreed.

After coming home from the hospital, Momma told me about Daddy's accident--brain injury the year before they married. His reasoning ability was getting worse because of the blow to the head. Momma and Merl had the best hand for winning their life's game of cards. Daddy was their Joker.

Something was changing, his mind, a fragile instrument broken, and sounding a bit out of tune. Merl was Momma's Ace in the hole, and Momma was the Queen of Hearts for both families. Their angry band played life's songs, out of time, slow tempos, and with no harmony. Their music, their songs were hard to follow for a four-year-old. Nevertheless, I knew something was not right.

I wondered if perhaps, it was true what Momma said. Daddy was losing his mind. Momma questioned everything he said and did, saying he was insane behind his back.

When she stewed, her anger surfaced like steam from a pressure cooker only for a few moments. She was always holding back something, never expressing her complete truth. She chose not to reveal her personal opinions without first weighing each phrase before she spoke. Her feelings around Daddy most of the time were subdued. On the surface, home-life overall was peaceful. Frustrations beneath the surface, a complex volcanic mix of emotions lay hidden, evolving for a massive implosion.

Why would he want Merl around again? Knowing Momma was a liar, concerned me deeply. Would it start up once more, and bring trouble into our home as in the past? I had viewed with my own eyes, and heard with my own ears. She was not innocent, but she had convinced Daddy that she was.

I watched them hugging and kissing. I knew their plans. I would not be their fool. I was not deceived. This was an adult game. I didn't completely understand their rules, but we all felt the effects of their deeds. My intuition revealed a turbulent future. What should I do to save my family? What could I do, if anything?

I decided to tell Daddy. Not wanting Chicken Thief Merl around us, I say, "He is a bit**," never explaining my reasons.

Both parents scolded me for calling Merl names. Realized, I could not tell the secret, cut off before expressing the full details. I dreaded what I somehow knew was about to become of the situation. Their common sense was gone. They gave me no opportunity to explain my reasons for the name-calling. The secret remained. My truth was swept under the rug, not heard.

Reconnecting with Merl blew my plan out of the water. How could I repair their marriage with Merl around to undermine all trust? He would be too much temptation for Momma. I wanted to tell Daddy about Momma lovin' on Merl, but changed my mind. Dared not for fear they would divorce as soon as possible. I am glad they cut me off. If divorced, adoption might be the next step. I did not want to be the son of a rich doctor. My young heart vacillated, while I kept my mouth shut.

Momma said she repented, over the intense arguments. That was water under the bridge as far as she was concerned. Nope, I would not stir that chamber pot and get it to stinking up the house again. Maybe things would be different this time. Despite my glimpse into the future, I couldn't tell Daddy what was to be, or share my feelings, what I assumed was coming.

During the coming months, Merl and Daddy worked together and our families socialized. Daddy's erratic behaviors worsened as he began to hallucinate infrequently. His sporadic jealous rages returned, triggered by the least things. Mental episodes worsened with every new outburst. This was the beginning of an approaching hurricane.

On the verge of a nervous breakdown, Daddy's delusional spells frightened me. I knew something was wrong, and getting more intense. Alcohol consumption heightened his problems. He infrequently broke into nonsensical speech, repeating the same phrases over-and-over. While he was driving one afternoon, he began to say, "No, no, howdy, howdy."

Being out-of-touch only lasted for a few seconds that day, but I cringed in fear. Shouted from the backseat as he ran off the shoulder of the road, "Daddy, Daddy, what's wrong?" I yelled.

Momma punched him. She harped, "Knock it off, you're a crazy fool. You're scaring the children."

He snapped to reality, and swerved onto the highway again. Terrified, Jane clung to my arm the remainder of the trip home.

Momma pleaded with Daddy, wanting him to sell the Bel Air. She said it haunted her after the accident. By Christmas, Daddy became fearful of driving and agreed to get rid of it. He sold the Chevy.

Using part of the money, he purchased for Momma a '48 rattletrap. The extra cash went to help buy a new logging truck. He and Merl went together on the vehicle loan as a business venture.

His emotions concerning Merl continued to oscillate. He was in a valley of indecision, between total devotion, confidence, and trust, too suspicion, and jealousy. Overriding his better judgment, he made the effort to keep the relationship. This was his way of showing Momma. He loved her, and did not want to destroy her friendship with Lilly. He would have to go slow with Merl and keep a watchful eye.

The effort to redeem his friendship with Merl was becoming his undoing. As time progressed, his nerves grew worse. Daddy trembled when he drove, and as a result, Merl or Uncle Joe operated the truck.

Financially, we were going in the hole. Something had to break. We needed more cash just to get by.

The daily warning-cry sounded: "Timber . . ." Then old-growth hardwood rumbled like thunder crashing to the earth on the surrounding hillsides. Majestic tall trees surrendered to lumberjack sweat, saws, and mules' brute physical strength. The mill saws, and blades spinning, ripped through giant white oak logs ten hours a day, at Chad's sawmill.

The trees had no voice to moan. The blades raped the life from the hardwood jungle. Machines did their jobs and cried for the forest with loud mechanical sounds. These were the implications of prosperity and economic good times. Yet, good fortune for my family faltered as Merl failed to show up for work half the time. He refused to pay his part of the truck payments, and bled Daddy every week, for more than his share of profits.

The timber jobs provided regular income, meeting basic needs was security enough when prices for lumber were reasonable. Just to survive was good. The prices dropped. These were hard days, and the pocket book came up short by the end of the week, time-and-time again.

When Bobby was a month on, Daddy said, he and Merl needed to work closer to train service. They would get a better price for the railroad ties, and cut down transport overhead. He sold Betsy, and the other livestock. We were moving away from Loafer's Glory.

Daddy bought a track of timber near Seligman, Missouri. Merl's clan and my parents decided we would move and harvest trees there, after the holidays. Together they rented a large house. Momma brought all our new furniture.

Two months after relocating, Daddy, Merl, Joe, and the others ate breakfast together as usual. The men left for work and Momma took Jane, Bobby, and me to the laundry mat. Returning home, Momma unloaded the wicker basket, putting away our clean clothes.

I noticed all the Judas children's toys had vanished. Lilly and her three kids were gone. Bewildered, I asked, "Where did Lilly and April go?"

Momma said, "Oh, Lilly probably took them out to have a coke."

I sighed, and said, "No Momma, all their toys are missing. Even April's bike is gone."

Momma scolded, "Saul stop making up stories. Her bike is in the backyard." She strolled to the door, poking her head out, "Well, it is gone," she happily said.

She turned, racing toward Merl and Lilly's bedroom. She checked Lilly's closet. Her garments were not there. The children's clothes were gone, only the empty closet remained. Their dressers were empty. Merl's attire remained in the closet on the other side of the room.

Momma glowed. Laughing, she fell backward onto Merl's bed. "Thank you, God," she said, while wiping a tear from the corner of her eye.

Why did Lilly leave us? Maybe she caught Momma and Merl smooching again. No, they didn't do that anymore. Maybe they were. I regretted not taking the opportunity earlier. I should have told Daddy.

Again, I doubted giving any knowledge of the sort to Daddy would have changed what was to be. His mental illness worsened as every day passed. His mind confused by delusional indifference and denial. His love for Momma kept us under the cursed friendship with Merl. He was crazy in-love with Momma. If it meant keeping Merl around in order to have Momma at his side that was his reasoning.

Were we, being deceived again? Manipulated by Momma and Merl, I thought, maybe. He had not caught them in the act. His truth was different from mine. My truth came from their past behavior.

Daddy was emotionally weak. Momma and Merl were his crutches. Why did Daddy lead us back into this Judas friendship? His jealousy and suspicions were not enough for him to truly, sever the ties. His heart would have to be, ripped out by the roots, and losing Momma's love would do him in.

Perhaps Lilly caught them kissing? Why didn't she tell Daddy? He was unpredictable in a jealous rage. He might kill Merl, maybe Momma. Lilly was probably right to keep the secret? I would never tell. Their affair was in the past. They didn't do that anymore. Why did Lilly abandon us? Were they kissing each other again?

Lilly fled, Merl remained in the house to help Daddy and Joe. I continued to keep my mouth shut hoping Momma and Merl's romance was actually over forever. Deep inside, I knew it wasn't, but I had no current evidence.

They told Daddy, Lilly got homesick for her parents and returned to Florida. She would be back. I could not believe their lies. My gut spoke something different. Yet, I had no tangible proof the flames of passion between Merl and Momma had indeed rekindled. I had not caught them kissing again. Despite the argument inside my head, I knew. I simply knew it was so.

Now, that Lilly was not in the picture. Their desires became stronger. Passions slowly began to roar as a destructive blaze in the lives of those who truly loved them. The hurtful flames of their lust would not, be quenched this time.

Paul E. Treadwell

The Burning Mule

Daddy brought the mules, Blaze and Mabel to Seligman. Several years our Mabel labored hard for Daddy. Gentle as could be, she was medium-tan with a white star on her forehead. Standing fifteen hands, she was massive compared to small children. Jane and I had no fear of her. Often we groomed and fed the beast, with Daddy's help. Blaze and Mabel were part of our family.

A few weeks after the move Mabel's strange sickness grew worse. The country veterinarian told Daddy about the mule's seizure condition. He said she needed to be, put down. Daddy didn't have the heart to kill her. His decision was partly, influenced by Jane and me.

The day he led her into the woods with a rifle in hand, he could not do it. To our delight, he came riding her back. We stopped our wails of pain, gleefully darting out of the house into the barnyard. We hugged her massive legs, and stroked her velvet snout.

Dismounting, he says, "Saul, I'll let her live a little longer. The vet says she is only going to get worse. You know. One day I will have to put her down. I'm doing this for you and Jane. One day you will wake up and she will be gone. It's, for the best. I don't want her to suffer. You children are going to have to learn not to be so selfish."

Pleading, "Daddy, you can't shoot Mabel. She is part of us. She belongs here. Please don't ever kill her," I said.

"Son, she'll have to be put down. For now, I won't," he said.

Agitated, tearfully, blowing my nose on his shirttail, "You must promise," I shouted.

He nodded. Daddy's eyes were bloodshot when he went inside and told Momma. His tender heart hated the thought of her inevitable death, as much as we did.

Harsh vibrations traveled through the open door. Jane and I heard Momma cursing him again. "You're such an insufferable, wimpy fool. Too kind for anybody's good," she yelped.

Mabel was faithful and docile, never failing to pull her load of logs out of the forest. Sometimes she would fall to the ground as though asleep. Five minutes later, she would roll to her feet and finish dragging her burden of timber. Late during the Missouri days her condition worsened. The seizures began with episodes once a week and were becoming more frequent as each day passed. After Lilly left, the seizures increased to three times a week, each episode lasting a little longer.

The Blue Goose train tracks ran through the property where Daddy purchased the timber. Some days, Daddy allowed me to ride along to work with the men. On the job site, I sat inside the truck cab watching them labor. I drank their big orange drinks, and snacked on canned Vienna sausage while waiting until the work was finished.

The day was grey, a cold, and windy working environment this afternoon in February, 1960. Merl hitched Mabel to a load at the bottom of a hollow. I observed as the train passed in the distance. Its whistle screamed. I plugged ears with index finger tips until the iron horse was gone.

Watching Merl, he was cursing Mabel to get up the slope. She strained and struggled, and then she flopped motionlessly to the ground. Merl dropped the reins. He kicks her. He beat her with a whip and threw rocks. His cruel blows did not faze her. She could not move. She did not flinch.

I yelled for him to leave her alone. I shouted, "Stop!" No one heard. My cries, muted under the roar of chainsaws. The horror of the scene unfolding before me was too great. I hunkered down on the cab floor under the steering wheel. I was peeking out again, when the saws unison ripping, grinding squeals stopped. I see and hear, a serpent, in the form of Merl Judas.

He stomped over a few yards to talk with Joe. "I need some gas. That lazy Mabel won't move again," Merl said.

I cranked down the driver's side window to hear a little better.

"Give her a few minutes and she'll be okay," Joe whipped, pointing to the gas can, and then cranked his saw. He went back to cutting down another large oak.

Merl carried the container over to Mabel. Joe had no idea what Merl was about to do, and neither did I.

Relieved, Mabel's beating had stopped; I stretched out on the seat, pulled my black-knit sock-cap over my ears, and closed my eyes to doze. I heard, nothing over the saws' raping teeth, and full throttle engines, as the roar grew louder.

I sat up again to watch them work, and I snacked on peanuts. Merl held the petroleum jug and sprinkled some gasoline on a rag. Then he poured gas into an empty Vienna sausage can. He bent over the sick mule's, behind. What was he doing?

Uncle Joe yelled, "Timber . . ." The majestic oak fell to the ground with a shattering pound. He shut off his saw, and turned around just as my eyes shifted toward Merl for a second time. Then, I glanced back at Joe. It was obvious. He and I both were no longer trying to figure out what Merl was doing.

Merl stepped a few feet away from Mabel. Dropping the empty sausage cup, and larger gas can on the ground, he lit a match, and tossed it on Mabel. Poof, the roar of fire from the ignited liquid, fed flames that leapt skyward. To our horror, we watched black smoke rising over her. The smell of burning hair, flesh, and toxic petroleum fumes were strong, drifting into the truck cab.

Joe ran toward Mabel. Panicked, he yells at Daddy who had just killed his saw. "Enoch, fetch the water." Joe shouted.

Joe hastened his pace toward the three-foot flares. He ripped off his coat and beat at the roaring cry of hot fire. The blazes refused to die. They raged high into the air off Mabel's hinders parts. He yelled again, "Enoch gotta get water. This brut has set her on fire." He continued to fight the flames on the haunches of the burning mule.

Locked inside the cab, not able to get the latch to release, I pounded the truck door, and screamed to no avail. I wailed, "You devil. I'll kill yah." I shouted.

Daddy sprinted across the forested slope. Reaching the truck, he grabbed something off the truck-bed, and flew down the hill. He flung the five-gallon thermos of ice-cold drinking water on Mabel. Joe continued to garrote the flames.

Daddy lunged for Merl, hitting him in the head with the empty 5-gallon thermos can. "You're a crazy ass demon. What in Hell is the matter with you? You've killed Mabel," Daddy raged. "Get out of my sight," He shouted, cursing and shoved Merl one more time.

Smirking, seeming to have no remorse, Merl backed off. He ambled up the hill toward me. When he opened the cab door, I leapt to the ground and ran for Daddy.

"Get your butt back here," Merl growled.

I was not about to stop. When I glanced over my shoulder to make certain, he had not made chase, he opened a bottle of coke and whizzed it down. Good, he wasn't after me.

My impressions of Merl at the beginning were wrong. I hated myself, for having ever liked him. He didn't need any second chances. I would not allow it to happen. I vowed, I would never again, be deceived by him. Always suspicious, never trusting a word out of Merl's evil lips. I was on guard, wondering how he would manipulation my family next.

What was this stirring inside of me? It was almost over powering. I had never felt any negative emotion as strong. I was no longer sitting on the fence concerning Merl Judas.

Resolute in my mind, he was no good. Merl was the human embodiment of pure evil. To know Momma wanted his kisses and embrace, repulsed me.

Joe's coat, ruined by the time the blaze snuffed. Moments later, Mabel awakened, and struggled to her feet as Daddy held me on his hip trying to comfort me.

"Now Son, look there," he said.

I turned my head to see.

"She's all right," he says.

Eased a bit, I watched. As trained without coaching, Mabel dragged the log hooked in the harness behind her up the gentle slope toward the truck.

Mabel severely burned. Her hair gone and the flesh smoldered on her hinder parts, tail, and back legs. Her privates seared with second, and third-degree burns. Merl had shoved the gasoline rag into an orifice, doused her with a good cup or more petroleum, and set her on fire during his cruel outburst. He was determined she would move the load on his command. He insisted she was just lazy and balked.

Daddy knew differently, he told Merl about Mabel's condition weeks before. There was no excuse. Merl already knew. Motivated by his demons, he intended to hurt the helpless beast.

Red faced with rage, Joe unhitched Mabel. She panted heavily, snorted, and brayed out her pain. Blood boiling, face flushed with anger he insisted Merl take the loaded logs to the mill immediately.

When Merl was gone, Joe and Daddy examined Mabel closely. They were horrified. The blood draining from their faces in a state of shock as the reality of the depth of depravity that possessed Merl's soul took hold of their minds. "That sorry SOB, I've a good mind to kill the bastard," Joe seethed.

He patted Mabel's neck and spoke gently to calm her. Daddy could not take it. He ambled off into the distance, leaving me with Joe and the mules. Daddy, collapsed behind a tree, weeping, shaking, praying, and cursing.

Joe glanced down and said, "Son, here's some candy." He reached into his shirt pocket, pulled out a chocolate bar placing it in my hand. He pointed. He says, "You sit on this log over here, away from Mabel and eat your snack." Handing me a half-full bottle of coke he says, "Here, finish drinkin' mine. I'll see about yah pa." As he walked away, he said, "Don't be getting up close to Mabel."

I nodded while wiping tear-stained cheeks, and stepped onto a fallen log. Joe trotted down the hillside to where Daddy was wailing uncontrollably. I turned toward the men, and sat to watch and listen.

He placed his hand on Daddy's shoulder. "I'm sorry, Buddy. Yah gotta get him out of your life. He'll be your ruin," Joe said.

Defeated, "I know. Gotta, find another hand to help. Ora will have a fit," Daddy says. Glancing up toward me, he says, "I wanted to keep the friendship. It's impossible."

Bristling, Joe says, "He's not a friend. He's a monster, not a human being. At the least, he is criminally insane. You don't need to think of him as a friend. He is a devil."

Daddy calms some, "You're right. I gotta get shut of him, once and for all."

Joe says, "Yah made a bad mistake puttin' his name on the truck. He's stealing yah blind. He ain't good for yah, and my sis. Enoch, anyone who would do what he just did is capable of anything. Merl has got to go."

Pounding his fist against the tree, Daddy barked, "My life, been hard all my life. He ain't any different from most others. The whole world is a chicken sh**."

Joe says, "I'm goin' back to Arkansas. I'll kill the monster if I have to be around him any longer." He added, "Yah gonna have to get another mule."

Daddy gazed up the slope as he heard and watched Mabel shaking and snorting. Silent tears were streaming down his face. "We'll sell her or trade. Can't, bring myself to put her down," he said.

His eyes shifted toward me. Splashing a brave, warm smile, he waved. I heard him mumble, "Don't tell Saul and Jane. Maybe I will set Merl's butt on fire. Pour gasoline down his crack. I'll make the bastard get us a new team. Blaze gotta go too, just too old. I should shoot Mabel, but I promised the kids I would not. Cannot lie to my babies. I need to put her out of her misery," he said.

Daddy lowered his face into his trembling palms. Unexpectedly he blurted nonsensical speech, "No, no, howdy, howdy. Captain, captain, I'm a navy kid captain sailor. No, no, howdy," he said.

It caught Joe off guard. He did not know what to make of the behavior. This man was not the Enoch he had known, since his preteen years.

I was gravely concerned, a few months earlier Daddy did the same, the day he ran the car off the road. Something was very wrong. This was not my daddy.

I thought, maybe, one of the demons cast out during the revivals might have attached itself to him. The image of Daddy being controlled by one of the devil's angels, sent shivers up my spine.

Daddy mumbled, and bawled uncontrollably as he began to tell Joe of the abuse suffered during his life at the hands of those he trusted. He spoke of the beatings inflicted by whippings with wire at his brother's hands when he was but a boy. He showed the scars on his legs, and shared the grief inside his heart, knowing Momma did not love him.

He told Joe how he thought Merl was his friend, but realized no friend breaks a man's trust. He revealed to Joe his troubles, and shook while slipping in and out of fear and rage. Banging his head against the tree, he said, "They say, not guilty as accused. They argue, saying they are innocent. I know they're liars. I know they are messing around. I just know it! No! No! Howdy, captain, captain! What could Ora possibly see in him?"

Joe yelled for him to snap out of it. Daddy took several deep breaths and they walked up the way toward me. They stopped work for the day, pouring hot coffee out of a black thermos Momma filled earlier. They filled tin cups until the coffee was gone, and they smoked one cigarette after another.

The mood was somber waiting for Merl to return. Daddy sat on the log beside me, and I crawled onto his lap. He held me ever so tight, as I wiped a silent tear from his cheek.

Merl arrived two hours later. The men loaded their tools, and the mules on the truck. Driving home, Daddy and Joe said nothing as

Merl preached about what they must do. He demanded Daddy give him more money to buy another team. He handed Merl the cash.

When we arrived home, I told Jane all I had seen. We feared Merl, after that day. He was no longer our beloved friend we wanted to forgive. He was Bertha's bit**, or was it, a witch. He was her offspring, her poison apple that didn't fall far from the Judas tree.

Merl Judas was our oxymoron. Loved, and hated by my family. Watching him unmercifully brutalize helpless Mabel, he became a King of Terror.

Wolf in the Camp

Daddy, fell into a deep depression for days, refusing to work or get out of bed. Momma harangued him, "You're a lazy, crazy jerk. You aren't much a man or husband. Men don't cry. Merl can work circles around you!"

Catching her breath, she shouted, "You shouldn't have been such an insufferable sissy hitting Merl on the head over ol' lazy Mabel. You and that mule are just alike, useless. Merl should have poured gasoline on you, and set your ass, ablaze too."

Daddy pleads, he says, "Ora stop."

As though he said nothing, she shrieks, "A man ain't, gonna hide in the bed and cry like a baby over an old sick mule. Get up and go make us a living."

He refused to work for the next week. Merl got rid of Blaze and Mabel. He purchased two younger mules, telling Daddy the money was enough with the trade of Blaze and Mabel. He said the man he bartered with was sending Mabel to a glue factory.

I did not know what that meant. I assumed that she would pull a cart at a factory loaded with bottles of glue.

Daddy was stuck in a dark pit of depression. Momma and Merl took charge, deciding we would move to New Glarus, Wisconsin where Ely and Fanny lived, and worked. They didn't reckon Daddy still had any fight left, to resist their plans.

Merl's slow brother Ely, married to Momma's homely cousin Fanny moved to Wisconsin the autumn of '59 before Bobby was born. Ely was not a feast to look-upon. Awkward, he was a righteous man, good at heart, near the opposite of Merl's character.

Their scheme was for Merl, Ely, Joe and Daddy to labor in the national forest. Of course, Merl would continue living with us. Daddy resisted, and informed them he had money invested. The Seligman timber harvest came first. Merl submitted to Daddy's commands. He would not have but Daddy had the small bankroll. We would stay until the end of March.

Momma . . . revolted by the idea of being around Fanny Judas, but she said nothing. Her reservations about the move stayed hidden. If that was what Merl wanted, then she was game on. Her true feelings and the best interest of her own family would take a back seat to Merl's wishes.

During the following weeks, she sided more often with Merl over Daddy. Pleasing Merl was her motivation.

Knowing Daddy would have to pay for the move, if it were to happen. She pressed to change his mind, to move immediately. Daddy was resolute.

Merl was penniless. He continually blew his check as fast as he was paid. Daddy said Merl thought money would burn holes in his pockets if he kept it for long. He spent it on hooch and women of the night. Daddy called them loose women.

I heard of those kinds before. They sucked the life's blood out of men. They were vampires, with sharp fangs. They are bats, pretending to be pretty women after dark. That is what Daddy called them.

The men returned to the woods, working sections near where Merl had set Mabel ablaze. In late March, tensions heightened for the adults. None of them got along. The Blue Goose whistle screams echoed, mechanical melancholy sounds. The irritation and frustrations undoubtedly caused by the power struggles going on between Momma, Daddy, and Merl. Their sounds were silent clamors, just barely above the human hearing. Silent screams radiated, grating on everyone's nerves. The fog of discontent was thick. The household was tense, on the edge.

The Blue Goose's treks were about to run out too. Her final days approached. Her end near, as she was being retired, the same as the Galloping Goose locomotive, back in Raccoon Springs. A way of life would be gone forever with the Blue Goose train line shutting down.

In time, the control issues between the adults were resolved as abruptly, as the train service. Again, we would journey afar, not returning to the old breeding grounds.

Uncle Joe told Daddy, he would be leaving, returning to Arkansas by month's end. Joe's brow wrinkled, concerned, he said, "Cover your backside, Merl is up too no good. He's gonna take yah for all yah got."

Momma informed Daddy, come April, they would be moving to New Glarus with or without him. Merl had good reasons for wanting to leave the area. Momma knew. My father would soon discover the crimes.

Merl was a common thief. He was stealing items from the neighbors. Worse, unknown to us, he traded Blaze and Mabel with the promise of cash later for the new mules. He pocketed the money Daddy gave him. Unbeknownst to Daddy the owner wanted the mule team back. He threatened to turn Merl over to the law if he did not return the mules or pay up, within the week.

Daddy's mental state worsened every day. Momma's visible disgust and loathing of him, spread toward her children. Her raging foul language revealed her heart's desire. Momma wanted freedom from her Hotmans, all of us.

Harvesting Seligman trees, the trio's last day together, a large gray timber wolf meandered by the work camp. Probably harmless, still the beast frightened the men. Joe seized a rock, the size of softball. He threw it for all he was worth, and cold-cocked the canine. The animal yelped, flopping to the ground, dead from the blow. Daddy was amazed.

I could not understand why Joe was so mean, and had to kill the big dog. I thought that he was showing off his arm strength again, at the expense of the shaggy pooch. The dead wolf was dark gray. It was as deep gray, as our Seligman days were grey.

Over the weekend, Daddy rode with Joe to Rooster Ridge, Arkansas. Joe now twenty-one remained there, courting his new girlfriend, fourteen-year-old pretty and petite Rebecca. They planned to marry soon. This gave Momma and Merl opportunity, time to be alone with only each other.

Dropped off at the old breeding grounds, Daddy boasted about little Joe's bravery. The Hotman clan didn't believe the wolf tale. They said it never happened. They surmised that he made it up. Here was another delusion, they decided, while ridiculing him. Despite the way his siblings treated him, he had to see them before hitchhiking back to Missouri.

Momma and Merl were kissing ceaselessly while Daddy was gone. They did not know, I had sneaked around and spied on them. I surmised, Lilly must have caught them, and relinquished her marriage, fleeing with the children. Their smooching stopped after Daddy arrived. Again, I could not bring myself to tell.

Momma was overly affectionate with Daddy when he walked in. Pretending she was thrilled to have him home. She wanted something. That was her way, when she was out to get what she wanted from Daddy.

The next morning during breakfast, Daddy mentioned he wanted to load up the furniture, and return the housekeeping goods to the old homestead, or take it with us to Wisconsin. Momma and Merl's carping attitude surfaced again. They would have no part of it.

Momma says, "You're a crazy fool. We gotta go now. Two trips are a waste of time and money," she said.

Merl joined in. "We need the mules to work. Don't need this ol' furniture. It won't put food on the table," Merl snorted.

Red faced, the veins on his neck throbbing. Daddy said, "I still owe, on the furniture. We gotta store it, or take it with us."

Not finishing our portions, Jane and I said nothing as we crawled off our chairs and exited the room. We huddled close on the sofa hoping their argument would cease soon.

Momma and Merl confronted Daddy's reasoning again. They ridiculed him, causing Enoch to doubt his own thoughts and wishes. Daddy conceded, but he was a very unhappy man.

Before sunrise, in the dark the next morning, the men loaded the mules onto the truck. Momma tossed a few of our clothes into a couple of orange crates setting them on the truck-bed in front of the animals, next to the cab. With Merl behind the wheel, Momma slid in beside him holding Bobby. Daddy, Jane and I all squeezed inside together on the passenger side.

Daddy pleaded one last time about the furnishings. He did not understand the rush. He was obligated to pay off those goods. More timber needed harvested off the plot he purchased.

They would not reveal the true reason for the rush to leave, and stealing away into the darkness. Merl got wind the day before; he was going to be, arrested that very day for theft of the mules.

I wondered why Momma had so much as tossed the new furniture into the trash by leaving it behind. She had been so proud of the house keeping items only weeks before. Momma also insisted we abandon her old '48 rattletrap. She said it wouldn't make the trip.

Momma and Merl defended their decision, yelling at Daddy as though he were a moron. Even at five-years-old, leaving the new furniture behind didn't make sense to me. I said nothing as I crawled into Daddy's lap beside Jane. It was a futile effort to try comforting him.

There is a Monster in the Room

April Fools, 1960, we made the trek to New Glarus, Wisconsin. Daddy and Merl found new jobs skidding logs out of the National Forest near town. This move was no silly joke for my family. We were the fools, the butt of one of life's harsh realities.

The adults around Jane and I were lost in a fiery confusing, deceitful web of lies, poverty, fear, ignorance, and lust. Coupled with Daddy's progressive mental illness, and his jealousy, the situation was on the verge of an explosive eruption. Soon unspeakable crimes began happening that would affect our lives forever. Daddy should never have allowed Momma and Merl to have control.

We rented a large farmhouse on the outskirts of the village. When we arrived at our New Glarus home, the property owner met us in the driveway. He brought two beds, loaded in the back of his pickup. We were to use them until we could afford our own. The men carried them upstairs, placing them in rooms on opposite ends of the hallway. Momma got busy covering the mattresses with bedding. She topped the beds with layers of Grandmother Anne's quilts.

The turn-of-the-century Victorian-Style two stories had majestic, tall white columns out front. Our bedrooms were upstairs and two empty sleeping quarters were on the main floor. We would decide who got which room later.

The place, owned by a dairy farmer, had a herd of fifty or more milk cows which roamed the fields surrounding the property. Beyond the back pastures were dense woods. The property's garbage-dump fell into a steep ravine, about a hundred yards from the house. At the bottom were mounds of trash, old furniture and household appliances. Items discarded by former occupants, for the past fifty years.

With no heat and temperatures continuing to dip into the twenties, outside the atmosphere was cold, but nothing to compare to the freeze inside. The nights were especially frosty, almost as biting and dark as Momma's heart toward Daddy.

We had no coal for the basement furnace while going without electricity for the first week. However, we did have indoor plumbing, which was new to me. I thought our landlord must be rich. Only the wealthy folks had indoor plumbing and running water in our area of Arkansas. The only commodes I had ever seen were in gas stations and hospitals, back home.

When we lived in rural Missouri from where we had just departed, that rental had only an outhouse. I was not accustomed to such convenience, found in the Wisconsin farmhouse. Impressed with the water closet, but I looked forward to heat, more. Warmth would be such comfort.

Momma got angry with me when I was playing, flushing the toilet, and running cold water into the bathtub. She squawked, "Stop frolicking in the water."

She swatted me on the behind. I giggled and flung sprinkles off the ends of my fingers into her face. Her demeanor changed quickly as she laughed, fuzzed my hair and chased me around the living room. For the first time in months, she was showing a flicker of joy toward Jane and me.

Rolling her eyes, and pulling back her locks, the hair fell to her hips. Again, she giggled. "You are a silly boy. But you're right, this is to be happy about," she said.

While tapping me on the shoulder, she says, "You're it," and we took off running in circles around the very large living room again. In pursuit, I was hot-on-her-heels catching her at the kitchen passageway. She raised me off the floor and pecked my cheek. Dropping me to the floor, she swatted my butt, again.

She said, "Now, don't waste the water."

Drawing her lustrous mane under her nostrils, she sniffed, frowning. She said, "Shewwww-wee . . . Guess I need to wash this mop."

Looking down, she grinned. "Running water is certainly going to make life easier. Bobby's dirty diapers. My hair, your baths, clothes," she said, and tickled me.

I flushed the toilet again. Another swat on the behind, she forced me to quit messing with water.

She snapped, "Now, Saul, I told you to stop." She strolled into the kitchen. "Come out of the bathroom, now," she says.

I pushed her as far as she would go. I best mind, or I'd get it good. Running into the empty kitchen, thinking the water was wonderful, I did a handspring, landing on my butt.

"Ouch." I said.

Momma glared down at me and shook her head. "Simmer down, Son. This isn't a barn," she said.

Jane giggled when I bounced to my feet. I say, "I won't do it again, Momma."

"You best not," she said, while opening the empty cabinet doors over the kitchen sink searching for something.

Momma seemed to be always seeking, as though she had misplaced an item. She was wanting, needing something, she was not sure of what she actually sought. Her spirit held a void, an empty place she longed to fill. Momma was never satisfied with herself or anyone else, other than Merl.

I was looking forward to a warm bath in the huge bear-claw-footed tub. That had to wait until the electric was turned on, no hot water.

Momma, Daddy, Jane, and Bobby shared one of the upstairs bedrooms. Merl wanted me to stay with him down the hall. Momma had no reason not to trust him. After all, she was his lover.

Daddy resisted the idea. He wanted to keep our family together. Momma took control. She was overruling his wishes. I wound up bunking with Merl. Her reasoning was I am the largest child and there was not enough space for five of us in one bed. Reluctantly, I submitted to her wishes. Merl held my hand as we strolled down the hallway.

Before crawling into bed, Merl and I stripped to our underclothing and then slid between the cold sheets. To stay warm in the briskness, I pulled the heavy handmade quilts Grandmother Anne had left us over my head, and snuggled close to him.

He spoke to me in gentle comforting tones and wrapped his large muscular arm over my shoulder. He held my backside close to his hearty chest.

I was shivering before, but now safe and cozy. Even though I did not like Merl kissing on Momma, he was warm as could be. It felt so good having his body heat against my goose-bumped legs and arms.

I remembered the burning mule. I cannot trust Merl. Still angry with him for hurting Mabel, but this night I had to submit, steal his warmth or freeze to death.

A week passed. I was beginning to think Merl wasn't such a bad guy. Maybe, I should forgive him. If my parents did separate, he might be my new dad. Hating him would complicate the scenario, if it were to come.

The second week we went through the usual routine for a few days. I would shiver, and he would pull me close with his arm draped over my chest. Late in the night, on the tenth day of the sleeping arrangements the routine changed. After falling into a restful sleep, I awakened.

He was rubbing his rough hands on my chest and belly. He patted my bottom and leg. Why was he doing that? Suddenly his hand was in my under shorts. He was fondling me. Terrified, I could not breathe. I could not move. I could not speak. What was happening? Why was he touching me there? No one had ever touched me liked that before. It did not feel right.

I thought, Stop! Stop! Don't touch me. This is my forbidden zone.

I wanted to cry out for Daddy, but had no air in my lungs to move over the vocal cords. I simply froze. Out of sheer terror, I stopped breathing altogether. He grabbed my hand and shoved it down inside his briefs. I blacked out from absolute panic.

The next morning, I was alone. Merl and Daddy were gone to work. I could not find my underpants. Naked in the bed, I was sore, spots of blood were on the sheets and I felt dirty. I could only remember pieces of what had happened, but I knew something horrible had taken place. I was still trembling.

I thought Merl was mean to me last night. I did not like him anymore. I was wrong to have ever thought I could trust him. Did he touch Momma that way? No, she wouldn't allow him. He would draw back with only a nub, if he placed his hand on her whoo-whoo. That was why Lilly left him? He hurt her too. Maybe, he did this to me because he knew I did not want him kissing Momma. I wanted their kissing affair to stop. He hated me. That was why he did this to me.

Merl's baby sister Della said he hurt her pee-pee, her whoo-whoo. No one believed it. Why would he do that? She told, and the Judas family said she was crazy. The Loafer's Glory community mocked her, laughing when the topic was mentioned.

Momma would not believe me either. I don't want labeled, nuts. That's what will happen if I tell. Should I mention this to Momma? No, she would only ridicule me, the way she did Daddy. She would call me a liar while she defended Merl. Just like the Judas family, did Della.

Daddy was losing his mind. Momma said he was the village idiot. Stupid or not, he would help me if he could. What could he do? Merl was stronger, now days. Daddy was smoking and not eating.

He was losing sleep, and weight. If they fought, Daddy was sure to fail.

Maybe he did not mean to hurt me. Was this, normal? Daddy never touched me that way. Why did Merl put my hands on him? I didn't want to. Merl was mean.

He was the son of a devil. What was that word? Oh yes, son-of-a-bit**, or was it a witch? That is what Bertha his mother claimed to be. He too was a mean witch. Or is it bit**? They were the same-kind of mean. I decided to sleep in the room with Momma and Daddy from then on, even if I had to sleep on the cold floor under the bed.

Frightened, I forced myself to move and search for my clothes. Relieved to find my pants, I sighed and quickly slipped them on. My search for underclothing was futile. I never found my underwear, never.

After dressing, nausea overpowered as I ran for the bathroom to vomit. I cleaned myself in the cold tap water. Just then, Momma walked in. She admired herself in the mirror, picking at hair framing her face, and pinched her cheeks. She sees I've puked.

Concerned, softly, she asked, "Is your stomach queasy?"

I nodded.

She said, "You might have a virus. Go back to bed."

I yelled, "No, I won't stay in that room again."

Scowling and rolling her eyes, she said, "Saul, don't get smart. Don't take that tone with Momma."

I dropped my gaze, and strolled into the kitchen searching for a glass. Momma followed and asked, "Did you have a nightmare?"

I nodded, and puckered my lips as my face wadded for a squalling attack, but I managed to hold back the tears. "There's a monster in the room," I whispered, head-down.

Momma handed me a glass of water, chuckled, and said, "There are no monsters, Saul. Only you and Merl sleep there. It was just a bad dream."

I say, "Merl is the monster."

She chuckled again, paid no mind, and went about her household chores, as though, my words are silent. I wanted to go home, to

Arkansas. I wanted to get away from the flesh and blood demon, the monster Merl. I was terrified of him. I thought he was the cause of all our troubles. I wanted him to go away. How do you kill a devil?

He and Daddy left before sunup. I dreaded the thought of Merl coming in at sundown. Spending the day quietly hanging around the house, I washed myself frequently. Feeling dirty, but I could not seem to wipe it away with soap and water. By late afternoon the bleeding stopped. The pain continued. The physical anguish could not compare to the emotional turmoil eating me up inside.

Momma scolded me again, shouting for me to stop playing in the water. I was not playing. I was trying to scrape the filth away.

I looked after little sister Jane, and baby brother Bobby the remainder of the afternoon. Momma worked to make the cold, empty house appear to be a warm, an inviting family place by cleaning. She hung some ragged curtains she found folded in a dusty box from the attic. Jane and I watched while cuddling close to Bobby on a pallet of Grandmother Anne's quilts.

The only furnishings were a player piano that was already in the living room when we moved in. Two beds upstairs, and now we had a dining room table the landlord brought early that morning. A couple of torn cloth-upholstery-covered chairs were setting by the big picture window. This seating furniture was also given to us by another friendly neighbor.

In front of the piano, Bobby played on a pallet sucking his bottle while sitting up to watch Momma. Jane napped beside him, and I huddled close for warmth. I could not sleep.

Momma's fickle heart was as cold as the room. I needed her comfort. She did not have it to give. I blamed her, but said nothing. I didn't know what had happened to me. There had to be a word for it. I did not know that word. In my mind, Merl was just mean. The pain, fear, and shame were all there, but not the understanding.

The word affair concerning Merl and Momma's relationship, I only connected as kissing and that was wrong. She was to only smooches with Daddy. Her kissing Merl in itself was turmoil enough.

His feelings were not suspect. Daddy's insane jealousy, fueled by suspicions, they were based on fact. I knew for certain. He was right on, in thinking, Momma was unfaithful. He had the right to be upset. They were breaking the rules of love.

I thought kissing and touching forbidden zones were not connected acts. Touching pee-pees was painful. Did Momma let him touch her whoo-whoo and bottom?

Bedtime came; I threw a fit, doubled my fist and wanted to hit Momma, but restrained the desire. I whined and pouted, crawling into Daddy's lap I refused to move. Merl glared down at me as if warning not to tell. Momma threatened to paddle me unless I did as she said.

"Get up and go on to bed," she shouted.

Wanting to blurt it out, but who would believe a five-year-old child? I felt shame and embarrassment. What would I be shouting? Merl hurt me. Then, he would deny it, calling me nuts like his sister Della. They would laugh, and Momma would spank me for lying.

I got myself into this dilemma, a frightening and painful situation by minding Momma. I should have resisted her commands from the onset, spanking or not.

I should have stuck up for Daddy, and this would never have happened. Daddy wanted me to stay with the family. There is where I should have slept from the first night on.

Merl might kill me. Maybe, it was my fault. Had, I made him angry. Yap, I threatened to kill him over Mabel. This was his revenge. What did he do to me? I did not understand. His touch hurt.

I leapt off Daddy's lap and bolted up the staircase. I slithered underneath their bed and held onto the slats, whimpering. Moments later, they all ascended the staircase.

When Momma discovered I was not in Merl's bed, but rather under hers, she shrieked, "Get-the-hell out from under there. You are not staying in this room. The bed is too small."

She lay Bobby on the mattress above me, and hoisted Jane standing beside her off the floor into Daddy's arms.

I bawled, "Momma, I'll sleep on the floor," I said. I could see Merl's feet, standing in the doorway. Fearful, I squealed louder.

Daddy sat down beside Bobby with Jane, and said, "It's okay, Ora. Let him stay with us."

Momma shouted, "Shut up, he's gonna mind me."

I clung to the bed slats with all my might as Merl raced over, reached underneath, grabbed my ankles, and yanked. I lost my grip while being dragged from under the bed and flung over his shoulder. Merl was quiet, saying nothing as I kicked and screamed when we exited the room.

She followed us out into the hallway. "You're getting a whipping' in the morning. Now, shut it up or it will be worse," she said.

I reached for Daddy as he stepped into the hallway and stood by Momma. He said, "Ora, you should let him stay with us."

Ignoring him, she raised her hand and flung her wrist, motioning for Merl to take me. She turned and disappeared through their bedroom doorway. Head-down, Daddy followed her.

I heard the springs rattle as she flopped down on their bed. She sighed, and said, "He has become too attached to me since the accident. Now, he acts like a spoiled brat."

Merl strolled happily toward the room of horrors, with his bundle of meat (me) tossed over his shoulder. That night, he abused me again, and threatened to kill Momma, Daddy, Bobby, and Jane, if I ever told. I had no one to protect me. I had to protect them.

I had to be brave. In my mind, I reasoned this too would pass, just as I got through the surgery. I would get through this somehow. Lying there, night after night under Grandmother Anne's heavy handmade quilts, I thought, I could feel her haunting prayers. Her quilts were my only comfort.

Many times, Daddy spoke fondly of his ma being in Heaven with Jesus. "Son, you be a good boy and we will all be together in Heaven someday. Ma sure loved Jesus. He helped her out of lots of troubles when I was a boy," he said.

I thought, maybe I needed to pray in her strange language. I didn't know the tongue. I could not. My cries, and whispers, would have to suffice.

Merl might kill me if I ever let the secret slip. I'm glad in a sense that Momma didn't get it earlier, when I called him a monster. I did not want him to kill them.

I wondered if he killed me, would I go to be with Grandma. Perhaps she could hear prayer since she was an angel, now. Hoped, I could keep the secret from the others.

I told Grandma, anyway. She did not count, because she was already dead. Perchance, she would send an army of soldier angels to rescue me from the night monster. I assured myself, Grandma Anne could see, and she would tell Jesus. I survived another night.

Two weeks later, I awakened early in the morning to the sound of a puppy playfully barking downstairs. Sliding into my pants, I raced barefoot down the staircase. There in the living room stood the property owner. Wrinkled, Mr. Nelson was tall, clean-shaven with gray-hair neatly combed. He held a lively Collie puppy in his arms.

He says, "There is the young man I came to see. I have something for you." A smile exploded across his face as he handed me the pup.

I ask, "May I keep him, Momma?"

She says, "Yes, you may. He is all yours, but you'll have to share with Jane."

Mr. Nelson chuckled.

I say, "Thank you, Mr. Nelson."

He says, "You're quite welcome. But say, my friends call me Otto. I think we're friends now. You can call me Otto."

I say, "You bet. You're the best friend in the world."

He says, "Nope, I have no right to take claim to that title. Maybe, I am the second best friend in the world," as he points to the puppy now uncontrollably licking my face.

I giggle.

"Let me know what you name him. Gotta tend to the new calves this morning. Best be going," he says, as he headed toward the kitchen door.

I say, "Thanks again, Mr. Otto."

He chuckles and says, "You're welcome, Son."

Momma walks behind him, she also thanks Otto as he exits the house. She latches the door when he is gone. Turning toward me, she asked, "What on earth are you going to name this noisy, playful fur-ball?"

I look into his eyes. Turning to face Momma, I say, "We will call him Buddy."

From the start, we became fast friends, and I found comfort in his presence. I thought that Buddy could actually understand my cries and whispers. His playfulness helped me to forget for a while. He brought great joy.

A few days later, Buddy and I buried ourselves inside an igloo of barn-loft hay. We fell asleep. I awoke to the sound of one of the mules braying. I peeked through the cracked loft floor to see Merl doing ugly things.

Buddy and I did not make a sound. We lay there, motionless, eyes closed most of the time. After he relieved himself, he hoisted the spare chainsaw off a shelf and left the barn. I waited a little longer. We heard the logging truck drive away, and we're certain the coast was clear. Buddy and I crawled down. We bolted across the barnyard toward the basement.

No place was safe from Merl's grasp. I thought, I will hide, but he will find me. No living creature was sheltered from harm with Merl around.

Inside the basement, we crept to the back of the coal bin, where I hunkered down, held Buddy, and softly sobbed. Fearful for my life, and the lives of my family members, I endured this netherworld for weeks.

Be brave, all things will pass, and indeed relief finally came one rainy Saturday afternoon near the end of May. The men could not work during the downpour days. Daddy was in the barn sharpening chainsaws. He brushed down the mules and gave them each a bail of hay, a bag of oats, and fresh water. When we returned to the house one hour later looking for Momma, I said, "Momma and Merl, probably gone into the basement to clean up the coal bin, and the area around the furnace. She said she was going to do that today."

Suspiciously, quietly, Daddy crept downstairs.

I hear Momma shout, "Crazy, sneaking son-of-a-bit**."

Merl yelled, "Oh sh**."

Flying up the staircase, Daddy stormed through the kitchen, hurt and anger gyrating down his cheeks. He mumbled, "Messing with my best friend. I am an ignorant fool. Why didn't I listen to Ma? Why didn't I heed Joe's advise? Intercourse, the sorry SOBs needs to be shot."

I thought, Momma and Merl having intercourse. Is that like smoochin' or touching pee-pees and whoo-whoos?

Furious, Daddy dashed out of the house, slammed the door, and stomped briskly away, headed toward town on the main road. I stood gazing out the front room window, stroking Buddy's thick soft fur as Daddy ambled out of sight.

This time I was siding with Daddy. He was right all along. Momma preferred the monster. I questioned, would Daddy be brave enough to stand up to them?

When he left, I am sure he would have driven despite his fear, but the only vehicle available was the new logging truck. Merl had the keys.

I smiled. No longer burdened to keep the secret, I planned to tell him about the affair. Now, he knew beyond any doubt. Maybe he would take us far away from this evil house. I hoped, a long way from Merl, forever. Maybe, he would go buy a car, and come back for us, his children.

Yap, Momma hated Daddy. I wondered if she felt the same about Bobby, Jane, and me. I resolved in my mind. Their marriage was over. We would live in different homes, just as Daddy prophesied the year before.

Renting a New Glarus motel room, Daddy was gone three days. During that time, Momma shared Merl's bed, and we children stay in the family bedroom together.

Huddling for warmth, we cried ourselves to sleep. The house had electricity now, but no coal for heat. Yet cool at night, the adults had decided warmer weather was at hand and they would not waste money on heating fuel.

Defeated, Daddy returned on Tuesday morning. Having made a decision, he humbly asked Merl to drive. Daddy, Jane, and I were leaving for South Bend, Indiana. Daddy's tall, very blond sister Lou, her four children, and husband Martin lived there. Aunt Lou would help take care of Jane and me while he worked. Jane and I could not recall ever meeting her.

Loving Momma with everything inside of him, I hoped Daddy would eventually use his brain and not act on his heart. Maybe, finally he was slowly accepting the fact that she no longer loved him.

It was a relief for him in a way. He now had the evidence. It was true. She was an unfaithful wife. He was not delusional. She had broken their covenant vows. He would work hard to overcome the treachery--a broken heart.

Uncle Martin had plenty of drywall jobs, and Daddy would not have a problem signing on with one of his crews to learn the trade. He had to go on, and make a life for himself, and his children. He had to get us away, or he would kill them.

If he did murder them, it was off to the chain gangs. He was sure to windup in prison for beating them near to death, if we stayed. Often he had spoken of strangling the life out of Merl. He said the thought of prison kept him from doing the dirty deed. He was thankful Grandpa Daniel Bip stopped him that day at Poojam's.

I was not sure about that. What exactly was a prison or jail? I heard it said bad people, are locked up there behind bars. I imagined it was a place like the zoo. Instead of wild animals in a cage for all to see, bad people made it home. Prison cages held mean spirited wild men and some evil women too. I was glad Daddy didn't kill them. I did not want him confined in a prison zoo. I was not displeased at the thought of Merl being behind bars. Monsters belong in locked cages so they cannot hurt people.

Daddy gave Merl the truck. Signing the title over to him was symbolic--Daddy washed his hands clean, of their childhood friendship, forever. We left six-month-old Bobby with Momma. She insisted.

Parting from Buddy was hard. Maybe, Momma would take care of him too. I could only hope that Merl wouldn't abuse my best friend, Buddy.

High Dollar Woman

Arriving in South Bend, three-and-one-half-year-old, Jane had her own secrets of terror from New Glarus. I would not know about her nightmares for some time to come. For the moment, as far as I knew, I was his only victim. She too fearfully kept her mouth shut.

I wondered if Jesus had heard me or not. Buddy could, but now he was gone. We would not see him, Mother, or Bobby for the next three months. Relieved to be out of Merl's grasp, I missed my own already.

I thought Jesus actually seemed like the story of Santa Clause. Was He real? Had He answered my prayers? Could Grandmother Anne actually see me, and had she told Jesus?

Daddy often said there was a narrow line between the truth, and insanity concerning spiritual subjects. I did not know about what he was talking. I wanted to believe an all-powerful God, and Jesus would help me keep my family. Despite any reservations I may have had at the time, I held fast to a belief that He did exist, because Daddy said Jesus was real.

Daddy called it Faith, belief in Jesus, but folks said Daddy was crazy. Maybe Faith was imagination, believing in unseen things as though they already existed, or hoping they would in time.

The religion was a little confusing for me at age five, but I had confidence Daddy knew what he was talking about when he preached, Jesus was God's Son. He said, "It is a crazy thing, foolishness to those who do not believe in the invisible resurrected Christ, or His Holy Ghost. The whole family is invisible. They are the unseen trinity. They are all powerful and very real."

Momma said she believed in Jesus, but He did not have a pa, named God. Jesus was His own Father. Momma called it the Oneness Doctrine. She said she loved Jesus, but angrily cursed Jesus' name when fighting with Daddy.

Everyone around me said they, believed in Him, except, for Merl. He said there were no God family, no Jesus, and no Holy Ghost. He says the only things with power on this earth were just the forces of nature, and the spirits of the ancestors. Merl said there was no God. What did that make him?

All said they believed in Santa, even Merl. I knew Santa Clause was not real. I had my reservations about this Son of God, Jesus. I had never seen him. I didn't know him. I just knew about Him. I thought, and hoped he did exist. Surely, Daddy would not lie about such a thing. Most everyone said Jesus existed. Merl was the exception. Even sinner believers say He lived in Heaven way above the stars. Some said He made His abode inside their hearts. I could not figure out how Jesus got inside them.

The professing Christians around me certainly did not walk the talk or keep His commandments, the law's Daddy preached. They were, double minded. Did they love Him? Perhaps they just believed in Him, maybe. I guessed, that made them sinner Baptist, and backsliding Pentecostals. They were moonshine drinking, smoking, cussing, fighting, carnal Christians.

They were not holiness like Grandmother Anne, or Momma's aunt Diana. These two, strived daily to obey the "Ten Commandments." Everyone called them saints.

Diana, the one who helped Grandma Iris raise Momma and her siblings, was married to Tex. Diana and Tex did their best to walk out in their lives, what they preached. Tex was Oneness, a Jesus Name Only Preacher. He was Grandpa Daniel's older brother. Tex told Pops he would split Hell wide open for divorcing Grandma Iris, and marrying Gert.

Pops said his brother Tex was already in Hell, bound by the chains of strict religious laws, impossible for any normal man to live, under. He wanted Tex to loosen up.

Diana was like a second mother for Momma. Two saints were in my family. One was living, Pentecostal Jesus Only, Diana Bip. The other was dead, Pentecostal Trinity, Grandma Anne Hotman. Despite their religious differences, the two matriarchs had been choice friends.

Their differences aside, this warm relationship was not the norm. They chose to find common ground in their religious doctrines. Most Oneness believers and opposing Trinity congregations dismissed the other's belief system, thinking they held fast to a false doctrine. Diana, and Anne genially loved, and respected each other. Momma resented them both.

Diana said she despised Momma's rebellion. She did not trust Merl, and had told Momma so, referring to him as an infidel. She scolded Momma, saying Merl would be her ruin.

Momma rebuffed those words. She held a grudge against Diana.

I heard Pentecostal folks, called sinner Baptist, hypocrites. Some said Momma was a sinner Baptist-Pentecostal-Jezebel, and Daddy was the lunatic preacher. What made them hypocrites? What is a hypocrite? Merl was not a hypocrite. He was a devil, Satan's angel, a demon.

Stories about Grandmother Anne caused me to believe she truly was a holy saint. Maybe, she was one of God's angels. I talked to her every night.

Momma was no respecter of persons when it came to her disdain. She hated Grandmother Anne. Out of respect, and to appease Diana, she conformed to some of the Pentecostal holiness beliefs, and dress codes. Her heart was not in it, especially when she got involved with Merl. Diana's stern words of warning, Momma warded off as the babbling of an old religious ignorant woman. If Diana had not been a second mom for her, she would have hated Diana too.

I thought; Momma hated Jesus. She said she didn't. Momma said He was her personal savior. She said she loved Jesus. Maybe her love for Jesus was kind of like the love-hate she felt for Daddy. Momma contradicted herself in saying God is Love, giving Him the sir name Damn.

She confused me. To curse God, the one she said did not exist and give His son who she said was God, the last name Damn. Then she tried to pin the same cursing name on Daddy. Was this Momma's definition of Love? Since she did not believe in Father God, I assumed Love had to be Jesus' nickname, or He would not put up with the name-calling.

Daddy's people cherished Anne's memory. Anne raised Daddy in the church. He gnawed on the backs of Pentecostal church-pews, while Anne preached. He never understood her tongues, and felt aversion toward the church antics. He said Ma had something from God that was beyond his reasoning. Maybe the tongues were real, but he didn't want them. He said he was crazy enough.

Delena said angels talked in tongues. That was the language spoken in Heaven. A few people on earth spoke that dialect, though not understanding the words that flowed out of their own mouths.

I questioned, why would anyone want to speak a language he didn't understand? I on the other hand, held by fascination at the exercise of others speaking in the unknown tongue. Delena said only a select group of two or three in any congregation understood the meanings of this babbling tongue. I certainly did not.

Daddy said devils talked in tongues too. How was any tongue talker to know if he was speaking the dialect of an angel, or devil?

Perhaps by the goodness that followed, maybe that was the sign one could know if it was from Heaven. Grandma Anne could not be a devil.

When we moved to South Bend, I continued hoping she would help me if she were an angel now. Maybe her tongues could cast a good spell on us to fix my family if I pray hard enough for her to hear. Maybe, it was not too late for my parents' marriage. I half-heartedly held onto that dim flicker of a possibility.

Aunt Lou, a tall, slender, blond headed woman, having long model legs in her mid-thirties. She was a polished, upper-middle-class, woman. She wore the latest in fashion attire, high heels, and matching accessories.

Diamond rings adorned her fingers. She wore sparkly earbobs and light makeup. Bright red lipstick with the hint of rouge, rubbed in to match on her cheeks. Her bottled platinum-blond hair was styled in the beehive.

Lou kept the books for Martin's drywall business. She had no idea what Jane and I had endured. We were not about to tell. Not even each other.

Jane was spotting blood in her panties when we arrived. She screamed hysterically when Aunt Lou tried to bathe and dress her. Hyperactive, high-strung Lou couldn't understand why the child made such a fuss. She thought the tiny droplets of blood from Jane's rectum were nothing serious. Perhaps Jane had scratched herself. The bleeding stopped after a few days. She considered nothing more of the problems as Jane began to trust her when bathed, and dressed.

August, the summer of 1960, Momma called Lou. She wanted Daddy to bring us back to her. Two and a half months had passed since the separation. She and Bobby were alone. Merl had gone to Florida to patch up his marriage with Lilly, abandoning Momma.

Against his better judgment, but driven by his love for Momma, Bobby, Jane and me, Daddy borrowed Uncle Martin's new Chevy Impala. He returned us to Leviathan's den, the Wisconsin farmhouse, where Momma waited.

Jane and I called the place haunted, a haunted house. Ghosts lived there; haunting memories without decency, ghosts of terror, a monster lived in that place.

Few words spoken between them as Daddy unloaded our clothes, packed in brown paper grocery sacks. He grabbed the pokes from the trunk of the car and carried them into the big white house. He held nine-month-old Bobby for a few minutes, then kissed him goodbye.

Bobby had grown a lot over the past three months, so had Buddy. I was overjoyed to see them both. Sadly, Daddy passed Bobby back to Momma. Hugging Jane and me goodbye, tears well in his eyes. "I love you kids. Now, mind your Momma," he said, and drove away.

I was happy Daddy overcame his fear, finding the courage to drive, again. Operating a vehicle was a necessary skill, needed for him getting to-and-from different job sites. Martin taught him how to finish drywall. He was making more money than ever before, but his heart was broken over Momma. My heart longed for him to stay with us as the Chevy crested a hill and fell behind it, out of sight.

We remained there with Momma for one week. She had no job and food was running out. The twenty-dollars Daddy gave her did not last long. Momma borrowed money from Otto, to make the trip back home to Arkansas.

We would go to her father's place. Jane and I would see Grandpa Daniel. We both agreed this was a treat. Momma took Buddy to a neighbor for safekeeping, until we would return.

Happy was our brief reunion. Now we were leaving him behind again. I did not know when we would be coming back, if ever. The possible reality saddened my heart. There were already too many goodbyes between us during our short friendship.

Paul E. Treadwell

Push Ginger into the Lake

Momma stacked quilts on the rear floorboard of her beat up '50 Ford until they were even with the backseat. She said Merl bought the car for her before he went to Florida, chasing after Lilly. Jane, Bobby, and I slept comfortably while she drove.

Hundreds of miles south of New Glarus, on the out skirts of Springfield, Missouri. I awoke and saw tears rolling down her cheeks. I wanted to ease her pain but did not know how. Momma seemed to have a black cloud of gloom hanging over her. I drifted off to sleep again.

The day was cloudy, and rain fell most of the long drive. The constant rhythmic clunk, splash, and squeaking noise of windshield wipers flapping during a heavy down pour. Sounds of rain, overpowered, by Momma moaning.

Her painful sobbing awakened me, again. Momma's crying, broke my heart. She was weeping uncontrollably while trying to hold back her groans of anguish. I crawled over the seat and sat down beside her. I patted her on the leg and looked up, trying to comfort her.

"Momma, why you crying?" I asked.

She sniffled, and wiped her face with a clean white handkerchief. She sighed, and took a deep breath. "I'm okay, Saul. You wouldn't understand if I told you," she said while searching for her cigarettes on the dash. The pack had slid to the passenger side and I handed it to her.

"Thank you, Son," she said.

I say, "You're welcome, Momma."

"Why were you crying?" I asked again.

Shaking her head, she sniffled, fighting back the tears, "Baby, adult stuff is too complicated for you to understand. Now, you don't worry. Momma is fine," she said.

She was not fine. "Do you miss Daddy?" I asked.

She frowned. "No, it's over between us. I do miss Merl. I love him," she whimpered.

Sadly, I leaned my head against her side. "Are you and Daddy getting a divorce?" I asked.

She sighed, and said, "Yes, Saul. He's crazy. I can't take it any more."

I say, "Daddy says you, and me, is chicken dookie." I snarled, "He's crazy, Momma."

Like a young elementary school-age-girl, she giggled.

I say, "He says Merl is hog sh**. I don't like Merl, Momma. He's mean to me."

Rolling her eyes as she did when Daddy said something disjointed from the conversation at hand. She says, "Oh, you are a silly boy. Merl loves you. Don't use the word sh** ever again. It is a bad word. Now, where on earth, did you ever get such a thought? There is not a mean bone in Merl!"

She scowled. "Yah probably got it from your lunatic daddy. Merl is a good man, and he says he loves me. Maybe one day he will come back to us. He will be your new daddy," she said, as she began to sob again.

I could not tell her. I decided that I would never tell her. She would tell Merl. He will deny everything, and call me a liar and then he will kill us all. No, I would never tell her.

Momma was more of a nut than, Daddy. I did not want Merl to be my daddy. Why would she think that would be pleasant news for me? I could not understand why she wanted to be with the monster.

Always, and vehemently she defended Merl in whatever he did. I could not change her mind. I tried many times in the past. She would not listen to my pleading.

I ask, "Where did Merl go? Why did he leave you alone in Wisconsin?"

Crying so hard, I could hardly understand a word she spoke. She said, "He went back to Lilly."

"God will work it out, Momma. Daddy says, He is help in trouble," I said, wanting to comfort her and myself. I stood in the seat, hugged her neck, and kissed her on the cheek.

She grimaced while patting my leg. "We'll be all right. Now, you crawl back and take another nap. We'll be in Arkansas soon," she said, sniffling and wiping the tears from her eyes again.

I crawled over the seat. Thinking maybe Momma was going to meet Merl. I wanted to go back to Indiana. I wanted Daddy. I wished Momma didn't love Merl. She loved Merl more than Daddy, Jane, Bobby, and me. What I thought in the hospital, it was going to come true. I just couldn't understand why he drove to Lilly's, if he loved Momma so much. I chose to think about it at another time, and drifted off to sleep.

Right around the town of Springdale, Arkansas, the clunker overheated when the water pump quit. After paying for the car repair, she was flat broke. Not having enough gas to drive the additional one-hundred-fifty miles, getting to Grandpa Daniel's place was going to be impossible without more money.

Momma tried to call one of her uncles who lived in Springdale, but his telephone disconnected. Next, she called Chad and asked him to wire her some money. She led him to believe we would be moving back to Loafer's Glory.

He says, all of father's siblings pitched in and remodeled the old homestead. They put new sheet-rock on the walls and linoleum on the floors. They finished it off with a fresh coat of paint. Chad promised they would help her raise us if she came back there to live.

She agreed, and Chad wired her fifty dollars by Western Union. Momma was to pick up the money in Springdale a few days later.

She lied to Chad, never intending on our return to Loafer's Glory. She loathed the Hotman clan, but gladly took his money.

Bean harvest was going on at full tilt in the fields around Springdale. We joined locals and migrant workers harvesting the crops. Having a little cash on hand was urgent, until we received the money from Chad.

No place to stay, and nothing to eat, Momma was worried. She decided we would sleep in the car near the fields over night. She parked under a broad shade oak closest to the patches.

Momma got out, and approached a big truck at the field's edge where a foreman stood. I toddled behind. He gave her a bushel basket. Smiling he bent down, ruffled my hair with his large hand, and asked, "Little guy, you want a basket?"

I nodded.

Momma smiled. She said, "Use your manners Saul."

Reaching for the top of a stack resting on the end of truck-bed, he grabbed a smaller straw container. When he handed down the basket, half the size of hers, I said, "Thank you."

He nodded, pointing toward the plants wanting us to pick. We strolled to the place, and set down our baskets between two rows. Momma headed for the car. She glanced over her shoulder as she trotted toward the vehicle. "Saul, you stay here and start picking. I'll get Jane and Bobby," she said.

"Okay Momma," I yelled.

The next row over we met a stocky handsome woman named Ginger. About thirty-five, Ginger had three children. Her youngest, Nina, was ten, blond, and pleasingly plump. Violet, twelve was tall, husky with light-brown hair and piercing blue eyes. The eldest, a boy named Robert. He was fourteen, robust, husky, handsome with coal-black hair, and dark-tan skin.

Jane and I tried to befriend them, but the children did not want much to do with us. Robert glared at us and mumbled, "Not another one." He sighed, and scowling Violet nodded. Nina stuck her tongue out at us when we waved.

Grinning, I said, "Howdy." When they did not respond, I crossed my eyes, crinkled up my nose, and stuck my tongue out too.

Momma took one of Anne's quilts out of the back seat and folded Bobby a pallet. She laid it in between the beanstalk rows behind her. Bobby lay on top and slept as she dragged it along while we picked our way to the ends of the rows.

The women conversed as they worked. Ginger had a bass voice with broad shoulders and light-brown hair, cut short and curled just above her shoulders. Quite taken with each other, they conversed, laughing and enjoying the socialization.

In some ways, Ginger's features reminded me of our good neighbor Mary back in Loafer's Glory. Yet, something about her that was quite different. I couldn't put my finger on what I perceived. What was it that made this woman appear strange to me?

Perhaps the likeness to Mary was why Momma took to her so quickly. She seemed as kind hearted and generous. Their ice chest at the end of the field near where we parked, contained milk, and sandwiches. When we took a break, Ginger filled Bobby's bottle. They also shared their food with us. When Ginger found out, we had nowhere to stay the night; she invited us to her house. Momma refused at first, but Ginger insisted.

Not wanting to be ungrateful, for the food, offer of a safe place to sleep, and a comfortable bed, the friendship that seemed to be blossoming between Momma and Ginger gave me a confusing distrustful feeling. I didn't understand why Ginger kept touching Momma's hands, and rubbing up against her as they squatted, picking the beans.

The women were not interested in the bean harvest, but happily shared highlights of their own lives, while getting to know one another better. Momma turned to see if anyone was watching. I scrutinized their every move and hung onto each word they spoke.

Momma seemed a bit embarrassed at Ginger's unruly touching. She rolled her eyes and blushed while I gawked. She quickly brushed off Ginger's hand from her leg and frowned. Turning to face me, she smiled, and continued giggling with Ginger. Something was wrong with this situation from the beginning. What was I witnessing?

Two days later, Momma and Ginger conspired to set Momma up with a local shopkeeper. He was successful, but a very married man. The new suitor and Momma were going out together for a day. I resisted the idea, and was quite troublesome, whining for Momma to stay. She ignored my antics.

Momma slips into her baby-blue chiffon dress. She looked like an angel. She painted her lips bright red, which she had never done before. She put on thick makeup and rogue. She curled her hair. She perfumed herself, with a-sickening-sweet cologne, Ginger gave her.

I had never known Momma to be extravagant in the application of her beauty aides, other than perfume. Diana's holiness background forbids the use of such things. Momma had always used a little makeup sparingly out of respect for Diana's teachings. In comparison, smearing blobs of the face paint on, Momma was looking like she fell into a vat of pink-pancake-batter. I was repulsed. She did not look like Momma anymore.

When the man arrived, Momma took Jane and left with him, leaving Bobby and me behind. I fretted the entire four hours she was gone. I did not like this stranger Ginger, or her snotty kids. Worse, I loathed the idea of Momma dating her married friend.

When they returned, Jane was wearing a beautiful, new, pale pink dress, and new black-paten-leather slippers. Momma stood in the yard with Jane on her hip, and kissed the man goodbye.

Her man friend was a short stocky fellow with thinning light brown hair, fifty, a potbelly and thick black-rimed glasses. He was ugly. I especially wanted to run out and hit him, when Momma let him feel her up. He slurped; suck face with his lips puckered forward like a huge carp's mouth a gasping for breath.

My guts rumbled with anger. Another affair, I didn't want her to kiss anyone but Daddy. The anxiety made me sick. I ran for the restroom, and vomited.

The same evening, I overheard Momma and Ginger talking in their bedroom while I eavesdropped outside the closed door. Momma got money from this man in exchange for her time with him. He wanted another date, and Momma decided to oblige him. I burst into the room begging her not to do it.

She scolded me for crashing in without knocking first. She says, "Peter Saul, use your manners. You know to knock before entering an adult's bedroom."

I say, "Yes, Momma. I won't do it again, if you promise not to go out again with ol' fish mouth."

She says, "Saul, I'm the parent. You are the child. There are no terms to negotiate. You will always mind me. My word is final. I'll go out with whom I please. Now, get out and leave it be."

I say, "Momma, that ugly man . . . You can't go with him, no more kissing. I heard you say you planned to see him again. What for? I hope his ugly don't rub off on you."

She did her best to twist the truth, making me think for a moment, perhaps I had misunderstood. I had not figured it wrong. She implied the kiss was only an innocent expression of friendship. It was simply a thank you for the day's outing, and for buying Jane the new outfit.

I trusted my own feelings from the observation, what I saw with my own eyes, and heard with my own ears. I had not, misconstrued. I figured she was trying to deceive me. Like, she did Daddy. She was attempting to hide another secret.

Daddy said women paid for their time with men are Jezebels. She was a liar. The money lay in a neat stack on the bed in front of them. She said it was the cash, Chad sent.

I knew better. I overheard them talking, planning, scheming. Oddly enough, she did not see him again. I forced myself to believe she had picked up Chad's handout.

By the end of the week, Momma received notice; the money Chad wired was waiting for her. I rode along to the Western Union office. After retrieving the fifty bucks, she got into the car, and I asked, "Momma, did Chad send you more cash?"

Sheepishly stuttering, she said, "Ah, yes. He said the fifty wasn't enough."

Her tone was suspect. Did she lie again? I didn't know if she was being untruthful. I had my suspicions. When we returned, I over heard her speaking with Ginger. Chad did not send two wires by Western Union as she had told me, only one. I had figured out her little white lie. They both chuckled.

It was a sultry Sunday afternoon, when she told Ginger we were leaving. The two women decided we would drive to the lake before we had to go. When we arrived, Robert and his sisters unloaded the picnic baskets from the trunk of Ginger's black '56 Chevy. They spread a quilt on the shaded beach, a few feet from the water's edge, near a large white oak.

Before eating, Ginger and Momma strolled toward the pier's edge, out into the deep part of the lake. Waves splashed against the support beams underneath. Ginger kept trying to hold Momma's hand, but she resisted.

The woman was up to her funny business again. I followed close behind. Ginger began to cry. She told Momma that she was in-love with her, and could not live without her.

Momma was gentle but firm in her refusal as she explained she had to leave. Ginger wailed hysterically at the rejection, reaching out to Momma several times. Continually, Momma pulled away.

Ginger says, "Ora, Honey, we can have a good life together. We can help each other raise our kids together. We won't have to worry about some sorry man breaking our hearts."

I moved closer toward Ginger.

She says, "Please stay. Please, I'm begging you."

Momma, held back her true emotions, a little fear in her tone. "Ginger. I thank you for all the help. Your offer is tempting, but we have to go." Waving her wrist, Momma motioned for me to get back to the picnic quilt.

I was not about to leave. I did not like Ginger and had to make sure Momma would go. If she didn't, I planned to push Ginger into the lake.

Watery eyed, Momma said, "I'm the wife of a minister. What I have done is wrong. I have ruined my life, and probably the lives of my children. Now, I am pregnant by a man who is not my husband. I love Merl Judas, but he left me and went back to his own wife and children. I have to go to my daddy's. Gotta decide what to do with my life. I need time to myself for a while so I can clear my head. Don't worry, Ginger, we will always be friends."

Ginger continued to sob, pleading with Momma to stay. When we finished our meal, she realized Momma was resolute in her decision. Ginger agreed to take us to the house. Pulling into her driveway Ginger said she could not bear to see us go.

Momma, Jane, Bobby and I got out of the car. They said their good-byes. As Momma leaned into the downed driver side window, Ginger kissed her. When we went inside, they drove away.

As Momma packed our things, she noticed a cigarette had burned a hole in her baby-blue dress. She glanced at me, shamefully, as if to say, I will never do this again. She nodded, and threw the dress into the trash. She fell to her knees in front of me and wrapped her arms tight around my chest.

"I love you Saul," she said, and kissed me on the cheek.

I smiled. "I love you too," I said, relieved that Momma was not going to play the Jezebel again. I was not sure exactly what a Jezebel was. I thought that it was a woman taking money for kisses. Many folks called her that, and I knew it had something to do with men other than my daddy. The two women kissing, maybe that didn't count. What was that word? Oh yes, affairs, kissing other men when married to someone else. What category did Ginger fit in?

Daddy said women paid for their time with men are criminals. So I knew what Momma did was against the law. I knew it, and so did she. Nevertheless, she justified her actions as an act of desperation to take care of us. Even so, the fruits of sin fell all around her, for she had indeed shamed herself in the eyes of many, and ruined any future of a life with my father. She was a troubled soul, too complicated for me to completely, figure out.

Losing Daddy didn't matter. She never loved him. He was only her way out. He bought her for fifty dollars and she resented that. She said she was too young, and stupid for believing the matchmaker Fanny. Their union was never holy. She was glad to be free of him. She is most happy to be free of Ginger.

I loved both parents, and wanted them together. That day, I gave up completely on the plan. There was nothing, I could do, to fix them. There was too much bitter water flowing under their bridges. It would take a miracle to mend their relationship, and my family.

We loaded our things, and drove to Grandpa Daniel's, Rooster Ridge home.

Momma's Blue Party Dress

Despite her promise to Chad, Momma never returned to Loafer's Glory. She made her choices. Now, we would live with them. No going back, to the life we led there.

When Pops and Gert married, they rented a house near the town of Timbo where Jimmy Driftwood was born and raised. Jimmy owned a cattle ranch there. It was here that Pops and Jimmy continued their plans for Rack 'n Sack to perform for the President one day.

Returning to Rooster Ridge for the winter months they stayed at Momma's childhood home. The old smoke house where she was born remained on the property but no one occupied it any longer. Pops built a comfortable home closer to the road. After the local springtime strawberry harvest, they followed the seasonal crops north, until cotton-picking time in the fall. When we arrived, they were preparing to travel, heading for the cotton fields around Grubbs, Arkansas.

Joe married his fourteen-year-old sweetheart, two months after he returned to Arkansas from Seligman. They were building a one-room shack down the road from Daniel's house. I could hardly wait to see Uncle Joe and meet my new aunt.

We stayed at Grandpa Daniel's for about two weeks. Daniel was sick with a rotten chronic cough. His strong breath smelled of rancid meat. His lungs were infected. Gert was worried. She thought the affliction might be contagious, possibly consumption.

Sensing, Pops Daniel did not want us there I was uncomfortable. A grouch, he glared at me over meals as I stared back at him. The loud annoying slurping noise as he sucked the coffee off the edge of a saucer while holding it to his face was grating on my nerves. His black-sharp eyes frightened me as he frowned during meals. Momma said that was his relaxed, natural expression, and for me to pay it no mind unless he growled.

Our playful laughter while running through the house put Daniel on the edge. He said nothing about wanting us to leave that I overheard. However, Momma moved Jane, Bobby, and me to Joe's house when Gert asked her to get us away Pops. Gert was genuinely concerned for our health as well as Daniel's.

Joe and Rebecca married less than three months. Small in stature, stout little Joe had no schooling. He could not print his name, other than using the X. Nevertheless, he knew how to deal with people. The man possessed major horse sense, and was a whiz with numbers.

Rebecca was naturally beautiful, rosy cheeks, tall and slim, with long golden-brown wavy hair to her hips. Her spirit was angelic. She showered upon us smiles, and kindness. Unfortunately, she suffered from an incurable ear infection that left her fatigued and dizzy most of the time.

Surgery would have alleviated the health issue. However, she was extremely shy, and did not trust doctors. Ultimately, she refused any type of proper medical treatment for the condition. As a direct result, would be permanently deaf if the issue was not treated.

Rebecca was unable to keep up with Jane and me, as we were inquisitive. Daily we were getting into cupboards, and shuffling through their boxes of personal items. We scattered cherished family photographs, and important papers around the house. The end of the day, worn out Rebecca struggled to prepare the evening meal.

Uncle Joe had a special place inside his heart for me. I was his first nephew, and he had donated blood, saving my life. To Joe's reasoning, that made me more like a son, than a nephew, since his own blood now flowed in my veins.

Momma was gone six days. We didn't know where. Cotton harvest was coming on. Joe and Rebecca were planning to move on. Rebecca prepared, packing for the trip to Denton Island, within the next few days. First, Uncle Joe had to finish the twelve-by-twelve rough plank cabin. He was building it located on the acreage he purchased in Rooster Ridge. Their property connected behind the rental shanty land where they currently stayed. He bought the ten acres a month after they wed. When they returned from the cotton harvest, they would live there for the winter.

Numerous local migrant families traveled to the Bottoms every fall. They worked the fields of white, stooped over from sunup to dusk. Laden heavy cotton-sacks strapped on their backs. Canvas bags the width of two feet, and length of eight, up to twelve feet long, they packed the bags with the pickings. Two full sacks, three, and maybe four for the day, they dragged the harvest out of the fields to the weight scales where the field overseer stationed. The heavier the loaded cotton sacks were, the more cash that was the day's pay. Often the adults individually picked at least five-hundred pounds a day.

The money saved by Thanksgiving would keep them through winter. Three children were too much responsibility for Rebecca to handle during harvest. They could not afford to keep us. She called Chad to have Daddy come and get us.

Two days later, Daddy pulled into the yard driving a brand new '61 Pontiac Bonneville. It shone like a polished black agate in the autumn sunshine. He purchased it the week before. Joe's eyes gleamed with envy as he walked outside to greet Daddy and saw the new car.

Momma arrived the night before while Jane and I were sleeping. When we woke up, she was packing our clothes in the same brown grocery bags that Daddy had when we left South Bend. She finished filling the pokes with the bundled clothing when Daddy and Joe stepped into the plank shack.

Joe motioned for Rebecca to follow him out the front door. They left us alone, taking a stroll into the woods behind the shanty where there new house was under construction.

Momma and Daddy alternated between calm discussion and raging arguments. He placed me on his lap. She pulled Jane onto hers. We sat on the edge of the bed where Bobby was lying with his bottle. Emotions were high as they discussed getting back together.

"Ora, I forgive you. I don't want our home busted up. Please come with us to Indiana. We'll start over. I love you. I can't live without you," Daddy said.

"Enoch, I'd give anything if that were possible. Too many harsh words and lies have flowed under our bridge. To forgive and forget all is only a fantasy. The truth is I simply don't love you anymore. I haven't for a long time," she said.

Daddy sobbed, pleading, he says, "Honey, please don't do this. You'll regret the decision years from now. Please, reconsider." Not wanting to reveal his grief--he placed his hands over his face.

I put my arm around his shoulder, I said, "Don't cry Daddy, I love you."

Momma scolded him. She said, "Hush, act-like a man! Besides, what I have done, you'll never be able to get past my betrayal."

Daddy flew into a rage yelling, profaning Merl.

Desperate to put an end to their quarrels, I lifted Daddy's hand, and Momma's, putting them together on my lap. "You kids stop fighting," I said, "Kiss." The action cooled the heat of rage for a time. Moments later, they were back at it again.

Realizing their differences couldn't be resolved, Daddy hoisted Jane and me onto his hips, and carried us outside, placing us on the backseat. Momma followed and handed him the sacks containing our few clothes.

Once we were inside the car, Momma hugged us. She turned racing toward the house. Tears streamed down her face. She stood at the door of the shack watching as the car began rolling forward.

Jane and I see her sobbing bitterly. She continued waving goodbye. We waved back at her through the rear window as Daddy pull out of the drive onto the main road.

Momma must have changed her mind. She came running in a futile attempt to catch the accelerating automobile. We heard her shout, "Come back, this is wrong. Maybe we can work it out."

Daddy did not notice her making chase as he drove us out of sight. However, he must have heard. He said, "It's too late my love, too late."

Once again, we left Momma and Bobby behind. We would now stay with Daddy's cousin, Hatty and her family in Landis, Arkansas.

Merl returned to Momma that day. Waiting at Pop's, for her to come to him. They despised the Judas. Pops loved Momma and reluctantly allowed them to meet there. Gert said Momma was foolish, if not stupid. They tolerated his presence only for Momma's sake.

The afternoon we left, Momma took Bobby to an elderly babysitter's house down the road from Joe and Rebecca's place. She asked her to keep him for a couple of hours. Momma gave an excuse. She said she needed time alone to grocery shop.

She never returned. Momma abandoned Bobby. The local Bip clan loaded their things and headed out for the Bottoms. The elderly sitter called Daddy's sister, Sonny, after two weeks past with no sign of Momma.

Free of all her Hotmans the day she left Bobby, Momma had only one option. Freedom to have her fantasy life with Merl became a cold reality. The life she longed for, all those many years, now, she had it. Her new truth was with Merl Judas. Off to Florida, a new direction, a new destination to start a life with Merl and his son, the baby Rambo, she now carried inside her womb.

Pretty Sonny, took Bobby in, her brood was already sizeable with three of her own children, and husband. They all accepted baby Bobby as if he was one of them.

We drove past the Red Wood Baptist church where Daddy was the pastor only eighteen months earlier. Expressing regret, his head dropped. Shame of knowing Grandma Anne would be disappointed, he held back tears.

Jane played with her red-haired doll. I crawled over the seat and stood beside him. "Don't cry, Daddy. God will send an angel someday, and fix our family," I said, as I kissed him on the cheek. Accepting the reality, I could not fix it. Only a higher power could intervene to soften their hardened hearts.

He chuckled and put his arm around me. "You're the only angel I need," he said and continued, "Your momma looks like an angel in the blue dress."

"I know. She kissed an ugly man in Springdale, and burned a whole in it with a cigarette. Momma threw her pretty, party dress away when left there," I said.

Daddy winced. Neither of us spoke again for the remainder of the trip. Both, losing all hope we would ever again be a complete family.

What's an Orphan-Jug?

Daddy left us in the care of Hatty. He and Momma's cousin Eddie drove to southeast Texas. There, they worked the logwoods.

Eddie, age twenty-two was a devoted Pentecostal Jesus Name Holiness believer. He would sneak around dipping snuff, and take an occasional chaw-of-tobacco. The use of nicotine was taboo in the holiness church. Eddie, a wiry fellow, and his short fat wife Lawanda seem unmatched.

Lawanda was eighteen and domineering, vulgar mouthed, and had a voracious appetite for sweets and coke. She wore round green earbobs, cheap costume jewelry, and bright red lipstick. Her glistening coal-black wavy-hair parted in the middle hung to her shoulders. From time-to-time, she made the trip with them, needing to be near her Eddie. Once in a while they drove their own '48 Chevy truck.

She was a Baptist. The woman enjoyed being argumentative with her husband. Squabbles happened over church doctrine, especially the clothesline religious dogma. The topic of once saved, always saved by grace brought some resisting shouts from Eddie. Hatty smirked at her antics with Eddie when they dropped by with Daddy to see Jane and me in-between trips.

The first day at Hatty's, she read nursery rhymes. I imagined Eddie and Lawanda when she shared the story about Jack Sprat and his fat wife.

Hatty shined, having great compassion. She was twelve-years-old when her mother and father both died a few months apart of Tuberculosis. At the wishes of her deceased parents, a court judge ordered her placed in the home, along with her three younger siblings. She and her siblings grew-up, as wards of, the Batesville, Arkansas Masonic Home Orphanage. Finished with high school at age eighteen, she returned to Loafer's Glory. Two years later, she married her husband Derk.

She had experienced great loss also. Sensing what we were going through, she was a comfort. Hatty at forty-five-years-old was a large-boned handsome woman. She spoke with slurred speech caused from a stroke ten years earlier. Her motor skills were not impaired other than being slow in movement. Intelligent, cheerful, kind, and extremely demonstrative with her five stair-step children. She was no-less attentive, and loving with Jane and me.

Derk reminded me of Pops Daniel. They had the same build and colorings, but completely different personalities. That booming bass gravelly voice coming out of his small dark form just did not seem to fit. He smiled a lot, never giving himself over to anger, or fits of rage. He had a father's heart for Jane and me.

The evening we arrived, she tucked us in. Sitting on the edge of the bed, Hatty said, "Children, I understood your situation. I was orphaned at age twelve when my parents passed away of Tuberculosis in '28."

Bewildered, I shook my head, and asked, "You mean you had no parents?"

Lips together in a thin line, Hatty grinned. "That's right. Not since, I was twelve. I was raised for six years in an orphanage."

Jane asks, "What's an orphan-jug?"

Hatty chuckled at Jane's pronunciation. She says, "Oh, the ragamuffin home for orphaned Mason's kids is where I lived. It was a place of safety for children, suffering the lost of both their parents."

I turned to face the wall, whimpering. "Momma and Daddy are getting a divorce. Does that make us orphans?" I asked.

Tilting her head, compassionately she patted my back, "No, your parents aren't dead," she said.

Hatty kissed us on the cheeks, and then she caressed our hands. "Yah knows, I think divorce is worse than death. Nothing is final in divorce. The heartache just seems to linger. The children suffer most. You know what I'm talking about. Don't you, Saul?" she asked.

I nodded, and so did Jane.

Hatty stood. Towering over us, she continued. "You and Jane are brave, strong children. You will overcome the curse of divorce. The struggle will give you compassion for others, and make you powerful adults some day. Hotman blood flows in your veins. You will understand one day and have the strength of character to forgive when you are adults. You come from good stock. The heartache won't kill you, though it may feel that way sometimes. With God's help the struggle will make you better human beings," she said, and sighed. "Now, get some sleep. We'll have a big day tomorrow." Hatty flipped off the light and exited the room, leaving the door cracked.

I thought that I was right. Ol' Judas witch Bertha did cast a spell-- the curse of divorce. Then I drifted off to sleep.

Derk, Black Dutch Cherokee, in his mid-fifties was a chain smoker and often coughed, like Grandpa Pops. Pops' lung disease would not allow him to smoke. He chaws the tobacco. Unlike Pops, Derk was in quite good health.

Jane was bleeding again and needed medical attention. Hatty became quite concerned and tells Daddy about the problem on several occasions. Daddy's alcoholism had worsened; he drank on a daily basis when returning from Texas to see us. Neglectfully, Jane did not get the treatment she needed.

The men were gone two weeks and sometimes a month before they drove to Landis. Eddie's home was in Rooster Ridge where Daddy bought moonshine after dropping him off. On many home trips the hooch being more important, he hid out at our old home place for lonely drunken weekends. After two days break from their jobs, they drove back to Texas.

Daddy's depression deepened as he continued to hit the sauce. During the first year after the separation, he became a full-blown alcoholic. His episodes of erratic behavior and nonsensical speech came and went during the coming months.

Often he would not put forth the effort or time to see us, only checking in with Hatty after we were asleep. Maybe we reminded him too much of Momma? He was tipsy on the few occasions he did pause to be in our presence. That was no holiday for us. The name calling, we were his little dookies. Constantly reminding him, we are not little chicken sh**s, brought him laughter.

We spent most of the autumn, through Thanksgiving with cousin Hatty's family. Her brood was older. They helping us to feel we belonged. What was theirs was ours as well. Hatty insisted they share. She did not have to be forceful as they were gracious, good-hearted people. This family lived the Golden Rule: "Do unto others as you would have them do unto you." Fanny's version of the rule was not like Hatty's.

Momma said her cousin Fanny reminded her of a turkey-chicken. She wasn't able to determine what was her breed, or her attitudes. Fake Fanny said one thing but did another. Momma did not trust her. Often she spoke of how she hated herself for listening to Fanny's advice.

Long before she and Daddy married, Momma babysat Fanny's children. Momma said Fanny was selfish, and never paid Pops for her help after Fanny gave birth to Ely's fifth child, Agnus. That was the year Fanny introduced Momma and Daddy.

Anne was holding public prayer meetings in the Hotman home. Invited by Fanny to attend, that was when she met Enoch. Momma thought, maybe Fanny assumed her matchmaking was payment enough for the hours of dirty diapers and house labor.

Momma said Fanny's version of the Golden Rule was a joke. Hatty's was not. Momma loved Hatty, so did Daddy, and Jane. Fanny was a different subject. Uncle Chad often chuckled, smirking he said of her, "Fanny is so ugly, maggots crawl off the carne cart, avoiding a glance."

I had heard about Fanny, and her split personality. I could barely recall seeing her but once. It was the image of her long crooked nose, stuck in my memory.

Momma stayed her distance after I was born. We did not visit the Ely and Fanny Judas family, after we moved to Wisconsin. When very young, I see the woman at a distance, after the accident. I could not recall everyone who came to the house during those days, as I was quite sick. However, I remembered her distinctive nose.

Momma said Hatty's Golden Rule was genuine. I am confused about this Fanny, as much as the separation. Momma said she loved Fanny because she was family, but she had no respect for her. Momma had the upmost admiration for Hatty.

Having no desire to come in contact, with Fanny, I was glad Hatty's Golden Rule was not twisted. I guessed that meant Hatty was just a good woman.

Hatty's youngest son, John was a year older than I was. He too lived by the Golden Rule, being considerate of our feelings. He and I played daily with their Red Bone and Blue Tick 'coon hounds. Derk liked to run his dogs every night. We liked frolicking daily with the pooches.

Roasted raccoon served the next evening after he would bring home a kill. My taste buds, never took the opportunity, to savor 'coon. Imagination ran wild. The baked beast resembled a skinned cat--just could not stomach the sight. Beans and cornbread were the trusty staples at every meal. From those bowls, I found my portion.

When John, six and a little bigger than I, got off the school bus we romped in and out of doghouses. The four hounds loved the attention. John laughed aplenty and we wrestled having great fun with the canines.

There were pooch slobbers from head to toe and sometimes dog feces on our shoes when Hatty called us to dinner. Daily, Spotted Dog Ticks embed themselves into our bellybuttons. Often she found crawlers on our heads, legs, and in our armpits. Hatty cleaned us up and checked our bodies for the sucking tormentors before we could eat. That was the rule.

I detested a sponge bath every day. Hatty heated an enameled dishpan full of cistern water on the potbelly stove, located in the living room. Water was hot when we came in from playing outside. After she bathed us, we slipped on clean clothes and sat down to eat. Family members took turns asking the blessing. The older kids detested the ritual of seemingly useless prayers over the food.

Once-in-a-while the bigger boys tried to buck up against Hatty's rules when Derk was not there. Frowning, she would say, "I'll tell your Pa." That was the end of that . . .

Experiencing the love and respect for others displayed in the character of this poor Arkansas family was a childhood blessing. They had something, all the money in the world cannot buy: A real family, love, and security. I wanted to live with them forever.

Before Christmas, Hatty and Derk drove us to Sonny's because they did not have the extra money for Jane and me during the holidays. They did not want us to feel, we were left out having no gifts under their Christmas tree. We would not see Daddy again until after Christmas.

Sonny and her husband Dan were poor, but they shared what little they had. Dan, a short handsome man, combed back his light-brown hair like Elvis Presley. He was a friendly sort, but a lady's man.

His gambling and fooling around with other women caused family problems. They kept their arguments confined to the privacy of their bedroom while trying to never, expose the household children to their marital disagreements.

I had the habit of eavesdropping, and knew all about his philandering indiscretion. Sonny was having quiet rages over the matter, not airing their dirty laundry for the community to behold. I guessed he was kind of like Momma, but he was kissing other women. Unlike Daddy, Sonny did not buy his lies, and became cold natured toward him. The recompense of her distance worsened their problems.

Christmas came and went. Sonny said Santa left Jane a set of paper dolls, and for me, a small red racecar. I knew she had put them under the tree. Jane believed her. The gifts were slim for all in the house.

Snow fell heavily, leaving a foot after Christmas. We made snowmen. Sonny prepared hot chocolate and a large dishpan of snow-cream every day until a melt the next week.

After the New Year, I developed a chronic cough. It was not horribly bad at first, but changing weather, lack of food and rest, made for sick with fever, and the hack intensified.

Had I caught Pops' rasping disease? Gert said his consumption might be contagious. I wanted no hospitals. Making every effort to suppress the barking, I was afraid Sonny would tell Daddy if he ever came back. Sonny could see I was getting worse. Would she take me to the doctor? I refused to complain for fear of another hospital stay.

When Daddy returned, Sonny insisted I see a physician. I trembled at the thought. She quickly changed the subject to Bobby. I am relieved.

Aunt Sonny bonded with Bobby and him to her. Motivated by a mother's love, she asked Daddy to let her keep him. Subject of a doctor is not brought-up again.

Emotions were strong; being a victim of theft surged throughout my being. Surely, Daddy would not give Bobby away. The adults were stealing our time. Time we could spend with baby brother, Bobby. Seemed some folks were always out to take one of my family members for themselves. I didn't want us split up.

Daddy worried about letting Bobby stay, but he could not drag a one-year-old around the country as he sought work. He already had his hands full with Jane and me. He did not wish to return to South Bend and drywall finishing. Liking the out-of-doors, he chose laboring in timber. He would take Jane and me with him when he returned to Spurger. That way he would not have to make as many trips, pay Hatty, or go out of his way to see us. Daddy reasoned this would be best for Bobby, to let him stay-put with Sonny and Dan, until he got us settled again.

Sonny said there was something wrong with a woman who throws away her babies. It was not natural. Dan felt he could not afford to raise another child. At first, he reluctantly accepted Bobby because Sonny intently coveted him. Soon Bobby's cuteness won him over. Jane and I returned with Daddy to Texas. Once again, we left Bobby behind.

Had Momma thrown us away? No, she left us to Daddy. I didn't know she abandoned Bobby until I overheard Sonny telling Uncle Dan the reasons for wanting to keep him forever. Her words were harsh and cold when she spoke of Momma. That was reason enough for me not to like the proposition. Why was she calling Momma a harlot? What is a harlot?

Paul E. Treadwell

LEVIATHAN KINGS OF TERROR, a memoir

Gone to Chicken Heaven

We moved to the swampland outside of Spurger, Texas near the Neches River. Total population was 120, with as many cats and hound dogs. Daddy worked in the swamp forest cutting trees for the local paper mill. Eddie, and the old man about sixty-years-of-age, named Mr. Roberts, were members of the small Spurger Pentecostal church. Eddie and Mr. Roberts attended services often as possible.

Mr. Roberts also worked with Daddy and Eddie. He was a scruffy, skinny, and whiskered man, a hard laborer. During the workweek they harvested, and loaded short logs on Mr. Robert's flatbed. They made sometimes three trips a day, delivering the wood twelve miles to the paper mill.

Dad, Jane, and I lived with Mr. Roberts and his tenderhearted wife Glenda, who reminded me of step-grandmother Gert. Dad paid them room and board. Mrs. Roberts cared for Jane and me during the day while the men worked.

I liked kind, but stern Glenda, most of the time. She forced us to nap every afternoon. I was not accustomed to daylight sleep, and fussed over the matter. However, she insisted.

The damp, rainy weather aggravated the respiratory weakness. Sharp pains speared through my chest as I began coughing up a tiny bit of blood. The congestion made breathing difficult. Tormented at the thought of hospitals, I never wanted to ever, go back to another one. Doc Nix and I became best buds there. I prized him, but not the infirmary, or his torture tools. Fearful of being, strapped down to a table again, I continued attempting to hide the illness. The afternoon naps actually helped.

Having no energy, Mrs. Roberts insisted I was not active enough. She shoved me out to run and play until naptime, locking the door so I could not get inside. Too fatigued for dashing about, I wandered around inside the chicken coop, out back.

The first day, I am hoping, to collect an egg or two. There, I cornered the featherless-butt hen. She was the rejected one, the pitiful fowl at the bottom of the flock's pecking order. She was an easy catch as I scooped her into my arms, and hand fed her grains of dried corn. Over the days, we became fast friends. I named her, Baldy.

While forbidden from entering the house for a couple of hours, I occupied the outdoors with my new pet. Baldy and I would meet at the coop gate each afternoon. She followed me around like a happy pup.

I thought that my presence caused her to feel safe. She was never fearful of flogging, or having her ass feathers yanked out when I was around. I threw rocks when other chickens aggressed.

Before rescuing her, squawking Baldy ran for her life as the entire flock ganged up. Singled out, I could not figure why. They would make quick pursuit, pecking and flogging as they yanked. Baldy's feathers flew.

I thought the other rude birds were as foul as some people I knew. Our clans picked on Momma and Daddy. I would not allow the other hens to harass Baldy in my presence but I could not rescue Momma or Daddy from their house. Maybe people were like chickens. Perhaps, Daddy was right to declare the whole world a chicken sh**. Maybe, the human pecking order was what he meant.

The smell of chicken litter and feathers deepened the respiratory affliction. Mrs. Roberts and Jane were dozing early one afternoon. She forgot to unlock the doors. Cold and soaked during a downpour I sought shelter inside the leaking chicken shack. Chilled to the bone, I collapse, passed out from heaviness pressing in on my lungs.

On my bed, I awoke the next morning. The sheets were drenched from broken fever sweats. Mrs. Roberts meant well by wanting me out for fresh air, she had slept through the storm. Her guilt over my worsening health tormented her after that.

She had found me in the coop unconscious. Not, fully recovered, but her home remedies and poultices helped. I pleaded with her for no doctors. She shrugged, as her gaze fell to the floor.

"Maybe not this time," she said.

Weak, I crawled off the bed and slipped into clean dry pajamas while she replaced the bed linens. Slithering under the covers and adjusting my head on the pillow I smiled and asked, "How's Baldy?"

She grimaced and said, "You broke her neck when you fell. She was lying underneath you when I carried you inside yesterday."

She handed over a hot bowl of chicken soup. I did not make the connection as I gobbled down the nourishment. "How is Baldy?" I asked again, grinning. "This is good," I said.

Mrs. Roberts smiled and said, "Gone, to chicken heaven."

I thought, that was okay, Baldy was with Grandmother Anne, and the old hens would not yank out her butt feathers ever again. Having a sudden voracious appetite, I requested a soup refill.

Paul E. Treadwell

Hog Wild

The swamp environment was not for the fainthearted. In dangerous working conditions, the men waded up to their knees in murky water during the rainy season, crossing low places in the forest. Pine and scrub oaks fell at the will of their chainsaws.

The dry season was not so bad, other than the mosquitoes were a constant nuisance. The men also had to be watchful of cottonmouth snakes, timber rattlers, and copperheads. Neighbors warned them to look out for alligators, but they never happened on one.

Aggressive wild hogs occupied the forest and kept the men on continual vigil. The hogs crossbred between native Red Razorbacks and escaped domestic pigs from local farms. They were large like the domestic animals and mean like the Razorbacks. Some purebred smaller Red Razorbacks still foraged in the woods. The men's worst fear was the possibility of tangled up with a herd of wild pigs or a sow with a litter of piglets. Some of the larger boars had tusks, four inches long, and they were razor-sharp, true to their name.

A sunny mid-March, warm afternoon, Eddie finished his labors for the day. He strolled alongside the muddy logging road, toward his vehicle. When he heard rustling in the undergrowth, he turned around. He thought, maybe Daddy was there, playing a prank, and set down his chainsaw.

Throwing a broken tree limb into the moving bushes, squeals rang out. He had hit a wild Razorback boar, and it was after him. Eddie ran, flat footing it as hard as he could go toward the vehicle. The hog was less than ten feet from him by the time he jumped into the truck bed. Now safe, but the native swine would not skedaddle.

Eddie yelled and waved his arms in an effort to frighten the animal away. This only aggravated the hog. Taking a different approach, he lies down motionless in the carriage box. After a few minutes, the pig snorted one last time and ran for the dense woods.

Daddy and Mr. Roberts finished for the day and strode out of the forest to find Eddie's abandoned saw. Daddy hoisted the tool, and carried it along toward their vehicles. They found Eddie had shut himself inside his truck-cab.

That was all for Eddie. He had enough of the Spurger swamps. Eddie and his obese wife Lawanda packed their things and returned to Rooster Ridge the same evening.

Daddy laughed for a week after the incident. He chuckled every time he thought of the expression on terrified Eddie's face when they found him sitting there mumbling and shaking. He said Eddie had gone hog wild, out of his mind for fear of happening upon another one.

I howled with Daddy every time he told the story. It did my heart good when Daddy's spirits were jovial, for those times were seldom.

Virginia, Oh Sheese

Daddy embarked upon a new relationship with a beautiful young woman in Texas. I was elated. Now we will have a real momma again.

Virginia had a striking resemblance to Momma. Though I thought, Momma was prettier. Virginia was divorced and had a two-year-old son of her own. Daddy wanted this to work, hoping to find a wife to help raise us, and someone, too truly love him.

Shuffled around often in the last several months, Jane became frightfully attached to Daddy, she screamed every time he got out of her sight. Some days he took her to the woods with him and she rode his hip while he tried to work.

Daddy cried a lot. He worried and continued to grieve over the loss of his marriage. Concern about the welfare of his children tormented him. He knew, he could not raise us alone and hold down a job. He was drowning his sorrows in the bottle. He had to have help. Virginia fit the bill.

One rainy night they took me out on a date with them. Jane stayed with Mrs. Roberts. Missing my own mother desperately, I looked into Virginia's eyes. "Miss Virginia, will you be my new momma?" I asked.

Virginia squirmed in the seat. Fiddling with the ends of her long beautiful dark-hair, she cleared her throat and gazed out the car window.

The night showers ceased. Other than the hum of the motor, there was dead silence as Daddy continued to drive. My question just hung there in the thick, humid air. Sadly, she took a deep breath, patted me on the head, and then she smiled and said nothing.

Virginia liked Daddy, but after this night, she no longer wanted to see him. It was my fault. I should not have asked the question so soon.

Daddy was drunk again as he sipped on his beers before driving Virginia home. He was talking nonsense and weaving over the road. He pulled off the paved highway onto the gravel lane leading to Virginia's house. Nearly running the car into the muddy ditch, he gunned the engine and swerved to the center of the byway.

Trembling with anger and fear, she yelled, "Stop the friggin' car! I'd rather walk than to ride with a drunk."

He kept going, mumbling, "No, no, howdy, howdy, no. I'm a Navy Kid Captain Sailor."

Horrified, Virginia reached for the keys in the ignition. He grasped her hand. Forcefully held it on his leg as her arms reached out in front of me where I stood between them on the front seat.

Wild-eyed, he let go of the steering wheel to pat her hand. He said, "I love you, Ora Honey."

Virginia shrieked, "You maniac, stop the car, now!"

At her screams and the car veering out of control. He let go of her hand and slammed on the brake. The car fishtailed, sliding to a fast stop and we lurched forward. I fell over into Virginia's lap.

Virginia badly shaken, helped me to my feet again. I slid down and sat close to her. "It's Okay, Virginia. Daddy does that some times. He's fine now," I said, while reaching over to grasp her hand.

She yanked it away. She clutched tight to her purse straps while breathing heavily as silent rage and fear churned inside her widened eyes.

Silvery moonlight beamed through the passenger's window. I could see her face turn bright red. The sound of Virginia's fearful, labored inhaling let me know she wanted away from us. She worked to smooth out her nerves and calm down. The smell of Daddy's stale beer mingled with her sweet lilac perfume. It was the scent of clashing aromas.

We sat inside the car on the edge of the country road three miles from her house. Daddy stepped out to relieve himself in the ditch. I am embarrassed. My father's crude behavior when he lets the vapors release in front of my potential new mom.

Calming some, she sighed. "You, poor-child, no wonder your momma left him," she whispered.

Looking around behind us out the back glass into the silver-dark she said, "I hope my brother comes this way. It's about time for him to get off work. I'll ride with him." That did not happen.

Troubled, she didn't like me anymore, and dread of losing her, I asked, "Miss Virginia, are you gonna marry my Daddy? I think you will be a good momma."

She turned her head, and gasp, "Oh Sheese," she said.

Daddy eased into the driver's seat and apologized. He told us he would not drink anymore, and drove Virginia home. Walking her to the front door, I heard them arguing, but they kissed a goodnight and she went inside.

Daddy staggered back to the car. He got in and said, "The whole world is a chicken sh**. She dumped me, too. I don't want to live."

I whipped, "Well Daddy, you are a chicken dookie when drunk." I giggled and he laughed with me.

True to his word, Daddy fell into an inescapable depression after this night and lingered in bed for a week. He stayed perpetually drunk.

Paul E. Treadwell

He Fell Asleep

Some days later, I toddled along with Daddy into the swamp. He has me sit on a fallen log a few yards away for safety. Happily I am observing the men going about their daily routines. Jealous of Jane riding to work with him, I threw a fit like hers that morning, and got the opportunity to be there. Jane had to stay with Glenda.

The men cut down trees until midday. Before breaking for lunch, Daddy was sawing down a larger oak when he slipped in the mud. The saw kicked back onto his right leg below the knee.

Gnawing through flesh and bone the sharp chain ripped out a half-inch wide, by three inch length gash before he managed to shove it away and shut off the loud machine. I watched as blood sprayed into the air.

Earlier, Daddy had insisted I stay put, no matter what. I wanted to run to him, but dare not. I yelled for Mr. Roberts.

Daddy was bleeding profusely as Mr. Roberts glanced up from his work fifty paces away. We watched Daddy taking off his shirt and wrapping the wound. Mr. Roberts dropped his heavy saw and dashed to help.

They hobbled out of the thickets, as I ran behind carrying their lunch pails. Mr. Roberts loaded Daddy into his truck. I slid inside and sat on the middle of the seat. Mr. Roberts sped out of the forest onto the main road. We raced toward Woodville for medical attention.

After the doctor sewed up the leg, Daddy limped into the waiting room where I sat with Mr. Roberts, eating a sandwich from Daddy's lunch box. The doctor followed him out as Daddy stood at the receptionist desk to pay the bill. I was listening to them converse from the other side of the room.

Doctor said, "Mr. Hotman, you're a very lucky man. There must be an angel looking out for you."

Daddy said, "Yes sir. Ma's prayers are still working."

Doctor said, "You need to stay out of the swamp until the wound is healed to prevent infection. Don't get it wet, and change the bandage every day. You can use some antiseptic on it before putting on the clean bandage. Come back in ten days and we'll take out the stitches."

Daddy thanked him, and made an appointment for ten days later. When he paid the bill, we loaded into the truck.

"I've had all of the Spurger woods I want in one lifetime," Daddy said, after slamming the truck door shut.

I wondered if he was planning to leave Texas. During the drive back to the forest to retrieve their saws, Daddy said, "Mr. Roberts, I'm not going to be any good to you as a helper for several days. Guess it is best if the kids and I go back to Arkansas until I recover."

Four days later the paper mill sent his check. He thanked the Roberts' for their hospitality, and loaded the car. We were leaving, heading out for the long drive to Arkansas.

Before we pulled away, Glenda stuck her head inside the downed driver's window and told Dad, I needed professional medical attention. She said Jane was leaving blood in her panties and she couldn't tell what the problem was but she needed to see a doctor too.

Daddy assured her. He would get us to a physician. We rolled out of the driveway; the destination was Loafer's Glory. The Roberts waved until we could no longer see them through the rear window.

Daddy drove all night. I stood in the front seat beside him. He fell asleep at the wheel. I screamed as loud as I could and shook him. The Pontiac careened off the road, nearly crashing into a tree as he missed a curve before he woke up and took control again.

I talked to keep him awake after that. I told him I would not allow sleep. He had to promise not to wreck the car. He had to listen to me, when I yelled to rouse him. He had to promise not to get angry, and not to fall back to sleep. He agreed.

He was not as good as his promise. Rolling down the window for cold air, his head slowly tilted and rested on his arm positioned outside the car on the window ledge. Then he dozed. The cool, April night air could not wake him. Again, I yelled and shook him.

Dreadfully frightened, I wanted sleep myself, but did not dare. I begged Daddy to pull off the highway and nap. He refused. He nodded off several times before dawn. During the long journey, I shook him or pulled his hair numerous times. The car swerved often, and went off the narrow road shoulders. I always managed to wake him before we crashed.

Finally, darkness gave way to light as sunrise approached. We arrived at Sonny's without a major collision. I was relieved and exhausted. The cock began to crow as the first rays of morning light stabbed through the scattered clouds when we crawled out of the Pontiac. We strolled toward Sonny's front door.

Perched on the roof of the outhouse, an old Road Island Red rooster sang his morning song while a Whippoorwill echoed from a nearby red oak tree. Smoke bellowed up from the chimney into the cool, dark-blue, morning sky. The lights blinked on one by one in every room of the old plank shack.

Daddy knocked. Jane was sleeping in his arms with her head resting on his shoulder. I wanted food and slumber for myself. Jane had slept the entire trip. She would be bucking to play in no time.

Wheezing, I struggled to keep from coughing. I did not want Sonny to know I was ailing. She was sure to send me to the hospital.

Sonny welcomed us in. After a sumptuous breakfast of chocolate gravy and homemade cathead biscuits, she gave me a dose of cough syrup and aspirin. She put me to bed, on the sofa near the wood stove in the living room. Nearby, Jane and Daddy fell asleep in the rocker.

I awoke by afternoon to the sound of Bobby crying. Sonny said Daddy had gone out, and would be back later.

Hank, five, (Sonny's youngest son) was playing with his battery-operated puppy. He had gotten it for Christmas. The toy pup caused me to long for Buddy again. Hank and I were chums but he was younger than I was. I always took the lead showing him the rules of our games. He did not like my bossing him, now that he was five-years-old.

He would not allow me to touch the mechanical pup. No pleading or begging softened his heart enough for me to have a moment of play with it too.

Sonny's eldest girl, pretty, blond Janice, twelve, and ruddy-faced Derk, ten, caught the big yellow school bus after breakfast. I am, fascinated, by the sound of their voices as both spoke with a rasp. They rang much older than children their ages because of the full voices.

Daddy was gone. Would, he come back to get us? Had he gone to the bootleggers for more moonshine? I hated booze. What liquor did to my dad, I disdained his ignorant drunkenness. The

alternative was worse. Having a drunken daddy was better than no daddy at all. At least he was not dead like Hatty's parents, and I was not an orphan.

A full week past, and Daddy had not returned. No one knew of his where about.

Crazy White Trash

Sonny sent us to Chad's family. He had four children. Lance, the oldest son earned a basketball-scholarship, and was on his way to college the next fall. Randy sixteen-years-old was preoccupied with girlfriends and fast cars. Bossy Danna, thirteen-years-old and the only girl, no one, could do anything to please her. Stan, only a couple of months older than I, was as bossy as Danna. They all had blue eyes and blond hair with freckles. Danna's long curled locks had a strawberry cast like Daddy's hair.

Stan was fun to play with if we did what he said. That got old fast. When Stan grew tired of frolicking, he simply did not want us around anymore. He was a Dennis-the-Mentis type, but with a cruel selfishness in his manner. I shared his room at night, though he did not want me in the house. Our last evening there he yelled for me to get out.

All business, dish-water-blond, and short, Aunt Vanny told him I would sleep on the bottom bunk the same as all other nights before. I would sleep there whether he liked it or not. Face to face, Stan politely smiled and agreed to obey his mother. He said, "Okay Ma."

Vanny had a passive aggressive type personality. She took Jane by the hand and led her down the hall to Danna's room. She said, "Jane, you should stay with us forever. Danna needs a little sister."

Whimpering Jane said, "Nooooo, I live with my daddy, and brother Saul."

Vanny, sighed. She said, "Danna, help Jane get ready for bed."

Danna said, "Okay Ma," and I heard the door to Danna's room slam shut.

When Vanny strolled toward the kitchen and was out of hearing range, Stan glared at me. "Your ol' daddy is crazy. Your momma is nothin' but cheap white trash. They got not a thing, but dumb, white trash kids," he said. "You're nothing but pond slime, and I don't want you here. Jane's okay cause Ma and Danna say so. No body in my house loves you. We don't want you. Daddy's gonna gets rid of you for me."

Loathing him, emotions of hidden rage washed over me. I swallowed the lump in my throat and held back my tears. I thought for a second, and then mumbled, "You're chicken dookie."

Wanting to hurt him, yet held back, knowing his parents would protect him. Fighting was not an option. This was their home. Why didn't he like me? I was not my parents. What was white trash? It must be like the garbage dump down the hill from their home. Maybe it was because I was not a girl, the reason they all hated me.

I wanted Stan to be my friend. He would have no part of it. He shoved me down on the bottom bunk. "You're only here because Ma says so for tonight. I want you out of my room tomorrow."

Biting my tongue, I crawled between the sheets. Stan climbed up to the top bunk. He had hurt my feelings. Be brave. Never let them know. Crying silently with my head under the blanket, listening to Vanny and Chad whispering in the next room. I drifted off to sleep.

I awoke to the hum of the diesel motors turning the huge, circular saws at Chad's mill a few hundred feet from the house. The blades squealed mournfully as they ripped through the giant, white oak logs. The noise was grinding on my nerves.

My nostrils burned from the pungent smell of burnt diesel, fresh sawdust, and soured wood scent that filled the air. Dust billowed across the yard as the first banged-up logging truck rolled past the house with a load of fresh timber. My eyes watered from the acrid fumes and dust.

Coughing uncontrollably for a couple of minutes after awakening, then I noticed a spot of blood soiled my pillow. I flipped the cushion over to hide the stain. Not wanting breakfast, I asked Vanny to take Jane and me back to Sonny.

Randy packed the younger siblings into his car. Vanny stood in the open doorway waving, she says goodbye to her children. Once they were gone, cold distant, silent Vanny loaded Jane and me into her vehicle and motored us away. I did not think she was unhappy to see us go, any more than we were to be leaving.

Spending as much time as possible with little Bobby when we returned, I realized somehow he now belonged with Sonny. I didn't know where Jane and I fit. What was to become of us? Not wanted, by most of our relatives. The ones who did, had too many children of their own to afford taking in two more.

The night before, I heard Chad and Vanny confiding in each other about an orphanage, and some woman named Leve. They were trying to decide what would be best for Jane and me if Daddy broke down under the stress and grief. The thought of a ragamuffin home horrified me.

To our surprise that evening Daddy came to us. He was clean-shaven and sober. He held us on his lap and rocked with great gusto. He said we would return to Indiana. He'd work for Martin again taping drywall.

The dread of an orphanage lifted as did my frown when I raised my head from his shoulder and giggled. Laughing, Jane grasped my hand and we wrapped our free arms around his neck. He chuckled and pecked us on the cheeks.

Almost a year ago, Lou and Martin were good to us when we stayed there the first time. Though Lou was grouchy, she made it a point to hug, cuddle and laugh with us every evening at bedtime. A time when all transgressions were forgiven during those moments. I could not hold a grudge against her.

The thought of this move, it was a comfort. Lou and Martin's children, our cousins accepted us. They were not hateful like Stan, and I looked forward to being with them again.

Don was a year younger than I was. He was rowdy and spoiled, but fun to play with. He was not belligerent, brazen or cruel, and he didn't make fun of Daddy or pin ugly labels on my family. He liked sharing his toys, and I liked his company.

Patsy ten-years-old giggled a lot and made all satisfactory marks on her report card. She could read, and liked sharing book stories with us. Maybe I would go to school there. Patsy could help me learn how to read.

Alvin, tall, and dark-headed was thirteen-years-old, a bit rebellious, and sneaky. He seemed too constantly be in hot water with Lou. Cousin Alvin was always coming up with fun games of tag, and hide-and-go-seek with the neighborhood kids.

Jimmy was seventeen, and he just thought about girls. He was not any fun. Hardly ever did we see him as he held a job, and was out with his friends much of the time.

The relationship between Patsy and Alvin was that of best friends, not just siblings. Closely attached, their cooperation was essential when they organized our fun risky games and joy filled playful days. They were my favorite cousins, always considerate of us younger children.

Lou would be a temporary mother for us again. Jane and I got along well with her children. We felt safe there, but Lou was strict. She griped incessantly about the least of things. We would just have to live with that. It was okay because we knew she loved us.

Best of all--Daddy would be with us every evening after work. Great anticipation and happiness about the relocation kept my spirits high until bedtime.

Early the next morning Sonny and Bobby were up to see us off. She cried while kissing our cheeks, and then waved to us from the front door as we drove out of sight. Smiling, Bobby waved too. I crawled over the seat and sat next to Daddy.

"Daddy," I asked.

He glanced down. "Yes, Son, what is it?"

"Where did you go?" I asked.

"Fishing," he replied, as he ruffled my hair, and we laughed.

I did not believe him, but questioned him no further; at least he had not abandoned us. He and Momma might be trying to work things out. That was probably just my imagination. The thought was a pleasure.

I grinned. "I can't wait to see Aunt Lou, Daddy," I said.

Turning onto the main paved road heading north on Highway 65 out of Raccoon Springs, he smiled. With his heavy foot pressed down on the gas peddle, the accelerating car jerked onward at great speed, and away we went.

Embarrassed

I was six when we arrived at Lou's. Daddy returned to work for Martin and I attended kindergarten. The first day after our arrival Jane, and Lou went shopping. Lou bought us new clothes. The second day she took us to the doctor.

I was okay, other than the chronic cold symptoms. Jane was not so lucky. Months earlier, I told Momma. "Jane's poop shoot is falling out when she goes potty," I said. Momma laughed and seemed unconcerned.

Glenda and our other caregivers told Daddy about Jane's condition. I told him. Nevertheless, no one took the initiative to get Jane the help she needed other than Lou.

Daddy worked all the time. Frequently his mind slipped in and out of two different worlds. He didn't focus on the immediate needs of his offspring. He was lost in his own world of torment and sorrow.

Momma was preoccupied, obsessed with Merl. Momma's concern for her children was not strong enough to notice the seriousness of Jane's condition. Her detraction was Merl. He was everything to her. We played second fiddle. Her lack of money to pay a doctor for services was a serious issue. Lou had the cash. Momma did not. Jane just never got the medical attention she needed until Lou had us checked out.

The doctor listened to my chest and had me breathe deeply. Immediately on came coughing. It was a longer spell than usual. I gasped for breath. The doctor pulled out a pad from his lab coat and wrote down something. He handed the paper to Lou.

He said, "Your nephew has a bad respiratory infection. Have these prescriptions filled, and follow the directions."

Lou glanced down at the scribbling. She said, "Doctor, I can't make out your writing."

He said, "Just give it to the pharmacy. They'll know what it is. It's cough syrup and penicillin."

She nodded and poked the prescription inside her purse.

The smiling doctor's demeanor changed to frowning suspicion when I began wailing as he told me to take off my pants. I resisted fiercely when Lou yanked them down and held me while he poked my butt with a long needle.

He said, "Big Guy, it's over. It won't hurt for long." He stood me upright on the exam table, turned me around and began examining my pee-pee.

I wailed louder, but not because of the painful shot. I was afraid. Was he like Merl? My innocence was already, stolen, gone forever at too young of an age. What was he going to do? How was he going to hurt me? Merl was the giver of pain. Was this doctor too?

I thought he was going to do to me what Merl did. Embarrassed, I did not want Lou to watch. I despised her for bringing me to this man. "I hate you," I yelled as he held my pee-pee between his fingers. The pain was next, I thought.

He whacked the head with a flip of his forefinger. That, was not the kind of pain expected. I bawled louder.

The grimacing doctor said nothing as he glanced up at me. He turned to Lou who was trying to calm Jane as she began screaming with me. He strolled toward the sink and turned on the water.

His back toward us, "You can put your nephew's clothes on now," he said.

I am confused, was that all? He didn't hurt me. He just embarrassed me. I felt, violated. I did not like him. Why did he play with my pee-pee? I was pleased that was all he did, and glad it was over. Feeling dirty, and powerless I was grateful he did not mess with my poop-shoot.

I thought, am I like other children? Am I? Is this normal? Were all children touched the way Merl touched me? I did not want anyone touching me.

I am a child. I could not comprehend such things. I was innocent. I was ignorant. I was vulnerable. What were the strange monstrous emotions Merl stirred inside of me? Feelings all mixed with rage, hate, anger, and fear. I didn't want Merl touching me, ever again. I felt dirty from the doctor's touch, too.

I thought Merl, was the adult. He was to be my protector. Nevertheless, he violated me. Now, I suffered the after effects of the trauma. I had no trust for any adults. Somebody needed to be responsible and love me, to build my confidence again. Help me understand what happened. How could they? It was a secret horror of the night monster. I refused to tell, too young to understand the disrespectful acts against me. I had no trusted guardian to explain.

I thought, Merl Judas, your touch caused me feel like a blob of slime, nothing. I loved you before you did this to me. Now, I abhorred you. I hated myself because of what you did. I would never trust you again. Merl took all my self-esteem. I would look at the world of all adults with loathing, fear, and mistrust. Merl should never have touched me that way. I would never be the same again because of his crimes against me. I thought why you did this to me, Merl Judas? Daddy did not. He was my friend. Perhaps crazy was easier to trust in a limited way. He did not hurt me.

I was ashamed. People made fun of him. I was his son, the first child of a village idiot. I refused to wear the labels. My heart cried I was not white trash as Stan says about Momma and me.

I thought, crazy was better than dirty and mean like Merl. I would never allow any of them to know the depth of my pain. I wanted my daddy to take me away from this doctor.

Across the room, the doctor washed his hands and shook his head again. I assumed he was going to ask a question as Lou helped me slip up my pants, and worked to calm my sobbing.

Jane continued to whimper.

Lou smiled and chuckled. "Saul, stop making such a fuss. The doctor didn't hurt you. He just wanted to make sure you're healthy."

I shrieked louder. His examination left me feeling powerless again. Jane frightfully bellowed too.

Lou's brow wrinkled, she says, "Now, hush before I give you both something to really cry about." She slapped my leg and turned to Jane. She says, "Shut up Jane."

I was experiencing extreme nausea. I do not allow myself to vomit. I wanted to go home. I wanted Daddy.

The doctor was annoyed. "Never mind," he said while tossing a brown paper towel into the trash can next to the examination table where Jane sat, softly whimpering.

I stopped bawling as Lou pulled down Jane's panties for the doctor to check her.

I thought I have to protect Jane. No one else will. I will kick them. Jane and I will run out of this dreadful place.

I thought, no, not Jane. He was goanna hurt her whoo-whoo. I was afraid. What was he going to do to her? I was too small to defend her. I could not defend myself. They will kill us. Why did Lou bring us to this place of pain and sadness?

I wept silently as the doctor continued the procedure. He checks her poop-shoot.

Jane screamed and fought like a wild tiger. Screeching uncontrollably she yelled, "No." She moaned, "No. Please don't do that," she pleaded.

Finished, he stepped back, shook his head, and glared at Jane again, and then he glanced at me. He turned facing Lou. "Your niece has a growth and pocket of infection inside her rectum. We will have to do minor surgery. She must have fallen on something. Have you not noticed blood in her stool? This growth probably drops down and is visible when she has a bowel movement. It's been there a long time," he said.

I was relieved. He did not hurt Jane. I did not want Jane hurt like, I was by Merl. This doctor man was not a bad guy. He was going to fix Jane's poop-shoot. Like Doc Nix repaired my leg.

Surgery was the word I remembered. That was bad, but it mended people. Jane would have surgery on her bottom. He was a good person. Maybe we could trust him.

Lou nodded. "Not really doctor. They came to stay with me for a couple of months last summer. I noticed some blood then. But it stopped, and I didn't think any more about it. I thought she had scratched herself," she said.

"We'll schedule her for surgery tomorrow," he said.

Jane and I never wanted to see another doctor after that. Jane's rectum surgery was successful. The doctor corrected it with the operation. Jane recovered quickly.

The Snake Pit

Lou and Martin fought constantly. Martin was an alcoholic. He thought nothing of sharing a shot of hooch with his children. Offering the booze to me, I declined every time. I had seen enough drunkenness, wanting no part of the beer or whiskey. His youngest son, Don, nine months younger than me, loved the stuff.

Lou dressed Don and me as twins. We were as different as light and dark. In fact, he was husky, a cotton top with pale skin tones, and rosy cheeks. I was a beanpole, and had an olive complexion with brown hair. We certainly did not look like relatives.

Lou did not know Martin would give in to Don's morning temper tantrums, whining not to attend kindergarten. Martin insisted that I go into the classroom. Don spent his time with Uncle Martin, on the job. He sipped on his dad's beers the daylong. Martin picked me up at school in the afternoons and I was to lie, pretending that Don was in class. This went on for weeks.

Kindergarten graduation approached, at the end of May. I let it slip one afternoon when talking to Pasty, Lou overheard. She and Martin got into a loud, cursing argument. Martin grabbed Don and tossed him into the automobile, then, they drove away. They were gone for three days. Martin had a girlfriend on the side, and spent a lot of time with her after that. He was hardly ever home. Lou cried seemingly without interruption. Wished, I had kept my mouth shut.

Lou was angry and short-tempered. No one could please her. She could spank hard and did so frequently. To that point in my youth, no one whipped me as hard as Lou. Daddy never paddled us, though Momma often threatened too, and did, once-in-a-while. Momma's punishment was never more than harsh words, glares, slapped faces, or a swat on behinds and hands. She never really hurt us.

We children walked on eggshells around Lou. Afraid we would displease her and she would pull out the belt. Her spankings hurt.

The end of May rolled around and school was out for summer. Daddy fell off his drywall stilts and broke his shoulder. He was unable to work for many weeks. Early June, Lou, Daddy, and we children piled into her new station wagon and drove to Loafer's Glory for vacation.

Twenty minutes after arriving at Delena's, Daddy began to cry uncontrollably. He said his head hurt. An awful pain throughout his body felt like someone had beaten him with a baseball bat. He said he had to see a doctor, and ran out. He jumped into Lou's car, and fired up the engine. Daddy sped down the highway around the winding curves toward Raccoon Springs. Doc Anderson attended him.

The next time I saw Daddy, he was a patient in the Arkansas State Hospital for the Mentally Ill, The Lunatic Asylum.

Daddy was not crazy. He does not belong here, I thought, as two strong male Licensed Psychiatric Technician Nurses dressed in white guided us through the maze of breezeways and corridors. The visiting area was marked off in one corner of the dining room. We sat at the tables as a nurse poured the adults coffee. The other technician went for Daddy, locked up, in another part of the hospital.

Delena sipped her coffee and set the paper cup on the long table. She turned and watched as several patients marched in and stood across the room.

"Look there in the lunch line," Delena said with a smirk.

"What?" Lou asked as she clutched tight to her red purse that matched her high heels and pleated skirt. She turned to see behind her.

We gazed across the large dinning hall to where patients from Unit 1, lining up for their noon meal.

"Well, I'll be hush puppy chewed up by a hound," Chad said while slapping his large hands on his knees and chuckling.

We watched a husky red-faced wrinkled elderly man fumble with a sanitary napkin wrapped around his neck. Delena and Lou's hands flung over their mouths, as they squirmed to hold back their laughter.

I did not know what it was. Their laughter stirred up anger inside my soul. They were making sport of the man. Now, they would make fun of Daddy since he lived here with these strange people. I did not see the humor. I assumed the patient had a white bandage covering a neck wound.

The tall male nurse noticed the commotion and promptly relieved the delusional one of the article, tossing it in the trash behind the kitchen counter. The patient turned his back toward us and banged his head against the wall.

Escorted by the other stern-faced male nurse, Daddy stepped into the visiting area. He did not seem any worse than when he and

Momma fought. Daddy was sad, browbeaten, like after their arguments. My heart broke, not that he was unhappy, but at knowing, he was a prisoner in this wretched place.

Someone across the room squealed, and Daddy blushed, embarrassed. We watched as a skinny man stole another patient's dinner roll. He ran for the corner and began wolfing it down.

The other patient, with cold empty brown eyes, frowned angrily, and then calmly walked over holding a carton of milk. With a full bass voice, he asked, "Would you like some milk with my roll?"

The other, timidly nodded.

At that, he promptly opened and dumped the milk on his head. He said, "There, you, you, you . . . scandalous thief. Enjoy it." He punched the hunkering patient.

Our attendants took notice. They ran to the scene dragging the aggressor out of the building as he kicked and yelled.

Observing the sight, nervously, "Enoch, are we safe? What if, one of those people notices us?" Lou asked and paused, placing her hand high on her chest. Fearfully, she added, "And, you know," she whispered.

Daddy said, "They lock up the violent ones in Rogers Hall across the street. These guys are pretty much harmless."

"Hell, that didn't look innocent to me." Chad scoffed.

Daddy bowed his head. "I should never have checked myself in this place."

Jane and I crawled onto his lap. I wanted to cry, but would not allow myself. "I love you, Daddy," I said as I kissed him on the cheek. Then I placed my index fingers on the corners of his mouth and pushed-up. "I knew you could smile." I said and giggled.

Daddy chuckled.

Jane did too. "I love you, Daddy," she said, and lays her head against his strong chest.

Smiling, Daddy raised his gaze and hugged us.

His doctor, a large-boned tall man with salt-and-pepper hair, dressed in a black business suit, stepped into the room and said Daddy was going to be all right. He explained. The separation had triggered a severe depression. Daddy had asked him to talk with us.

I learned Daddy was having something called a nervous breakdown because of all that had happened between them. In addition, he had some brain damage from a blow to his head.

After the doctor left, we strolled outside and sat at a picnic table under a huge oak. The hospital grounds gave me the creeps. I felt ashamed and embarrassed that my own father was in this place.

Two men were kissing, three tables down the way from us. Shocked, his eyes popping nearly out of his head, Chad yelled, "Look at the friggin' queers!"

I thought, queer? What was that? They were touching each other like Momma and Ginger had touched that day in the fields. What did this mean? I was confused. Was Momma queer? What was a queer? They were a two-daddy couple. Maybe, but Momma had not kissed Ginger like that. They just touched, except for the day we left, when Ginger pecked her on the cheek. No, Momma was not a queer.

Another patient was pulling tiny, imaginary things out of thin air and poking them into his shirt pocket. Three men walked around glassily eyed, hopped up on medication, and were begging for coke money.

Some patients approached us to mooch cigarettes. Chad pulled out a pack and Daddy shook his head. Chad caught the signal. "Sorry boys, I only have enough for me today," he said.

One jolly soul jumped on top of a picnic table and began singing off key. Smiling, he turned to us and introduced himself. "Thank you. Thank you, my dear folks. They have made a dreadful mistake, yah knows. I don't need to be here," he said and ran his fingers through his greasy hair while bounding off the table and stepping toward Delena. He fell to his knees in front of her and pleaded. "I'm Elvis Presley; yah just gotta help me escape. I'm gonna be late for the gig this evening. Yah gotta help me get out of this prison," he said.

As she swallowed, nearly choking on coffee, fearful Delena nervously strangled, gasped for breath, and began coughing.

Chad shouted, "Beat it, yah crazy jackal."

The wide-eyed delusional Elvis leapt onto his table again and continued performing.

I winced, as that one reminded me of Merl.

Turning to Delena, Chad asked, "Are you okay?"

Delena nodded, and her hacking subsided.

We saw other patients who were much worse off than, Daddy. They frightened me, and I wanted to take Daddy out of that dreadful place. I could not save him. I wailed as the nurses led him away when it was time for us to leave.

Now, it was just Jane and me. Great sadness overpowered as Lou drove us to Loafer's Glory without Daddy. In back, Jane and I sat on either side of Delena, saying nothing while we listened to the adults' conversations.

"Poor, Enoch, that trifling whore did this to him." Delena seethed as she applied more lipstick while looking at herself in the small compact mirror she pulled from her purse.

Chad lit a cigarette. "Hell, Delena, the boy's been sick all his life. He ain't ever been right."

Delena says, "I can't stand the idea of him being locked up in the snake pit."

Lou fiddled with her hair while glancing in the rear-view mirror as she drove. "Ma always said he wasn't right. It's the cow-horn curse, yah knows."

Jane and I were humbled with grief and shame. She crawled past Delena's lap and snuggled close to me. We slept the remainder of the trip.

Jane and I, along with Lou and her offspring stayed with Delena a few more days. While in, Loafer's Glory, Jane and I visited with Bobby. Lou and her clan sought out other relatives. After a week, Lou decided we would return to South Bend without Daddy.

Daddy remained hospitalized several more weeks and underwent electric shock treatments, thirty-three in all. The therapy didn't help. The remedies only worsened his condition.

Paul E. Treadwell

What's This?

Back in South Bend, Martin was waiting when we arrived. He missed Daddy too. Daddy became so proficient at his job that Martin put him in charge of the crew working on show homes in the new building additions of town. The bankers and realtors liked Daddy's work when they toured the houses he finished, and consistently gave Martin the money he needed for future projects. Now, those days were gone for Daddy.

Martin genuinely cared about Jane and me. He was good with children, playful, and happy, but ignorant of the effects of alcohol on us. He thought it was cute when Don staggered and acted silly when drunk. He would regret his ignorance years later.

One evening Martin drove Don and me to see his mother Bonnie. She lived in a mobile home park that Martin owned. He provided her with a free house after she moved from Loafer's Glory. She hugged Don, and Martin. He gave her two-hundred dollars. Then she demanded an extra one-hundred-eighty dollars.

Browbeaten, shamefully, Martin bowed his head. He promised to give her more the following evening. Bonnie, harsh-spoken, fat, a brazen woman in her mid-sixties. I decided she did not care whose feelings she hurt. Maybe she was a good woman. I was not sure. Martin loved her, but she was not kind toward me. I did not like the way she spoke to Uncle Martin.

She wore her long graying hair in the holiness roll around the top of her head like a doughnut. "That ol' woman you're married to is going to take you for everything, Son. If you don't get rid of her," Bonnie said.

She glanced down at me with her never ceasing natural scowl. "What's this? Are you running an orphanage and taking in all the woman's foundling kinfolks and their kids too? You need to get rid of him. You have enough kids of your own. If they are yours. Take care of your own--your poor old sick mother, Son. You do not need this added responsibility. Besides, he's probably the reason you don't have the money to help me."

Red faced, Martin's sad embarrassed gaze fell.

I smiled.

He smiled back and winked.

I winked back.

He took a deep breath and exhaled. Martin told her again he would be back with the money.

I decided not to come along the next time. She did not like me, but Martin loved me.

When we got back inside the car to leave, Don asked, "Daddy, why is Grandma such a bit**?"

Uncle Martin refused to answer. He laughed.

Humiliated by Bonnie's insults and knowing she had hurt my feelings, he bought a bike the following week, and presented me with the gift. I could not have been more delighted.

August whirled around. Martin and Lou were fighting endlessly. He stayed drunk and the children were out of hand. Lou was constantly angry.

Martin paid off the loan on Daddy's new Pontiac. Then he sold it.

Chad got the old home place after he paid the back taxes. He made plans to give Daddy five hundred dollars for his loss.

There was no hope of my family returning to Loafer's Glory. The old homestead, a symbol of constant stability as my early childhood home was gone forever. It now, belonged to Chad and Vanny. Our mode of transportation was gone too. I Liked the Pontiac, but the '57 I missed worse. Blue was my favorite color. The Chevy may have held negative memories for Momma, but it was a symbol of happier days for me. I wished Daddy had not sold it.

The second week of August, Lou said Jane and I needed to be closer to Daddy for more frequent visits. We needed to be there for him if ever he got out of the hospital. She loaded our things into the station wagon, along with the bicycle, and drove us to Delena.

I suspected her true reasons were to dump Jane and me. She simply did not want the added responsibility. I did not want to leave.

I thought, maybe Bonnie had something to do with this surrender. Perhaps Martin didn't want us after all.

Lou's marital problems kept her grieved and stressed. I reconciled she didn't need us. We would only add to their family problems.

In a sense, I was happy to be with Delena and familiar community surroundings. I longed for my own family.

Paul E. Treadwell

Don't Repeat This

Delena married a gambler. He was fifteen years younger. They wed after we returned to South Bend the first time. Saul was his name, just like mine. If only for that reason, I liked him from the start.

Delena ran the restaurant from sunup to eleven p.m. Jane and I spent a lot of time with Saul. His gentle nature bestowed a genuine love and affection for us. He hugged us, while telling silly jokes and giggled along as we children laughed.

We forgot our losses when around Saul. We grew to love him. Saul, at thirty-three was husky, with a dark olive complexion, coal-black hair, greased back. His piercing blue eyes were mirrors of happiness. He was a handsome man.

His large bright smile, jovial laughter, and protectiveness made us feel loved. Every night at nine o'clock, he took us from the restaurant to the house next door and put us to bed. Faithfully, he told a bedtime story and tucked us in. Then he stayed until we dozed off.

For us, this was heaven. In the past year, Momma and Daddy left us to live with ten different families. Now we felt we were wanted and safe for the first time in a long while.

Enrolled in the first grade at Raccoon Springs Elementary school, and not having the social skills to truly interact with children my own age other than my cousins, I didn't make many friends. The six-mile bus ride frightened me, especially when the older students got a little rowdy at the back. I sat behind the burley bus driver, feeling safer there.

The first weekend after school started, I found out the reason why Lilly left us. Saturday she dropped by to visit Delena at the restaurant with her oldest daughter April, and the two younger siblings.

They sat at the counter eating hamburgers when Jane and I came running indoors. We did not recognize them at first. I spied pretty, blond April, now eight, sipping on a bottle coke with peanuts floating around inside.

She looked grown up, being taller and talking with the adults at the counter. She was a stranger. Lilly slid off her stool, smiling as she raced toward the doorway and gave us a hug. We pulled back.

She sadly asked, "You don't remember me?"

We nodded.

"I'm Lilly. And this is April," she said and pointed to the counter.

Wondering, not certain for a moment, then we happily realized who she was and threw our arms around her.

"How are you babies doing?" she asked while embracing us.

We smiled. "Fine," we said in unison.

"Come have a soda with us, this will be better than old times," she says.

She took us by hand, and hoisted us onto the stools next to April. She glanced across the room to check on her younger children asleep in the booth. She pulled out her coin purse and poked a nickel in the Juke Box. Selecting a happy tune, she sashayed to the beat toward us and took her seat again.

Looking up from her plate of food long enough to greet us, April smiled. "Hi Saul, hi Jane," she said, and waved with her pinky finger, then went back to sipping her pop.

Other customers paid their bills, and then it was just Delena and us.

"Can they have a soda?" Lilly asked Delena.

Delena smiled and nodded. She opened two six-ounce cokes and set them on the counter as Lilly began to share with Delena why she left Merl.

Lilly said, "The weather turned exceptionally warm the week before I left Seligman. Merl says he is hot at about two a.m. and takes a quilt to lay on, in front of the open kitchen door. I didn't think anything of it at first, until a few minutes later when I heard Ora shuffling down the hallway toward him."

She lit a cigarette, puffed, exhaled and then coughed. Composing herself, she said, "They were whispering, but their words weren't distinct. I waited, thinking she would go back to bed soon. She didn't. Thirty minutes later, I heard them giggling and moaning. Some months before, I had suspicion something was going on."

Lilly paused, took a drag, exhaled, and tugged on her earlobe with her right index finger and thumb. She says, "They were rotten deceivers. I just didn't want it to be true. I pushed my gut feelings aside all those months, even before we left here. Intuition got the best of me. I crawled out of bed and peeked around the corner.

Caught them in the act," She growled for loss of words, as strong emotions overwhelmed her. Trembling as she raises the smoldering cigarette to her lips.

She exhaled and banged her fist against the counter, after downing a sip of soda. She says, "The gossip was true. They were lying on a quilt, naked as two picked birds. Their naked butts were a shinin'! They were," she snorted, and leaned forward, whispering into Delena's ear. "Having intercourse," she said.

Lilly cleared her throat and glanced over at us. The look adults give kids when they hope they do not understand. She rolled her eyes, smiled and smashed the cigarette butt into the ashtray putting it out.

I heard the last word. Daddy caught them doing that in Wisconsin. I wondered if they were naked then. My brow wrinkled for a second as I concentrated, searching for a definition. What had it meant? My brain had no file under that topic, yet. It didn't matter. I reasoned intercourse was just another, one of those angry games adults played. Figured, I would never play that game. It hurt too many people.

We smiled.

Relieved, Lilly nervously yanked her earlobes and commenced whispers loud enough for us to hear, again. "They're beasts, immoral beasts. No more scruples than alley cats," she said.

Sullen, Delena sighed. "I could have told you that. It has been going on for years since shortly before Saul was born. Ma caught them meeting down by the pond many times," Delena, mumbled.

Lilly sipped her coke then continued, "There was no explaining. They didn't know I caught them. My only regret is I never told Enoch," she said, and sighed, head down. "He wouldn't be in the friggin' Lunatic Ben now, if not for their treachery. I think Merl was poisoning Enoch. His herbal sh** weeds, spikin' Enoch's moonshine," she says.

Delena gasped, and flung her hand over her mouth. "No." She whispered.

Lilly nodded. "My mind was made up. I wanted to just get-to-hell away from them," she says. Her lips, trembled, her eyes were watery.

She said, "When everyone was gone, I gathered the kids and drove to my parents' home in Florida. I didn't even leave Merl a note."

Delena said, "I can't blame you. I would have killed them both."

Lilly motioned for Delena to lean closer over the bar as she hissed, "Merl molested April in Loafer's Glory before he and Enoch moved us to Missouri."

Delena gasped.

Lilly shot to her feet, and banged the counter top. "Damn that son-of-a-bit**," she snorted.

Her face was grief struck. She sat, whispering, into Delena's ear again, "He got to April for the past four years. I never knew until April spoke up a few weeks ago. I want to kill him." Lilly's gaze fell to the floor.

I heard but did not understand. I thought, what is molesting? That must be bad too if she wanted to kill him, probably as bad as setting Mabel on fire.

April blushed. Tearfully she slid off her stool, and ran outside. "Momma, don't tell. He'll kill me. You embarrassed me. You promised not to tell. I want to go home," she said.

Lilly shamefully glanced up at Delena. She stuttered, "Don't repeat this to anyone. Please."

Delena stared in bewilderment at Lilly, and then raised her gaze toward April standing outside the open door. Suspiciously, she turned, her laser eyes burned through Jane and me as her chin fell, and she nodded, no.

The younger Judas children sleeping in the booth awakened as Lilly hoisted them into her arms, fleeing the restaurant. April continued bawling as they piled into their car and drove off.

Delena never questioned us about molestation by Merl. Just the thoughts of such abominations were too despicable for her to speak.

Lilly's, Loafer's Glory reunion was to court Mr. Bronze, a neighbor up the road. After a few short weeks they wed. She, Mr. Bronze and her children returned to Florida. Eventually Mr. Bronze landed a job in Ohio, where they permanently relocated. We never saw them again.

Cold Black Hearted Ol' Witch

Sunny and warm the first Saturday in October of '61, Jane and I were playing in Aunt Delena's yard. I was giving Jane's "Chatty Kathy" doll, a bike basket ride. A strange yellow and white '58 Mercury pulled into the cafe parking lot near the front of the house. Tall, and thin, a beautiful woman with slicked back raven-hair and dark sunglasses opened the door. She got out of the passenger seat.

Wearing white peddle-pusher pants, and sandals, the woman walked over and sat down on the yard swing under the century old red oak that shaded the house. She smiled, and asked, "Hi Saul, hi Jane. Do you know who I am?"

Jane and I peered at her with questioning eyes. We shook our heads.

"Why, I'm your mother," she said and patted the seat. "Come over here, sit with me, and let's talk."

Apprehensively, I gaze upon her for a moment. I say, "Ol' Gal, you're not my momma."

She smiled and took off her dark shades. "Don't you remember me?" she asked.

I thought, I did, but was not certain. Her hairstyle was different. I had never seen Momma with a short ponytail. Momma's mane was always very long, right down to her hips. Momma wore dresses and skirts to please her Aunt Diana's holiness teachings. If this was my momma wearing pants, and had razor chopped off her glory, she would go to Hell.

Jane and I sat down beside her on the swing. Despite our misgivings we wanted her to be Momma. She asked if we would to go with her to Raccoon Springs for an ice cream cone.

I said, "Delena has plenty of ice cream in the restaurant. She'll give us some."

When I jumped up to run inside the cafe, the female stranger grabbed my arm and pulled me back onto the seat. She said, "I like best, the strawberry flavor in town."

I said, "We have to ask before we go anywhere."

She said, "Delena wouldn't mind. After all, I am your mother."

She finally convinced us to get into the car. Jane and I wore shorts, tee shirts, and we are barefoot. That was okay. We would only be gone a few minutes. Maybe, Delena would not find out.

The petite woman lifted Jane onto the front seat by Merl's twenty-eight-year-old nephew Jeb. He nervously sat behind the steering wheel. Jeb was the younger image of his dad Ely except that he inherited Fanny's witch nose. I stared at his large crooked snout. I had seen one like that before. For the moment, could not remember whose.

I slid across the seat and sat beside Jane. The slim dark woman was looking more like Momma. She squeezed in beside us, slammed her door, and locked it. Her kind, sweet demeanor flipped one-hundred-eighty-degrees when she shrieked, "Put it to the floor, Jeb. Let's get the f*** out of Arkansas."

He shoved the transmission into reverse, speedily backed out of the yard, and rammed the gearshift into drive. He floored the gas-peddle. The back tires flung parking lot gravel and dirt around the automobile as they made their speedy get away. We zoomed out of Loafer's Glory at eighty miles per hour.

"Guess we showed those domineering, crazy bastards," Jeb shouted.

"Fight Jane! This is not our momma! She is stealing us! Kick, hit, and bite," I shouted.

We did exactly that. Jane bit Jeb's ear and he nearly ran off the road. I grabbed the woman's ponytail, pulled as hard as I could and held on. The screaming woman squirmed around and slapped my face. I let go.

Cursing, she grabbed Jane and flung her into the back seat. Jane held on, yanking Jeb's hair. The woman slapped her hands, forcing Jane to release.

I kicked her with bare-feet, while hitting them with fist. Terrified, we screamed and yelled, behind a flood of tears.

Kidnapped, taken by force from Delena, by our own mother. We hardly knew her anymore. We had once again, been taken from safety into the arms of strangers and evil.

On the straight stretches, Jeb ran the Mercury as hard as she would go. He only slowed enough to keep from losing control as tires squalled when the car leaned into the sharp Ozarks' mountain curves. He sped through Raccoon Springs, St. Joe, Pindall, Western Grove, Valley Springs, Harrison, then across the state line into Missouri. After an hour, Jeb finally slowed down. Then he and Momma relaxed a bit.

We continued our haunted fueled trumpeting. Jane was in the back seat alone. I wanted to crawl over to comfort and sit with her. The woman full of malice would not allow it.

"You cold, black hearted ol' witch," I yelled, repeating what Delena had said of Momma. She did not respond the way I expected. She simply held my face tighter against her breast.

After another hour, our bawling subsided to whimpers. They stopped at a drive-in restaurant a ways north of Branson, Missouri. Momma ordered strawberry ice cream cones. She had forgotten I am allergic to strawberries. I threw mine on her lap, soiling her white peddle-pushers.

Jane watched and followed suit by tossing her cone onto the back of Jeb's head. The woman threatened to paddle us. I thought that this vile person could not be Momma. Never leaving us alone, one at a time they cleaned themselves in the cafe restroom.

I did not want to believe this woman was my mother. Jane and I referred to her as "Hey Lady." Not once did we call her mom, or momma. Just, "Hey-Lady," was all would come out of our mouths. We drove through Missouri and into Illinois. Late in the evening, we stopped at another restaurant. There, standing outside the ordering window flirting with a young teenage-waitress, stood Merl Judas.

Now, there was no doubt. She was Momma. We continued to refer to her, "Hey Lady."

Merl strutted over, opened the backdoor, and slid onto the seat with Jane. "Oh no, it's you again." Jane painfully wailed, and asked if she could climb over the seat and sit in front.

Momma shouted for her to stop whining. She turned around and glared at Jane. "Merl isn't going to hurt you. Now stop your f***in' bawling." Addressing Jeb, she growled, "I'm so glad we stole my kids away from those crazy mother f***ers."

"Hey Lady," I said and tugged on her blouse.

She glanced down smiling. "What, Saul?"

"What is that name you called them and said to Jane?" I asked.

"What?" she asked.

"What's a mother f***er, lady?" I asked, not knowing the meaning of the word and having lost any memory of Momma or Daddy using it before. The adults roared with laughter. Jane and I squalled again.

Attempting to wipe the smirk off her face, Momma glanced down. "Son, that's a bad word. You don't need to know the meaning. Don't ever say it," she said, chuckled, and mussed my hair.

She playfully tickled me in the ribs. We stopped whimpering, and giggled for a moment. Soon, Jane was whining again.

As we drove over the next three hours, Jane continued to whimper. Suffering alone in the backseat, from time to time, Jane asks Merl to stop. I thought maybe she was weeping still over the trauma of kidnapped. Not knowing Merl was hurting Jane. I was not the only child he molested. Merl fondled her, the entire trip. She was barely five-years-old.

Late that night, they rented a motel room. The next morning Momma and Merl left for food. Jeb was showering. I picked up the telephone and told the motel operator I wanted to talk to Delena or Uncle Saul in Loafer's Glory. She asked if I knew the number. I didn't. I told her that a woman who claimed to be my mother had kidnapped Jane and me, and I wanted to go home.

Momma and Merl strolled in, carrying coffee and donuts. Momma tossed the box of donuts on a dresser, and yanked the telephone out of my hand. Placing the phone to her ear she asked, "Who the hell is this?"

Realizing it was the operator, contrite Momma said, "Oh, I'm so sorry. This, boy of mine isn't used to telephones and he was playing. I was afraid he had called someone long distance and was running up our bill. Please forgive me for being so rude."

She glared down at me while hanging up. Momma yelled at Jeb to get out of the shower and into the car. Jeb hopped out of the bathroom, quickly strapped on his artificial leg, threw on his clothes, and limped out the motel door with his uncombed hair dripping wet. Momma and Merl tossed us into the vehicle and we sped out of town.

Jeb drove for two hours until we came to a small, dark-green house surrounded by fields of tall drying stalks of popcorn plants. After Momma, Jane, and I got out; Merl and Jeb drive away. I did not like being with Momma. This woman was now a stranger. Nevertheless, I was glad the two of them were gone.

We were alone for two weeks. The weather was getting cold. Jane and I still had no shoes and only the clothes on our backs. Momma washed out our shorts and tops at night after we went to bed.

One cool morning I ventured outside, crossed the barbed-wire fence, and explored the popcorn field. I pulled the largest ear I could find off a drying stalk nearest the house, crawled under the fence, and carried the cob of grain inside to Momma.

She put it in the window directly catching the morning sunlight and left it dry there for another week. The day before we departed, Momma shucked the kernels off the cob and popped the corn for us.

Jane and I accepted the fact that we might never see Delena again. Our only security now was in this woman, who looked and acted a little like the mother we once knew. Now, Momma had an all-consuming hardness about her. She was different, I was not accustomed to her moment by moment, endless on edge gruffness. Perhaps it had always been there, and I never saw it before.

Driving his dark-green '53 Chevy, the next morning Merl returned. Noxious clouds of dread engulfed me as we crawled into his car and headed for the nearest town. We stopped at a shoe store where Momma and Merl dragged me inside. They forced crying Jane to stay in the car.

Momma found a pair of black patent leather dress shoes for Jane and handed them to Merl. She told him to see if they would fit her.

Merl was gone a long time. Momma had me try on several pairs before she decided on red tennis shoes from a sale rack. I deplored them.

She strolled to the door and yelled at Merl down the street. He was in the backseat with Jane. Jane was kicking at him and screaming.

"Do the shoes fit?" Momma asked, seemingly unfazed by Jane's antics.

Poking his head out the back car door, smiling, he replied, "Just fine."

Momma paid for both pairs. When we left the store and were on the highway traveling again, Momma scolded Jane for making such a fuss.

Jane had another secret to add to her list of traumatic childhood memories. Merl had raped her again there on the public street inside the car.

The Matchmaker

We drove several more hours arriving on the outskirts of New Glaus as the sun was setting. Towering in front of us was the big white rental house in Wisconsin where we lived before. This was Leviathan's lair.

Cold brisk winds whipped from the north when we got out. The temperature was not below freezing, yet the wind chill cut to the bone on skinny naked legs. I shivered, and pointed toward a large dog in the yard.

The woman grinned. "That's Buddy, Saul," she said.

Amazed and a little fearful, I said, "He is so big!"

He was now a full-grown Collie. Overjoyed to see him but reserved because of his size. Timidly, I called his name.

"Buddy," I said.

He whined.

"Buddy it's Saul. Don't you remember me?" I asked.

He wagged his tail, came closer, and sniffed. He recognized us and began running circles. Leaping onto my chest, he knocked me to the ground while happily barking, wagging his tail, and licking my face.

Jane crawled out of the backseat and came racing to pet Buddy. His long pink tongue, dog slobbered her cheeks and she began to wail. He then focused his attentions on me and we wrestled. If I had a tail, it would have been wagging too.

"You boys can play later; right now you need to get into warmer clothes. Let's go inside," she said, as she took my hand and pulled me from the ground.

Sniffling, Jane grabbed my arm and held tight. Buddy growled when Merl reached to pick her up. She screamed for Momma.

Letting Jane's hand drop, he kicked Buddy's gut, knocking the dog off his feet. Seething, Merl mumbled, "Damn dog, I'll teach you to bristle at me."

Buddy whimpered as he followed close behind to the front door and lay down on the porch.

When we walked inside, I wanted to boot Merl. Angry and fearful, I took a deep breath and sighed. Once again, we are captives of the King of Terror's unmerciful evil. We returned to the house of horrors, and brought the monster with us.

The house was warm. Someone had finally purchased coal for the furnace. Merl's older brother, goofy Ely and his homely wife Fanny now rented the house. They were inside waiting for our arrival.

Jeb, their eldest son, our kidnapper pulled down his pants to remove his artificial leg. He rolled off a stomp sock soiled with tiny spots of blood and yellow fluid.

His leg had been, crushed as a teen in a logging accident. To save his life, doctors amputated high-mid-thigh. The wooden limb did not fit right and irritated the end of his stump. He may have been a naive, gullible, good fellow like his father Ely. For me, he was as evil as Merl for helping Momma kidnap us.

Wanda, Jeb's young wife applied ointment from a green bottle to the open sores and blisters. She placed a clean stump sock over the end as he cringed.

Ugly Fanny and Ely sat beside them on the living room sofa listening intently to a fervent Hellfire and Brimstone radio preacher. My eyes bugged out as I gawked. I had never seen such an unattractive woman. Fanny was as homely as Uncle Chad said. Then she spoke. Her screeching voice was grating on my nerves.

Late-forties, and graying, Fanny's small crossed, beady-brown-eyes and razor-sharp-long nose, crooked on the end. She resembled a witch. Jeb got his nose from her gene pool.

Fanny's voice sounded like the calling of a crow. Frequently twitching her head, and checking to make sure her bun was in place, she repeatedly says, "Praise the Lord," while softly and constantly humming a gospel tune.

Staring, I thought now I meet the matchmaker. No wonder I could not remember her. She had the face one would want to forget.

Indeed, she arranged many young marriages back in Loafer's Glory, and prided herself on the endeavors. Pops, Daniel Bip gave her a good cussin' when he found out she was secretly arranging meetings between Momma and Daddy, when Momma was only twelve-years-old.

Despite his efforts to stop Fanny's matchmaking for Momma, Fanny went right on. She believed she was doing God a service. It was God's work, she did. Fanny's husband Ely obeyed her every command and supported her match making endeavors.

I thought he was a catch for her.

Ely wanted to be like Elvis. The poor soul, though he tried--not endowed with the better natural genetics, as was his brother Merl. He was more of a Gomer Pyle, religious and fearful of not pleasing God. Ely was afraid he might not make Heaven if he didn't obey Fanny.

I recalled how much Delena loathed Fanny. She called her ignorant white trash. Laughing, sarcastically she had said, "To Fanny's way of thinking, a girl should marry and start a family as soon as a gal becomes a woman. When the time of a girl comes to an end and womanhood arrives through the blood. A virgin who is fourteen and unmarried, is in danger of becoming an-old-maid. She is in need of serious intervention. The matchmaker is of course, always Fanny. After all, Fanny is a religious woman and wants no bastard born. She thinks she is doing God a service. The young folks around her needed to be moral. Getting them married, stopped any form of fornication. Fanny reasons matrimony will keep them from sin."

Delena's voice rang disdain, as she added, "The bit** is confused. She claims to be a Christian. Pentecostal Holiness her choice, and she wears the bun in public. Hell, she is no more holy than the hypocrite pastor's son, Newton. Only a nut marries off her ten-year-old daughter to a thirty-year-old man. Her religion is the clothesline only," she says.

Fanny squawked, "We've been expecting you children. Now you behave yourselves while you're under my roof."

I snapped out of the rubberneck reminiscing trance, and thought, I am glad Momma was not that ugly.

Jane and I nodded.

Pretty Wanda sat on the sofa next to Fanny. Wanda, twenty-two, admired her beehive hairstyle in a mirror. She dressed in the drab Pentecostal holiness clothing like Fanny. Her dark-hair clashed against her pale white pious face. Ely's other daughters, Angel, thirteen, retarded Agnus, nine, and their rowdy son Donny, seven, all were there.

Everything about that house had changed. It had nice furniture and pictures on the white walls. It was warm, and the smell of fresh baked bread drifted from the oven. Across the room, dark-curly-haired Angel held a six-month-old baby. He looked a little like Bobby.

Momma held our hands, and led us to the infant. Smiling happily she said, "This is your brother, Rambo. Merl is your new dad."

We didn't say a word. I frowned.

Merl strolled over, hugging Jane and me, real tight. His breath smelled of chicken dookie, tobacco smoke, and booze. When he kissed us, I pulled away.

Jane escaped his deceitful embrace, and held tight to Momma's leg while making the effort at hiding behind her.

I thought what a fake. He wants everyone here to believe he is a good person. "He doesn't love you, Momma," I mumbled under my breath. No one heard or understood my muttering.

Moving away from Merl and hoping the child belonged to my daddy, I motioned for Jane to come closer to Rambo. One foot away, we peered down into his face. Sure enough as far as I could tell, he belonged to Merl. He had Merl's ears that were distinguishable by the long fat lobes on the ends, and Merl's thick plump lower lip.

He was my half-brother. He got here from Momma and Merl's kissing affair. The stork dropped him on the front stoop. That stork dropping, story did not make a lot of sense to me. I had no other explanation.

The same afternoon Fanny donated Donny's castaway clothes. Donny, a year older, smiled when I put them on. The garments he had outgrown, fit well.

We had not met before. Fanny and Ely moved to Wisconsin from Loafer's Glory after my leg was injured. I knew they lived up the road but before this day, I could not recall seeing any of Ely's immediate family, up close. Except for Jeb, the day he helped Momma kidnap us. Of course witch nose Fanny, I recalled from the day she came to visit after the accident. However, that memory was vague.

They all come to the house the evening of the accident. I had seen Fanny then, but thought I was having a nightmare. I did not recall the others at all. In spite of not recognizing them, I had heard much gossip about them.

Right off, Donny and I became friends. So did Jane and Agnus. Agnus was three-years older than I was. She was developmentally delayed and closer to our age mentally.

Fanny boasted about getting Momma and Daddy together--though disappointed that my parents' marriage was not working. Worse, there was no Hotman' gold to be had, as she originally told Momma. Loafer's Glory gold was but an old wives tale.

When supper was almost ready, Fanny cornered Momma and Merl as they necked on the sofa. Like a pissed off Turkey-Chicken-Rooster she flogged them, screeching, "Ora, you should have stayed with Enoch. Divorce and adultery are sin. You and Merl both are goin' to Hell if you don't repent. I pray over my matches. God wants you with Enoch. Praise the Lord."

Momma's killer eyes turned into flamethrowers of silent rage as she bounced to her feet and flouted off into the kitchen. She poured a cup of coffee while mumbling profanities, and stepped onto the porch. Smirking, Merl followed her out and they shared a smoke.

Fanny stuck her head through the cracked door opening. "Shame is on both of you. Now you got a little bastard Judas baby because of your selfishness. Both of you should repent and go back to your mates. Neither of you have any scruples."

They ignored her preaching, and sat on the steps sipping coffee. Fanny continued speaking her mind, and bragged about the successful unions she instigated.

The same year Momma and Daddy got hitched, she married off her ten-year-old daughter Bella. The groom was a thirty-year-old, single, neighbor. Fanny and Ely signed the consent forms. They lied about big Bella's age, wrote down that she was fourteen. Hardly anyone born in Loafer's Glory had a legal birth certificate. Court officials took them at their word.

Ely and Fanny's eldest daughter Bella, now eighteen was still with her mate. They were grandparents of Bella's six-year-old daughter, Pia. Pia's birth very nearly killed Bella, delivering at age twelve. Too much damage to her female organs. As a direct result, she could never conceive again.

Fanny boasted, she would find Angel a husband next year. She went on crowing. Fanny made it clear she did not approve of Momma and Merl's behavior. At that, I took a real liking to this strange ugly woman.

Henpecked Ely always went with Fanny's opinion. He stuck his head out the door to throw in his two bits. "You should listen to Fanny's advice," he said.

Momma and Merl snickered.

Fanny and Ely loved Merl. They would not turn him or us out of their home. They too lived with blinders. This situation became a witch's brew for disaster--a pedophile's playground.

Just Don't Look

Wisconsin's autumn Indian summer lingered during the first couple of weeks after our arrival. One sunny afternoon, Merl put on his scant leopard-design swimming trunks and flaunted himself on the porch as Momma happily had him posing with Rambo.

First, she positioned herself to the right side, then the left. Momma snapped the pictures as he postured. Modeling like a body builder with his paunch sucked in, he flexed his arm and leg muscles. He was aroused and the skimpy tight bathing suit bulged.

Momma giggled.

Annoyed, Fanny asked if I would help her gather the last apples of the season from the orchard about 200 feet from the house. I agreed. Fanny followed close behind, mumbling under her breath, as I dragged a two-gallon water bucket down the hill and set it under a tree.

She wrinkled her brow, and said "They're gonna split Hell wide open." She angrily stomped forward while fiddling with her bun.

I was gathering apples off the ground. Fanny tossed a few into the bucket. She continued to mumble. Hiding behind the largest apple tree, she peeked around the side watching Merl and Momma.

"This is terrible, shameful," she said.

Fanny seemed to be shivering. She shook herself, and then went back to staring at Merl. She moaned while rubbing her breast against the tree as she gawked, entranced over her brother-in-law's posing. She shook herself again, and squeaked, "How vulgar."

I wondered, what did that mean? Sounds like vulture--something is rotten. I stared at her, and assumed she was getting a thrill out of watching. Maybe it was jealousy of Momma, I perceived.

I could not quite put my finger on it. Perhaps, because she was so ugly compared to Momma. Merl certainly was better looking than Ely. Maybe she longed to be Momma.

She could not take her eyes off him. Forcing herself, she looked away. Quickly she turned to peek again. Immediately, she is captivated one more time. The temptation was overpowering her. I surmised she must have wanted to kiss Merl, have a kissing affair. Her competition was not too great.

Comparing Fanny to Momma . . . Momma was pretty as a movie star. It did not matter to Merl if anyone was good looking, as long as he could easily do his business. Momma was pretty, but the mules were not. Fanny was a little more attractive than the mule team. It did not matter to him, good lookin' or not, he would have taken advantage of Fanny if she had let him.

I laughed. "Well Fanny," I said, "If it is so bad, stop staring."

Her face beet-red, she snapped, "Child, don't backtalk or make light of your elders."

"I'm not back talking you, Fanny. Just don't look if it upsets you."

She broke off an apple tree switch, and whelped my legs' ten or twelve times. "Stop that backtalk," she scolded.

Up to this point, I believed Fanny was my hope of comfort. A member of the holiness Pentecostal church, she wanted Momma and Daddy back together. We had the same goal. The whipping changed my attitude toward ugly Fanny.

I thought, let her have her way, she can have Merl for herself. Let her take him away from Momma. Let him be her monster and not ours.

However, something about her demeanor, she really did not like Merl. She was confused. Was this temptation? He was not religious. Maybe that was it. She restrained in the chains of her religion but Momma and Merl lived out their fantasy. Perhaps, what I had seen were dark human emotions. Overpowering temptation, repulsion, and jealousy. I was too young to understand. It seemed the adult relationships were some form of oxymoron. I perceived them that way. Love and hate was mixed-up inside them all.

I questioned if Fanny was a godly woman. She wore her hair in the bun and never used makeup or jewelry. She prayed in tongues, too. Nevertheless, after that day I lost any respect for her. Why had she whipped me? I spoke the truth. I was not making light of her.

In coming days I see her force Agnus to crawl inside the burlap feed sack she had hanging on the kitchen wall. She kept it for discipline purposes. Fanny tied the top closed and beat Agnus with a belt while the child was bound. She whipped all her children this way over the years. She said they could not run from her until the punishment was over. "Spare the rod and spoil the child. Praise the Lord," she often says. We younger ones were never in danger of being spared or spoiled.

Starved for attention, Fanny did the strangest things. In the barn by accident, she scratched her leg on a nail. She intentionally caused more bleeding by squeezing the open wound. The red ran down from the knee to her ankle. She refused to wipe the clotted blood off her limb.

Instead, she let the crimson plasma dry and wore it for two weeks. When anyone came to visit, she made a point to draw his or her attention to the wound.

"Look there, see what I have done to myself," she whined in a pitiful voice while swinging her foot high above her knee.

Fanny was peculiar but something about her seemed to be more noble and moral than the rest of her family. Perhaps because her presence was forceful as she said, "Praise the Lord," when ending every other sentence.

Maybe it was her domineering character, self-assurance, and confidence in her beliefs and the way she religiously conducted herself while hammering all of us with scriptures. None of us wanted to make God mad, or go to Hell. Fascinated by the tongue talkers, I perceived Fanny as an expert on the subject since she spoke in the tongues when she prayed. Even ugly tongue babblers, had something I did not understand.

Soon after our arrival, Merl was up to his old tricks. One day he secretly made a pass at Angel. She told Ely and he confronted Merl. Angry, Fanny went through the roof, giving him a piece of her mind. She ordered Merl to get out of the house. Momma defended Merl, but he tucked his tail and rented a motel room in town. He stayed drunk for over a week.

Momma did not want him to drink. When we visited at the motel, she fussed on him for being drunk. I was thankful he was there and not in the house with us. Drunk or not, I did not care.

Tensions were running high in the household. About a week after Merl made the pass at Angel, Ely and Fanny moved their family to Belleville, and rented another house. None of us knew Merl had got to Agnus already and Jane again. They would not tell.

Momma and Merl fought continually when he immediately moved back in. Merl's drinking grew worse as he frequently stayed out all night in the bars. When he visited the local prostitutes, Momma's rage exploded. Eventually, she calmed down, reconciled herself to his immoral passions. She said she hoped she would be his only desire. She would have to try a little harder to please him, so he would not want anyone but her. She said she was a stand by her man woman.

Merl's other women were routine, but Momma was not about to give up. Once she took my jar of pennies buying gasoline for the car to hunt him down. In the parking lot of a tavern, I watched them argue, as she begged him to come home.

He refused, and took his new girlfriend down to Florida. He told Momma the trip was to visit his children. I suspected he also left to escape his brother Ely's wrath. It is just us, left alone, in the big white house with no furniture again.

After Merl left, Momma managed to get a job at the Frito Lay Company. She eventually purchased used-furniture at a junk store in New Glarus.

I Am Your Mother

I was calling Momma, Momma again, only because she forced us, shortly after Thanksgiving while Merl was in Florida. She says to stop playing on the staircase. I was not going to mind.

"Hey Lady, I don't have to listen to you. My momma is dead. You are a mean witch who stole us from Delena and Saul. I hate you," I shouted.

She latched hold my arm and busted my posterior with her hand several times. She paddled me harder than ever before. She shook me violently. Through my screams of terror, hate, and pain, she too cried and yelled at me.

"I'm your mother. You will call me Ma, Mom, Momma, or Mother. There will be no more of this, Hey Lady crap," she shouted.

"Hey Lady, you're not my momma." I bellowed, through defiant tears. She spanked me again.

Jane ran up the staircase, tearfully, she hit Momma. She squeaked, "You ol' stealin' witch, leave my brother alone."

Momma commenced spanking Jane. "Please stop Momma!" I yelled, at the top of my lungs.

She broke into sorrowful sobs and crumpled to the staircase steps. Momma held us in her arms and wept louder than our howls. We huddled together there for the longest time. Again, our tears mingled together and became one as they had the day of the accident a few years before. Now, I cried not for myself, but because of Momma's broken heart. From then on, we called her Momma.

Jane and I were happy. Merl was gone. His degrading words, often he said that I was stupid and ugly. He beat with a belt when he got frustrated that I couldn't understand simple arithmetic homework. Terrified of him, Jane withdrew into a shell.

Jane came out of her inner place of safety a little bit when he was gone. We were playful children again. The low self-esteem, hidden rage, and deep psychological damage he helped to create within us remained after he left. I began aggressively acting out against those around me.

Momma was so sad without Merl that sometimes I wanted him to come back, just to give her smiles again. I felt guilty for Momma's

Paul E. Treadwell

sake in that her joy with Merl was my pain, and her sorrow was my hidden joy when he was gone.

A Demon Named Trouble

Snow fell aplenty the winter of 1961-'62 in New Glarus. A foot covered the ground before school dismissed for the Christmas holidays. Buddy came up missing. I had not seen him since Thanksgiving. He was my only friend except for Jane. I terribly longed for him. The loss of Buddy hit doubly hard because I was having a tough time at school. The boys were name calling, and would not allow me to join in their games. They mocked my clothes and unkempt appearance.

Momma found a bargain at the local rummage sale. She insisted I wear the girls green mittens with feminine designs and beads stitched on the back. I hated them. Reluctantly I slipped them on. They were all I had, to keep my hands warm during recess.

The other boys pounded me with snowballs. They yelled, calling me, "sissy." I did not know what a sissy really was, while thinking it must be a bad thing since none of them liked me. They provoked me to near tears. I was not going to give them the privilege of knowing. I had a better plan.

One afternoon, three weeks before Christmas break, I challenged them all to a snowball fight. Alone, I was up against six of them. They agreed to give time for making snowballs first, since I had to fight so many.

Recess came. I went to make my stand on one end of the concrete playground. The boys stood thirty feet away at the other end of the playground where the snow banked up by the school's snowplow.

Digging down through the frozen white, I found the edge of the concrete slab. Uncovering gravels the size of quarters. Clutching a handful, I packed snow around each one individually, until there were a dozen ice bombs.

The bullies began yelling, "Wimp! Sissy! Pussy! You ready? Your time's up!"

"I'm ready," I yelled.

I stood, letting them pelt me with most of their frosty ammunition. When they called a time-out to make more, I charged and released my secret weapons with deadly accuracy. Two of the boys, I torpedoed their heads. One got it in the neck and the others on their hands and legs. All six foes were in tears by the time I finished.

Laughing, I ask, "What's wrong pussycats, sissies!"

Through their tears, they threatened.

I say, "Can't take a little snowball in the face, meow!" I yelled at them again, and kicked snow dust up toward their faces. Painfully, I was yearning, wanting them to be friends. I shouted, "Don't call me names!"

The teacher came running. Blood oozed down one of the bully's face where a rock had torn his flesh. It didn't take the teacher long to derive a conclusion. She sentenced me to spend recesses in the classroom, reading for the remainder of the semester.

There would be no more outdoors socialization with classmates for me. When the other children went outside to play, I enjoyed the isolation. This was not punishment. That was okay by me.

I could not read, but I liked the pictures in books. I would not be outside in the cold where the bullies could taunt, and ridicule the mittens. The teacher simply rewarded me. She did not realizing, I preferred being away from peers. She accused me of being the troublemaker.

I was only defending myself, playing their kind of game. Treating them the way, they treated me. As Fanny said, it was the golden rule: "Do unto others as you would have them do unto you."

I simply gave them what they wanted. I did unto them what they did unto me. If they didn't want to be cold-cocked, they should not have been so mean. Fanny was right. The Golden Rule sure did make a person feel good.

The aggressive behavior increased over the coming weeks. Parents of the bullies caused such a fuss the principle asked Momma to transfer me to a different school. She thought about it during semester break.

Momma gave us a sock filled with fruit, candy, and nuts on Christmas day. We had to share. Hoping Buddy would return soon, I saved some candy to divide with him, hiding it underneath the old scroll player piano.

Angel came to babysit over the holidays. Merl wasn't around, and she was safe, or Fanny would not have allowed it.

I grew to love dear sweet Angel. She was kind and affectionate. I thought she liked babysitting because Fanny did not allow dancing. With no adults around, she turned up the radio volume, locking in a rock 'n' roll station's signals. We did the twist, along with a few other steps she tried to teach. We giggled, burning up the floor with swift dance moves.

I was in charge of looking after my younger siblings when Angel went home each afternoon, while Momma prepared meals. The assigned responsibility brought feelings of all grownup. The twisting with our teenage baby sitter did too.

The chronic cough returned. Sick, and running a low-grade fever every day. On New Years day, unexpectedly Merl reappeared, and Angel abruptly stopped coming to the house. I missed her as much, as Buddy. They were my only friends except for Jane.

Merl's emotional abuse began again. He accused me of faking the illness. He said I was playing sick, for extra attention. Thankful, he had not messed with me sexually again. I was immensely grateful he did not even try.

I did not know he had been messing with the other children, except for the incident with Angel. I was not sure what a pass was. I strongly suspicion it had something to do with kissing? It had to be true or Angel would not have been so upset.

Momma and Merl verbally fought for a week. Then, he told her he was leaving again, returning to Florida to be near his children. Before he was gone, he shaved my head with his razor.

Momma transferred me to a different school in January after classes resumed. I was excited about the new start. However, it didn't take long for me to realize bullies were at the new school as well. Bald as an egg because I had gotten into his hair grease and globed the stuff on my hair to slick it back like Elvis Presley. All the other children in school made fun of my skinhead when I returned to classes, at the new school. They did not mess with me for very long. I became too forceful and efficient in exacting revenge.

A pretty, dark-haired girl who sat right in front of my desk was constantly making nasty remarks, and flipping her long braids into my face. I thought, she was gorgeous and I wanted her to be my friend. To great disappointment, she rebuffed the entreaties, acting as if she was a high-dollar-woman, better, too good for my friendship.

I asked her politely to stop slapping me with her hair. She refused. This went on for several days. I was holding back the anger until it exploded, unrestrained.

Late on a Friday afternoon during art class, I lost control. Enough was enough. While using India ink to outline pictures, we colored with crayons; Vicky slapped my face with her braids. Smugly, she giggled.

Why was she doing this? I thought, she probably thought she was being cute, causing me to mess up the artwork.

Angry, I managed to control myself enough to reach forward and gently take hold of her right braid. I shoved the end into the bottle of ink then threw the black ink-soaked braid against her back. Her white blouse was ruined.

Vicky turned around and snorted, "You are a nasty bald flea, don't touch me."

I smirked. "Keep your braids off my desk," I said, and went back to coloring.

The teacher told us to put away art supplies and gather our things to leave for the day. I grinned inside, knowing that Vicky had not noticed. The teacher didn't know either, and no one else had seen. It was the perfect crime, so I thought. I smiled all the way home. Smug pride over the act ended the next Monday at school when Vicky's mother arrived and talked with Mrs. Angely.

Her mother was a pretty-face, and fat, a woman with burned bottle-blond curly-hair. While they were conversing, Vicky turned around, stuck out her tongue, and crossed her eyes.

"My mother is going to make your mother buy me a new blouse and coat," she seethed.

Short, Mrs. Angely was all business wearing her new brown skirt-suit and jacket. She frowned a lot. Her pageboy graying hair neatly plastered to her head. Its texture was stiff as a board with hair spray. Once Vicky's mother was gone, she dragged me into the hallway, and shook my shoulders.

Wrinkling her brow, angrily she said, "Saul, this wasn't very nice. You ruined her new clothes. Why did you do it?"

I answered, smirking, "She wouldn't stop slapping me in the face with her braids, and she ruined my picture," I said.

Mrs. Angely sighed. "What possessed you to poke her braid in the ink?" she asked.

I say, "I didn't. She did it. It was an accident. I warned her, this would happen."

She placed her hands on her hips, sternly she says, "Young man, you are a liar. You did this on purpose, just to be mean. Now, I want you to march right in that classroom and apologize to Vicky in front of the entire class."

"I won't do it. I'm not sorry, and you can't make me tell another lie," I shouted. Feeling justified, I assumed no responsibility for the hooligan behavior.

All the time I was secretly thinking and planning. I will cut off Vicky's braids if she slaps me in the face with them one more time. Anger with Mrs. Angely, would be expressed as revenge. Retaliation against Vicky would come. She started this trouble.

Mrs. Angely pinched down on my ear, as we marched into the classroom. I was painfully squirming, on my tippy toes.

She said, "Children, Saul has, something he wants to say."

She let go of the ear and sat at her desk. Tap, tap, tap, the sound of a ruler held tightly in her hand, flicking against her desktop. I stood in front of all the classmates--the one place I did not want to be. They all hated me. I hated them. I wanted Daddy. I longed to be with Delena, back in Loafer's Glory.

Faking remorse, lower lip extended out trying to appear repentant. "Teacher says for me to say, I am sorry." I pretended to bow my head in shame.

"Now apologize to Vicky," she said.

I say, "I'm sorry, Vicky. I will not ever put your hair in the ink again. I promise."

The teacher asked, "Vicky, do you accept Saul's apology?"

Sweetly, innocently smiling, Vicky said, "Yes Mum."

Mrs. Angely stood shaking her index finger at me. She commanded, "Take your seat Saul. We will not have any more trouble out of you, or you'll be in the principal's office. Do you understand me?" she asked.

My head dropped, nodding sadly. "Yes, Mum," I said, and strolled toward my seat.

Vicky behaved herself for most of the morning. Afternoon art class began. About midway through, Mrs. Angely is summoned to the principal's office. She left us unattended. Vicky took advantage of her absence by slapping my face, again. Her braids, like a bullwhip when snapping against my eyes. At my irritation, she was laughing about it.

We happened to be using scissors cutting construction paper. Without hesitation, I calmly reached forward, and latched onto Vicky's right braid. Yanking it backward, I held on tight. I placed my free hand to the back of her head clamping down on the braid there. Freeing the other hand, I grabbed the scissors.

She struggled and screamed to get away. I hacked at the braid with dull school scissors while the other children laughed. Some whispered for us to stop before we all got into trouble.

Mrs. Angely must have heard the commotion. She raced into the room as Vicky howled. Every student in class watched Vicky's frantic struggle to get free of my grip.

I glanced up, catching sight of Mrs. Angely's intimidating presence. I refused to deter from the vengeful actions. I was not going to let go. Not until at least one of Vicky's braids sliced from her head.

The teacher's harsh demeanor didn't faze me. No, matter the consequences. I had absolutely no fear of Mrs. Angely's punishment that would be waiting when I had accomplished the dastardly deed. I continued to hack. I was determined to resolve the problem, for all of eternity. The obvious solution was to cut it off.

The aggressive enthusiasm that seemed to balloon, quickly deflated, when the teacher charged for my desk. The scissors were too dull. I only managed to cut off half the braid about six inches from the back of Vicky's head.

I had set into action the law of reciprocity. Mrs. Angely breathed heavily down the back of my neck. I resisted, but was losing my grip, as she wrestled the scissors out of my hands. She shoved me down onto my seat.

Vicky was crying hysterically. "My mother will get you for this," she shrieked.

I sneered. "Next time I'll bring a razor and shave your entire head like Merl shaved mine. Then I'll shave your momma's fuzzy bleached head," I shouted.

At that point, our tall, muscular principal walked in. He grasped my pant-waist lifting me out of the seat. He dragged me toward the hallway heading for his office. The entire class hatefully glared and snickered. Mrs. Angely tried to comfort Vicky as we exited the room. I was in big trouble.

Still holding fast to the backside of my pants, we enter his office. He opened a file drawer. Out came the Butt Buster. He leaned me over his desk, and POW! POW! POW! The loud sound of the wooden paddle against my rear, three swats on the behind.

Rubbing my butt, I say, "Ouch that smarts."

He forced me backward to a row of padded office chairs lining the wall across from his desk. He sat me down and asked what had happened.

I explained my reasons. I say, "It was the trouble maker demon. He is the same booger that had hold of Uncle Roscoe, when he shoved Momma."

He says, "Hogs wash, Saul. Tell the truth. What has caused such anger? Tell me the truth."

I say, "It had to be the demon. He caused Angry to surface. Vicky woke him, when she kept slapping me in the face, and by hitting my eyes with her long braids."

He shook his head, sighed, and picked up the phone. He dialed Momma at work. He talked with her in private for a few minutes, and then informed me that she would be dropping by to take me home.

Momma was angry, but when I told her my version of the story, she began to laugh. She says not to do that anymore, and if I had problems with the other kids to talk with the principal, before I fought with them.

School the next day . . . Vicky's hair cut short. Mrs. Angely moved her to the front of the class near her desk. Now, we were on opposite ends of the room. I was at the back of the classroom isolated from all the other children, forced to wear the dunce hat. Classmates were not allowed to speak to, or play with me the next few days. I am, shunned.

That was not a punishment. For them to say nothing was better, than calling me names. None of them wanted my companionship anyway. I was not missing out, on anything.

Little did I realize when we went home Friday, after wearing the dunce hat for most of the week, I would never see any of them again. I would not miss them. Over the weekend, a major winter storm blew in.

Denial

Snow fell heavily into the next week. A foot of white already covered the ground. Then more harsh blizzards dumped an additional good two feet, along with several more inches between the major storms. The frozen precipitation seemed to fall uninterrupted, continuing into the next week.

After one whiteout the first week of February, 1962, a snowdrift reached some twenty-five feet up to the peak of the barn and covered the rooster-shaped weather vane. When the snows finally stopped, accumulations were over the top of my head. School dismissed for several days as a result.

By the time the roads were clear enough to go back to school, I got chicken pox. No more than got over the pox when the weather turned cold again and we got another eighteen inches of snow, and school dismissed several more days.

The stress of having to face the bullies lifted, and the pox sores faded. The greatest tension reliever was Merl being gone. I am feeling much better. The time had come to enjoy the snow days. The mounds of white were an inconvenience for the adults, but Jane and I loved it.

I was not looking forward to going back to school. I need not have worried. Momma was making plans to move back to Arkansas. Once there, her decision was to file for divorce. She hoped to marry Merl someday. She longed for him come back to her.

Momma didn't want Merl to drink and she was even more upset about the other women. They had fought again about his affairs, the excessive drinking, and he wound up leaving us supposedly for good. That is what he said as he stormed out of the house late one night, and drove away. I was glad he was gone. I hoped he would never come around again.

Momma did not believe the accusations made against Merl by Angel and Ely. She defended him, to bitter end.

I knew they had to be true for I had my own dirty little secrets concerning Merl. I thought, privately, Momma knew. She knew about his pedophile, fetishes. She knew what he did to me. I did not have a name for his inappropriate behavior, the crimes. She had to know the word for it. I would never ask.

I thought she could not conceive the facts that the man she loved had these problems. To live in denial was easier than to face the cold hard truth. Perhaps she didn't know. I would not tell.

If she knew, and approached the problem head on by confronted him, she would have lost him forever, or be murdered. To admit he had these demons meant she had chosen the wrong man again.

She was not about to give him up. Not now, she had forsaken all to have his deceitful snogs. He was her god.

Momma held great remorse. Now, he was gone because she confronted him about the betrayal, his despicable actions with the prostitutes and the booze. If she wanted him, she had to take the whole package as is. She said she would lose herself, and compromise her own dignity to keep him. She vowed too never bring up his behavior again. Her only goals were to have him forever as her lover. If only he would come back to her.

Guardian Angel

I turned seven the snowy winter of 1962. Only days after my birthday, before we left New Glarus, little sister Jane and I bundled up against the cold. Heavy clothing cut the biting Wisconsin winds as we went out to play. We had snowball fights and built snowmen. We found a virgin snowdrift and fell into it, making snow angels. Feeling normal for a little while was wonderful. No playground bullies in our yard.

We were shaking the snow off each other as I looked down the long drive toward the main highway. I could not believe my eyes. Off there, in the distance, a ball of orange and white fur looked like Buddy, heading toward us. He had a striking resemblance to Lassie.

Overjoyed, Buddy, gone nearly three months and I was worried, sick, now a sigh of relief. As he drew closer, a finger of dread began to play with my insides. Something was unmistakably wrong with Buddy.

He staggered as he trotted forward. Drawing nearer, I could see froth spray out of his mouth when he violently shook his head.

Catching sight of us, first he growled, whimpered, and finally moaned. He stopped and let out a ferocious bark.

Part of me wanted to run and meet him at the yard edge. I held back out of fear. His wild-eyes fixed on Jane and me. Buddy grew most excited as he dashed onward in our direction. He leapt faster toward us through the deep snow, leaving a trail of foaming froth in his tracks.

He came within twenty feet, arched his back as fur bristled around his face. He snarled.

"Buddy, my puppy, you've come home," I said, my voice shaking.

He whined like a pup and wagged his tail. He snarled again, and howled as if confused. He sat down on his haunches. I took two steps toward him. He raised, his teeth shining as he crouched for a jump.

I glanced back with horror-stricken eyes. Jane was about six feet behind me. What could I do to protect us? Nothing! We could not move fast enough over deep, wet snow for safety of the house. We were at Buddy's mercy.

Momma was inside. I was afraid to call out to her for fear of rousing the dog's anger. Daddy had said Jesus was a help in trouble. Everybody said that. Now was time to test the statement.

I remembered Ely and Fanny telling me to pray when I needed God's help. Fanny prayed in tongues. I did not know that language. Shaking myself, I tried to muster-up what I believed to be faith. Heart, mind, and every fiber of being, I prayed like never before, though careful to keep quiet lest I agitate the dog further.

Hearing soft distant sounds of horn music, I thought that Momma must have the radio on. There it was again, another trumpet's blast. Horrified, we had no escape. Fearfully trying to believe God would hear me, I looked up to the sky and whispered my prayer again.

Just then, a beam of light, about eight feet in diameter, stabbed through the clouds and shone around Buddy. I was awe-struck, as a huge being, descended through the light and grabbed Buddy by the scruff of the neck. His massive hand held him still.

This giant human like creature, clad in medieval armor must have been ten feet tall. Buddy could not escape his grip. I stood motionless, not able too fully understand what I was witnessing. Was this an Angel? Maybe, He was God.

Daddy said we all had a guardian angel. Childlike reasoning persuaded thought, the giant was an angel sent from heaven, no more fear. Peace surrounded us, radiating from the strong heavenly presence.

Our eyes locked when he spoke, "Turn around, take Jane by the hand, and walk, don't run, into the house."

Without a pause, I did exactly as he instructed. When we were safe inside, behind the bolted backdoor, I looked through the window hoping to see him again. He nodded and released Buddy.

I smiled. I wanted him to stay. To my disappointment, he ascended upward. The light followed him into the clouds. He was gone as suddenly as he had appeared. I wanted Momma to see him. She would not believe if I told her, I thought.

I softly ask, "Jane, did you see my guardian angel?"

She giggled and asked, "Where is he?"

I say, "He held Buddy until we got inside. He went back to heaven, just now."

She says, "I didn't see him. You're fooling."

I sighed.

Buddy lurched for the back porch and leaped against the door. He snarled and growled, barking and howling as he banged against the door attempting to get into the house. Slimy froth smeared over the glass and ran down the door-panes.

The commotion brought Momma running. Terrified, she shrieked, "Oh my God, Buddy has rabies." She nervously pulled the door window blind and vocally snapped while pointing toward a different part of the house.

Momma followed us, as Jane and I raced out of the kitchen. Just in case Buddy was able to break through, she closed the wide French-doors leading into the living room. Using the crank telephone mounted on the wall, with two long cranks and a short, she called a neighbor and asked him to come shoot Buddy.

In a few minutes, things got very quiet. I looked out the picture window as Buddy stumble around the side of the house headed toward the main highway.

Jane and I cried. Buddy would soon be dead. I didn't want the neighbor to shoot him. He was out of his mind. He had frightened me. He was no longer my Buddy. There was no hope for him.

Why the angel did not help him, I could not understand. I did not want Buddy shot. Though I was grateful, Jane and I were safe.

Clutching Momma's trembling hands as we stood there watching Buddy swagger away, I say, "Momma, he couldn't hurt us."

Her voice shaking, she squatted to my eye level. She says, "Oh, but Son, he could have torn you to bits, and gave you rabies." Her eyes, watery, she pulled us close.

Smiling, I say, "No, Momma. The angel held him."

Her brow wrinkled as she tossed her hair back from her slim shoulders. Giving me a questioning look, her eyebrows rose. She says, "Saul, don't lie to Momma. You didn't see an angel."

"Yes I did. I am not lying. He had a shield and a sword and he wore a pleated skirt made from brass colored strips of metal." I shouted.

She questioned me, thoroughly. She kept telling me not to lie. My story changed not. I told her the truth. Disbelieving, she patted my head, and chuckled.

She says, "Angels do protect little children. Maybe you did see him."

Momma forever questioned, she was not certain my guardian angel existed. When discussing the incident later, she pondered if perhaps the episode was a figment of a child's imagination.

Momma says she was not playing the radio that day. She tilted her head, realizing I must have had some kind of supernatural experience. She said, "Son, the sounds of the trumpet's blare were perhaps Heaven's Shofar."

I asked, "What's a Shofar?"

She said, "Well, it is a horn, made from hollowed antlers of a goat. One of the instruments played in Heaven's Band."

I shrugged, not quite able to understand.

What Momma believed, or could not comprehend was insignificant. He was real. In my innocence from that time on I trusted with assurance God could hear my prayers. I presumed my angel was near, always. I had discovered a powerful secret. I realized that day . . . Faith in a person, named Jesus was a great weapon against evil. I planned to use it again.

His Bag of Tricks

A few days after Buddy was shot and killed, Momma decided we would head south where she would divorce Daddy. We left New Glarus. The destination was her pa's place in Rooster Ridge, Arkansas. The plan was to stay with them for a few days.

It was cold in Arkansas when we arrived on Momma's birthday, March of 1962. This was the year Stone county Arkansas was the second poorest of all counties in the lower forty-eight states. Economic times were tough for the poorest of the poor living in the Ozarks.

Short, plump, and gray, step-grandmother Gert despised Merl. She and Pops called him the "devil." Gert often said, "The devil will be slithering back into Ora's life. Coming back, like a hound after a bit** in heat."

The only word Daniel spoke when referring to Merl was "devil." He was glad the devil had left us. He also knew Momma would welcome him with open-arms if he showed up on their doorstep with his bag of tricks and sweet talk.

Daniel and Gert did not want Merl around Pete, mother's eleven-year-old younger brother. They are anxious, thinking Merl would eventually follow her to their home. After a couple of days, it was obvious we needed to find a place of our own.

During intense arguments with Gert, Momma defended Merl. She refused to accept the truth. Wroth motivated, she moved us down the road to Joe and Rebecca's abandoned honeymooner's shack. They moved to Michigan where Joe was learning the drywall trade. Rebecca was expecting their first born.

Their shack had a tin roof and its walls constructed of rough oak lumber. Square openings cut into three walls where the windowpanes should have been. Instead of glass, the holes had a tough clear plastic tacked over them. The floor was rough oak-planks. Gaping cracks between the floorboards were wide enough to poke fingers through to the other side. The crudely hung unfinished saw-milled slab door had as many long narrow openings where each board joined the other. This shack became our home until near summer.

The day we moved into the shed, a dank chill ripped exposed skin with frostbite. Strong winds bellowed from the north racing over the hills and hollows. It howled, and whistled through the shack cracks. The last blast of winter was upon us, spitting tiny snowflakes.

Two days after setting-up house keeping, Momma drove to a local dumping ground two miles from our shed. We rummaged through the junk and garbage to find anything that might make our life more comfortable.

I wore a ragged dirty coat three sizes too large. It was a gift from Pete. Slipping a pair of holey socks over my small hands, as an attempt to keep them warm, I helped dig through the rubbish.

Embarrassed, I could not make myself wear the green, girly mittens one more time. I told Momma, I didn't know where they were. I lied. I threw them in the trash dump back in Wisconsin. Being cold and having frostbitten fingers was better than enduring laughter from schoolmates.

Momma found old clothes, dishes, and a broken table with one of the legs missing. The most valuable prizes were rusted stovepipes and a burned-out King wood-heater. Momma gathered an arms load of rags to use for grease lamps since we had no electricity. We dumped our treasure into the car trunk, and headed for the shack.

Arriving at our new shelter, we carried flat field rocks from near the woods, into the shanty. We laid the gray stones on the floor under a window. There, it made--a hearth for the stove.

The heater's bottom is burned completely out, totally gone. The upper part of the stove was intact and functional. We placed the stove shell on the crude stone hearth. After setting smaller rocks around the outside edges, I poured five gallons of sand inside the corroded firebox. The stones around the outside edges kept it from moving and prevented the sand from sliding out of the rusted, jagged rim around the bottom.

Grandpa Daniel gave us the sand. He brought it from the Buffalo River where he fished the day before. He collected the sand just for Jane and me. Warmth was more important than play; a sandbox would have to wait.

The next day Pete brought scrap pieces of tin roofing. He helped us install the rusted pipes by cutting a hole in one piece and nailed it over a window opening. The flu pipe ran out the hole. Pete placed the metal inside around the walls of the heater, and another piece he placed on top of the sand.

After gathering small fallen tree limbs, and twigs, we broke wood to fit inside the heating chamber. Momma built a fire. Now the drafty shack was warmer. The sides of the heater and pipes turned cherry red as the fire roared. With no damper to control the blaze, the fire danced, thundering hot. There was no stopping it.

The shack air was sweltering. Rambo cried. Jane sweated. I am comfortable.

Momma's face was wet from perspiration when she opened the stove door and doused the blaze with our bucket of drinking water. Scalding steam and fiery smoke gushed into the room. Blistering water, wet ashes, and sand oozed down through the rocks and dripped out the cracks onto the ground under the house. I could hear the dying coals sizzle as they futilely struggled to stay alive. Momma killed the toasty fire.

I would not have cared if the house burned down--at least I was warm for the first time in three days. Nevertheless, she was fearfully compelled to put the fire out. My frustrations escalated further at her use of the drinking water.

I lugged it up the hill from the spring in the hollow behind our new home earlier in the day. She sent me to fetch another pail before dark. Out into the cold I ran, swinging the empty water bucket.

The shed had a bed and wood cook stove belonging to Joe and Rebecca. Momma cranked up the fire in the cook stove but it burned only an hour then the night chill set in again.

We slept one more night in the cold. Momma bought a pipe damper the next day. We had fire for a few hours every evening. Momma was cautious. She never let it burn until we fell asleep. Every evening at eight p.m. she doused the flames.

Jane, Rambo, and Momma shared the bed. I slept on a pallet of Anne's quilts lying on the drafty frigged floor. My weak lungs infected quickly.

To make matters worse a neighbor gave Momma a gallon bucket of hog lard used in making grease lamps for light at night. She constructed one in a tin can and lit it.

Smothering, the room filled with grease smoke, I lay on the floor my head near a crack to breathe cold fresh air drifting up from under the house. I coughed and wheezed every night.

I was sick, gasping for breath, and short winded most of the time. Some days were worse. Momma accused me of faking to get out of doing chores and going to school. My condition improved a little when the weather warmed up.

Shortly after we arrived, Momma enrolled me in classes at Rooster Ridge school. I am, far behind academically compared to the other children my age. That was not my only problem. Not getting along with peers followed us, all the way to Arkansas.

Chronic coughing and low-grade fevers were a good excuse for me to stay home. I did not fit in. Rooster Ridge had its share of bullies too.

Sometimes, I faked being worse, especially after sharing the angel experience with classmates on the playground. They laughed in disbelief, while nicknaming me, The Angel Boy.

I did not like the labels, Angel Boy or sissy. I decided to mute, never talk about Guardian Angel ever again. Even Momma didn't really believe.

The sadness and loneliness at times were unbearable. Rejection and I were well acquainted.

I thought no reason existed to go to school. I could not learn anyway. Knowing how to figure numbers or read and write was not important. None of Momma's brothers except for Pete could read, and they got along quite satisfactorily.

Tired of being sick, I did not know how to get better. None of the adults saw to it that I got professional medical attention. They gave me an aspirin when I ran fever.

Sadness ruled my life. Lack of social graces, learning disability, and the constant bullying by classmates made attending school quite an unpleasant experience.

Momma got government relief in the form of a commodities box, delivered to the shed once a month by welfare workers. I looked forward to the arrival of groceries, especially, the canned meats and powdered milk.

Someone reported Momma for neglect and abuse of us children that spring. Many afternoons she insisted we hide in the woods behind the house, fearing the state workers would come take us away. While hiding out, we gathered bundles of twigs and broken tree limbs for the night's heat. With the fading sun, we returned to the shed, built fires, and Momma prepared supper from the commodity foods. My favorite of the free food was powered milk, a real treat.

Within a few weeks of our return to Arkansas, Merl came back. Momma was happy again and I was glad for her that she was not sad. Merl's presence only increased the gloom for Jane and me.

Momma is reported again. Turned in, by someone else to state workers for cohabitation, adultery, and exposing her children to immoral lifestyles. The accusations also included failure to provide food and medical neglect. We continued hiding in the woods during daylight hours. Momma was paranoid.

Within a week of his return, Momma saw her attorney to discuss the divorce. She was hoping to receive some back child support from Daddy.

I looked forward to that. I was too embarrassed to eat the free lunches at school. I stayed on the playground at lunchtime but Momma never knew.

Once, in a while, she gave me a nickel or a dime and I bought candy at the country store across the road from the school during the lunch hour. Momma says many mornings, she wished she could give more money but she just did not have it.

Though I am young, I knew she loved us in a sad way. She did not want the responsibility of raising us. The worry over our welfare was weighing heavily on her soul.

Taking care of her needs was difficult enough. She had as many problems as Daddy. Hers were just different. She did not talk nonsense but she was obsessed with a man that was mean to her and us.

She worshiped Merl Judas. He was on her mind constantly. She often said, "I would lie down on a bed of hot coals and let him walk on me to keep him from burning his feet."

I wished she could have those same feelings of love, and respect for Daddy. She didn't. I was learning to accept the fact that she hated him.

A contradiction in terms, Merl was as sweet as candy, loving and kind. These facets of his personality always preceded the flipside of his nature when he turned into the selfish bastard from Hell. He was an evil, sexually perverted sociopath. He was the giver of pleasure and pain for all of us. The serpent was an oxymoron for all those, his life touched.

Momma took Rambo with her to the attorney's office and tried to pass him off as baby brother Bobby. Aunt Sonny had Bobby at her home in Loafer's Glory. Momma had not seen him since he was nine-months-old.

Momma told the attorney she had custody of the three children all this time and she wanted the back child support. The lawyer had no idea Rambo was her illegitimate son by Merl. However, he did make a comment about how small the child was for his age.

She tried to initiate the divorce proceedings some months before but had no money to pay the legal cost. Merl gave her the cash to retain an attorney this time. Now the final paper work filled out, and a court date was set. She thought, soon, she would be free of ol' crazy Enoch, forever.

It was mid-May 1962, during strawberry harvest when she went to court. That evening, she was sad. No, she would not talk about her case.

Later, during a crying jag, she spilled the beans. The judge could not grant her a divorce because Daddy was in the mental hospital again. Sonny showed up in court that day and the judge ruled temporary custody of Bobby to Sonny until Daddy could attend proceedings.

Momma's attorney was upset with her because she deceived him by pretending Rambo was Bobby, and for lying to him about other issues concerning her divorce and the separation. He dropped her as a client.

The next afternoon, Momma's aunt Diana and uncle Tex came to visit. Merl had gone to town to buy cigarettes before they arrived. He would not be back for a while. Their timing was perfect.

They pulled into the yard, driving their black 1950 GMC pickup. Momma held Rambo on her hip and greeted them. Smiling, happily, she said, "Come on in. I'll put on a pot of coffee."

She was overjoyed to see them. Diana wore her holiness flour-sack green attire and matching hand made cloth sunbonnet. Tex wore a new pair of bib overalls and pale blue shirt. They stood on the front step as Momma towered over them in the doorway.

"Honey, we can't stay, but just a minute. Don't go to the trouble. I need to talk to you," Diana said.

She poked her head inside and saw us sitting on the bed. We were playing with our toys. She fiddles with her bun. Then she raised her strong calloused hand waving at us. "Hi Saul and Jane, you have some nice toys," she says.

We smiled and went back to playing. I listened.

Slightly panicked, Momma asked, "What's wrong? Has something happened to Moms or Pops?"

"No, I just don't want the children to hear," Diana said.

"Okay, let's go to the truck," Momma said as she stepped out the door with Rambo on her hip. They walked together toward the pickup.

Curious, I dropped the toy car on the bed and ran for the door to listen. When adults excluded me from conversations, they only peaked my resolve to hear what they have to say. I was determined to eavesdrop.

"Ora, Honey, you know I love you," she said as she embraced Momma and kissed her on the cheek.

Tex hugged Momma too, and patted her on the back as Rambo began to whine. Tex spat, his chaw of tobacco on the ground. "I love you too," he said.

"Ora, you know I have loved you as my own daughters. I did all, everything I could to help your poor momma raise you kids. I've done my best to teach you right. You know that. But I am concerned about you, Dear Heart." She scowled. "Merl Judas is not good for you or your children. I know, you and Enoch will never be able to mend the fences now that you have this little one," she said as she smiled and tickled Rambo in the ribs.

He giggled.

Frowning, harshly, Momma snapped, "What's on your mind?"

Diana said, "You shouldn't be living like this. You need to pray and ask God to help you gets your life right again. This is wrong, Ora. Aside from the adultery, I can't put my finger on the evil I sense, but I know it is here, and it is going to destroy your life."

"Well, that's my business and none of yours," Momma shouted.

Diana shook her finger in Momma's face. "Now Ora don't let yourself get in a huff. I love you or I wouldn't be here," she says.

Fidgeting, Momma sighed as she hoisted Rambo higher up on her hip. Then she smiled. "Merl and I are getting married as soon as the divorces are final. He is divorcing Lilly this month, too," she says.

Her brow wrinkled, sadly, Diana said, "Ora, Merl is no good, and if you don't get away from him and do right, you will hear the cries of your babies upon your deathbed."

Diana was the most dedicated and kindhearted Christian, I had ever known. Merl was the only person I ever heard her openly speak of with an ill tone.

I thought she was right. Why was Momma not listening? Why was Momma so angry? Diana loved Momma. Should I tell her my secret before she married Merl? No, she would not believe me.

I knew the evil Diana sensed that she couldn't put her finger on. Merl was a devil, Satan's own angel from Hell.

I thought, maybe, she has that gift. Delena called it, a gift of discernment. Maybe God would let her discern that Merl hurts children.

"Just leave." Momma shouted while turning and racing back to the house in tears. "I never want to see you again. I love Merl. I always have. I never loved Enoch. This is my life and I'll live it how I damn well, please. It's none of your business. Leave," she said.

"But it's God's business. Your life is not your own. I love you." Diana shouted, sobbing as she and Tex crawled into the truck. He nodded and grimaced when he started the engine. Diana pulled a handkerchief from her purse and wiped her eyes as they drove out of the yard.

Momma lay on the bed and wept bitterly. Jane and I tried to comfort her as we all huddled close.

I handed her a handkerchief from out of a box of clothes under the bed. "Don't cry, Momma. We'll have a good life with Merl. I just know it," I said, wanting her to feel better.

At that moment, I hoped my words would come true. I did not want Momma to cry anymore. Her crying caused me to lose all reasoning ability. Why was I telling her a lie? I did not want Merl back in our lives. He was like two sides of the moon. One bright, and light, the other was darker than dark.

Merl tried to cheer her up that evening. They talked a lot, kissing and hugging. Merl caressed and kissed on Jane, Rambo, and me too. He assured us that he loved us, and we were going to be a happy family.

I wanted to believe him. After all, he had not touched us in an ugly mean way since his return, not me, anyway. I tried, but could not love him. I knew his true character. He could not be trusted.

He brought Jane and me a huge grocery sack full of chocolate candies the day he came back into our lives, weeks earlier. We were now finishing off the poke of goodies.

Having never brushed my teeth, my set-of-babies were rotting from sugar decay. The front ones were missing. I did not know what a toothbrush was.

They made plans to move.

Paul E. Treadwell

Chicken Thief

Strawberry harvest was over by the end of May. We relocated to the outskirts of Springdale. Following the seasonal harvest, picking beans and stealing turkeys would be our next jobs.

The day we arrived to gather beans, Momma's old friend Ginger and her children were working in the same field as us, no more than thirty feet away. Ginger appeared to have a new woman friend now. Both Momma and Ginger pretended they did not know each other. They did not speak.

Waving and smiling, I shouted, "How yah doin'?"

Ginger pretended not to hear. Her children hatefully stared at us. I heard Robert tell the others, smirking, "There is that squalling brat. He is such a momma's boy, a real sissy."

They laughed. I reached down and snatched up a rock.

Momma frowned. "Saul, put it down," she mumbled.

I dropped the stony projectile.

"Pay them no mind, Son. Robert is just a bully. He'll get his comeuppance one day," she said.

Almost in tears, but not wanting them to see, I carried my bean basket several feet up the rows ahead of them so I couldn't hear what they were saying.

My feelings seemed to always get hurt. I wanted Daddy, but all I had was Merl. "I ain't a Momma's Boy. I will be the best chicken thief, ever. I'm not a Momma's Boy." I mumbled, while yanking the long green bean pods off the plants and tossing them into the basket.

Merl watched what I was doing and frowned. I pulled the leaves out, and threw them on the ground.

I questioned, what's a Momma's Boy? Maybe a boy loves his Momma! What was wrong with that? Maybe he was a sissy. I was not sure, what it meant to be a sissy. I just knew it must be a bad thing. No body called Merl a sissy. Momma said he was a real man, not crazy like Daddy. I would try to be like Merl since he was good to us now. There was really no other choice, having lost all hope of ever seeing Daddy again.

We never lacked for poultry products living where mass-industrial chicken and turkey farming were the livelihoods for a majority of citizens. Springdale, Arkansas seemed to be a growing hub.

Merl had me tag along at least twice a week to steal chickens and turkeys. In the middle of night we stole from one of the big farms located a couple of miles from our house in the rural community of Lowell. Always fearful, someone would find us out. I watched as he used wire cutters and snipped holes through the tall fence. The opening was large enough, a passageway for slithering through. Our evening excursions to raid the chicken and turkey houses paid off. We didn't go to bed hungry when we lived on outskirts of Springdale.

I am short winded, and could not catch the birds, but sure held them fast with a strong grip, once Merl handed them to me. I shimming through the fence hole dragging the frightened birds firmly in my grasp. Before leaving, Merl folded back the cut fence and wired the opening, shut, so it would not, be noticed.

I held the squawking, flopping birds, one in each hand, by their feet upside down. They beat their wings in a futile effort to escape. I stood there behind the car, anxiously waiting to leave. Merl loaded them into an orange crate in the trunk. We headed to the house under the cover of darkness with headlights off, until we got a distance from the poultry farm.

Back home, Momma was boiling water. Swinging their bodies in a circular motion, holding tight to their skulls I wrung off the bird's heads with my bare hands. Once the heads wrenched off, the bodies took off flying across the yard, or they flopped to the ground and ran with blood spewing from the open necks. I carried the dead birds inside to Momma once they fell over dead.

She submerged them under scalding hot water for a few minutes, then pulled them out and placed them in a large dishpan. We stepped around to the back of the shack and plucked feathers. The blistering wet chicken feathers stunk worse than dookie.

Merl gutted the kill. Momma deep fried, or baked the stolen night treasures. Foul, fowls prepared for the meal, and we ate heartily.

I was happy in Lowell for a couple of months but soon our nightmare commenced again. Late in the night, Merl came into the bedroom where Jane and I slept. He had his way with us. Jane cried.

He muffled her screams with whispering threats, and slammed his large brawny hand over her small mouth and face.

This became a ritual for the next month. I wanted to kill him when he messed with Jane.

I wanted to forgive him when he was good to us. I tried to love him for Momma's sake. I simply, could not understand why he was so mean. How does one love the psychotic monster of his worst nightmares?

He could be kind and shower us with candy, sweet words, and tender hugs, especially in Momma's presence. Confusion, shame, and fear became our closest companions. Momma was going to marry Merl. That made him my daddy. I had to love him. I tried, while suppressing the internal rage.

The Devil's Booger Men

Migration came. We packed and moved on, heading toward the Bottoms. There we harvested cotton. I was seven when we took up residence in the shanty on the Denton Island cotton plantation.

Once we settled in, the molestations became worse. Now, Merl became physically violent with Momma, Jane, and me. The sexual abuse was a nightly horror. Hunger gnawed at our empty bellies.

His frequent fisting, and belting during drunken stupors insured our submissions to his will. We were growing numb. Knowing what to expect, but it did not stop the pain. We went on living, keeping our mouths shut we endured a secret, a private Hell on earth.

The emotional and sexual abuse was bad for me, but worse for Jane. I could do nothing to protect her. Jane and I just tried to survive until he finished with us and returned to Momma's bed. Then we would block the obscene acts from our minds until the next time.

Many occasions when he got drunk, Merl threatened Momma with ... he was leaving us. He would drive away. Momma bellowed all the time he was gone. He disappeared for two days in October, and Momma bawled so hard I could not bear her anguish any longer. I knelt beside her and prayed for God to send him back.

Six hours later, he drove into the yard with a grocery sack full of candy. He was sober. Momma rejoiced as she ran to greet him and fell into his arms.

Fear and loathing surged through me. Why did I pray for him to return? Momma was happy. In a sense my reasoning established, she was more important than Jane or me. Her happiness was all that mattered. I guess that I truly was a Momma's Boy. I could not bear her pain.

Merl was provoked easily, and slapping Momma around seemed to be a game for him. He beat us if we didn't produce what he expected of us in the fields. His psychological head-games and emotional abuse were worse than any physical harm he could inflict. We knew the rules. He was in complete control.

We suffered from malnutrition. Food being scarce many evenings, Momma prepared macaroni and cheese out of a box. Jane, Rambo, and I got one small portion each. She would have nothing to eat. A cigarette had to be sufficient to suppress her appetite. Merl got all the rest.

I enviously watched Merl wolfing down the mound of food on his plate. Whining at the dinner table, I said, "Momma, why does Merl get the whole bowl and we only get a couple of bites? I'm still hungry!"

Harshly, she said, "Saul, stop, you're bickering. Merl provides for us. He needs his energy to work. When you can pick more cotton than him, then you'll get the large portion."

I bowed my head for shame.

After many days with little food and no money, Rambo only had sugar water in his bottle. Feeling no-dishonor, I begged other migrant families in the camp for a slice of bread or sausage bit from a can. This was how Jane and I kept from starving that fall in Denton Island.

Momma, Jane, Rambo, and I were hungry, while Merl ate his fill of what we had, and spent the meager wages on cheap wine. His carnal pleasures, the booze, and smokes were more important.

It was Sunday, the week before Halloween evening when the closest neighbors were away at the Baptist church in Grubbs. I stole one of their laying hens. The head I wrenched off as the bird struggled and squawked. I brought the bloody fowl into the house for mother to cook. She scolded me for stealing, and Merl beat me.

I thought, Merl taught me how to steal chickens. Now, this was wrong. He instructed me to steal from enemies--the wealthy and strangers--but not from family friends.

The chicken's owners were good kind people. They were not my enemies. Hunger was our villain. However, Merl consumed the largest portions after Momma cooked. He burned the feathers in the wood stove, and buried the guts under the edge of the house. No evidence of the crime could be, found.

I was intimidated to keep my mouth shut about this to the neighbors, and lie to the end if ever questioned about the missing hen. Deny! Deny! Deny!

I just wanted to help feed my hungry siblings. That was the reason I stole. Jane and I got the legs, wings, and back pieces. I gnawed at the neck bone to scrap every morsel. Momma picked off small bite sizes from a thigh, and fed Rambo.

It was ineffable to expect such young children to work like adults. Long days, in the cotton fields were necessary. The sack Jane and I dragged through the rows of snow-white tufts became a burden.

It was heavy, beyond our combined physical strengths before we could fill it. Merl had to help pull the sack along as we continued to stuff cotton into the opening.

I abhorred picking in the early mornings. Warmer days, if there was no frost, the morning dew soaked our clothes as the leaves from the plants dripped the night catch of moisture droplets.

I could not recall ever seeing a black person before we arrived in Denton Island. As we worked the fields one afternoon, a new family of migrants moved into their shed on the other side of the field. Their black images were distant. I watched them, and noticed as smoke spewed from the metal stovepipe poking through the tin roof of their shanty.

A sweet appetizing aroma of bacon drifted across the way into my nostrils. My mouth watered for the taste of only one slice. I determined that I would visit our new neighbors when picking was done for the day. Mooch a slice and maybe a biscuit to share with Jane and Rambo. As the day went on, we heard hymns drifting over from a distant field.

Soulful singing, workers' songs, but I couldn't see anyone. By late afternoon, I saw the black family picking cotton on the far side of our field. They continued their delightful harmonies the day long. Ignorance and fascination ruled. I asked Merl what manner of persons were these dark humans?

He says, "Those are booger men." He chuckled.

Daddy spoke of booger men. They would get me if I misbehaved. These did not look like the monsters, I imagined.

Merl said, "They are the devil's boogers, headhunters! If you don't pick your quota this afternoon, I will hand you over to them. They eat little white boys and girls who misbehave."

The next day terror flooded our hearts, as Jane and I continued to suspiciously glance at the black pickers. They were moving ever closer as each hour passed. By near sundown they were a hundred feet from us in the same field where they continued to harvest and sing.

We hastened our pace. Frightened, not only of the blacks, but of Merl's threat, we stripped the cotton stalks of green boles, encasement pods, leaves, and stems. We quickly rammed them into the sack and then covered it with a layer of only pure white cotton tufts.

I was thinking. This would increase the weight in our sack. We would get finished faster, and could move to a different row further away from the Negro workers.

We had to be careful not to let Merl see the unwanted stripping we placed in our sack. He was working ahead of us in the adjacent row. Maybe, we would get away with our cheating deed, this once.

The day finished, Merl dragged our heavy sack to the weight scales. The plantation-foreman dumped the contents of our harvest into the gigantic wagon. When he saw the leaves and trash fall out of the sack, Merl distracted the fellow by offering him a tobacco chaw. Not deceived, or manipulated by Merl, he declined his offer. He glared at Merl and said, "I'm docking the weight because of the trash in the sack."

As he was paying Merl the day's wages, the black family pulled their sacks out of the field to the weight scales. Scowling, Merl shouted, "You're gonna be dinner for them there nig***s tonight."

I thought Jane and I were going to get a flogging if we got to the house escaping their dinner table. The blacks were coming. No! No!

Terror stricken, we shrieked. I grabbed her hand. We ran as hard as we could to the picker shed. I was wheezing and gasping for every breath as we hid under the porch until Momma and Merl insisted we crawl out.

We refused until their laughter, reassuring we would not be handed over to headhunters. We shimmied from under the porch.

Merl grabbed my hair when I poked my head out. He snatched me up and beat my behind. Punished, for putting trash in the cotton sack, he continued to smack my behind and back with his large strong hand.

Rage contorted his face, he shouted, "Boy, you're just lazy. Stop, that wheezing, you're puttin' on. I'll never give you any slack. I don't fall for playing sick." He tossed me to the ground. I hit my head against a wooden stilt holding that corner of the shack off the ground.

Then, he started in on Jane. He dealt several hard blows to her behind with his brawny hand. Momma turned her back on us and went inside. I pleaded with him to leave Jane alone, and said it was my entire fault. He dropped Jane and started in on me again.

Jane and I sat on the porch until after dark watching the black people's shack, fearfully curious as we dried our tears. We really did not know what to make of them. They acted like people but they looked different from us.

The Negro family built a bonfire behind their shanty facing ours. They played guitars, harmonica, and sang gospel hymns. We were entranced. I was wondering if perhaps, maybe these creatures were not booger men at all.

After our small ration of food for dinner, Jane and I returned to the back porch to watch our new neighbors again. Momma brought us a cup of coffee to share.

I asked, "Momma if they are the devil's booger men, then why are they singing praises to Jesus?"

She sat down beside us, rolled herself a smoke, and lit it, tossing a large kitchen match onto the black soil at the edge of the porch. A wreath of tobacco smoke swirled around our heads when she exhaled. Jane and I took a sip of the coffee and then Momma sips from her cup.

Through her chuckles she responded, "Honey, they ain't devils, or boogers. They are just poor folks like us. Just poor folk, trying to make a livin'. Their skin be black cause their people came from a land far away from here. Their great grandparents brought here. Bound in chains on slave ships, and sold to white men to work the fields. They do the white man's chores. There were slaves in this here country for hundreds of years, until President Abe Lincoln and the Civil War freed them," she says.

I asked, "Where is this land they came from?"

"Africa! I heard their skin is black cause the sun is so hot there. They are all born that way. Guess the black don't burn in the hot sun. Besides, you kids, Merl, and I got a touch of the tar brush. That's what I am told. Don't know it be true or not, but that is a hush! Something we gotta hides if it be so. It mostly bred out of us now, I guess. Maybe, it not true at all," she says.

Wide-eyed fright, I say, "But Momma, Merl says they are the booger men. They eat bad white children after wringing off their heads like a chicken. He said they save the heads as trophies, and shrink them over a fire. I'm, afraid." Jane and I snuggled close to her.

With a stern look she responded by rolling her eyes and scowling, speaking firmly and harsh, loud enough for Merl to hear inside the shack. She says, "Merl lied to you kids, Baby. They are just poor migrant workers like us. Their skin just happens to be black. They ain't gonna hurt yah. Cause they be black, they work on the other side of the fields and the white trash works on the opposite side. Truths be known ain't no migrant worker thought too highly of. We called poor white trash, and fruit tramps by the rich folks. Now, you kids don't worry yah minds one bit more."

She stood, smiling. "It's about bed time. We got a lot of picking to do, getting this crop in. Yah needs your rest. Finish your coffee and come on to bed when I call yah," she said.

We hugged and huddled together for a moment. She turned and walked into the shed. I heard her strong firm voice tell Merl not to scare us anymore. He slapped her and laughed.

Merl stuck his head out the back door. "Boo," he said.

We jumped out of our skins. I dropped the cup onto the ground. Luckily, it didn't break or that would have been another rump warming. Momma called us inside.

I picked up the cup and took it indoors, placed it in an enameled dishpan, and then we crawled to our bed. We pulled Anne's quilts over our heads.

Merl came into the room and stood in the open doorway smoking a roll-your-own. We peeked out from under the covers. He says, "You-ins didn't needs that coffee anyway, Son. Children who drink coffee will turn black before they're grown. That's, what happened to some of them nig***s you been watching all day. Yap, sure enough, coffee will turn a kid black and he'll stay that way." He laughed sinisterly.

I didn't know whether to believe Momma or Merl. He used the wives tale of coffee turning children black, as an excuse. From then on, he did not allow Jane and me to have evening coffee with Momma.

I'm Calling the Sheriff

I learned the meaning of hate and racism in Denton Island. I scorned the cotton. I abhorred the school. Despised the teacher and classmates, above all, I loathed Merl Judas.

Watching him rape six-year-old Jane, night after night, his lies and beatings stirred terror in our hearts daily. We were his innocent, ignorant play toys. He held no respectful value for us.

Seeing Momma slowly wasting away, gaunt, becoming very ill only added to our sorrows. She was lethargic part of the time. She had cancer but did not know. I could do nothing to help but try to behave, tend to younger siblings, and be kind to her.

November roared in like a Siberian Express. Temperatures dropped to the low twenties and teens. The cotton harvest was in. I was looking forward to moving away from this dreadful place. I wanted Daddy.

The plantation owner purchased a new diesel-powered cotton picker and informed all the migrant workers he would not need our help the following year. I watched him run the new machine over the last few rows in the field behind our shack one Sunday afternoon.

The roaring contraption sounded like a giant vacuum cleaner. Howling as it sucked the white balls of fluff out of the hard open bowl encasements in which the cotton rested. The sound, reminded me of Aunt Lou's vacuum cleaner, but it was much louder and more powerful.

The noisy apparatus did not pick cotton, as did humans. It left strings and torn cotton balls on the plant and some fell wasting on the ground. This new invention liberated us. I could tell from the brief demonstration that our cotton-picking days were over.

I hoped that somehow Jane and I would soon be liberated from our nightmare. Silently, I prayed every night for him to be gone, vowing never to ask God to send him back to Momma. I decided to resist empathy generated within me because of her tears.

New ways of living were coming, and they were concerned for their source of available migrant jobs. They discussed options, possibly having to learn a trade. They were fearful, weighing the opportunities of finding employment at a canning factory. Maybe they would work at sawmills, or chicken processing plants. They did not know what to do. Both were practically illiterate. All they were qualified to do was backbreaking manual labor. Merl attempted to find local odd jobs to see us through the winter. They were scarce, but we got by for a couple of weeks.

The Denton Island community was small, not able to afford a school of its own. When the harvest was in for the season, I was required to attend classes. Grubbs Elementary was where Momma enrolled me in first grade. The bus arrived at sunup. The trip took about one hour each way.

The same troubles in class and with peers followed from Rooster Ridge. I did not care if I learned anything or not. Part of me just wanted to die of shame. Every weekday morning I forced myself to get on the bus. I endured the cruelty of mocking, giggles, and derogatory remarks, while longing to be anywhere but there. I held my rage back watching out the bus window, daydreaming of more pleasant places, and better times.

The other students mocked because I smelled, and wore tattered dirty clothes. Merl shaved my head again when he found a nest in my hair. I am covered in lice that fall. I wasn't allowed back in school until they were gone. Once again, I am a skinny skinhead. This time, I was not alone. He cut off most of Jane's hair too.

If Momma had not pleaded with him to leave at least a couple of inches, she would have been a burr head too. Then he smeared motor oil on our scalps. We had no self-esteem. We felt no self-worth. Merl liked it that way.

Death was not a true heart's desire. I simply wanted the pain to go away. Hopes of moving are crushed when they decided to stay for the winter.

The black folks were gone. I missed their nightly songs, and family laughter that echoed across the field to our shed. Jane and I had apprehensively considered asking them to take us in, until we discussed the possibilities.

Life with them might be better if they were not the devil's boogers. I was not sure. The one thing we did know for certain, they sure could cook delicious smelling meals. The sweet savor of their food preparation made the thought extremely tempting.

Fearful uncertainty flooded our young minds. No, they are cannibals. That was the smell of roasting kids. We decided not to take the chance.

Cold north winds chilled to the bone inside the drafty shanty. I could not get warm, no matter how many layers of clothing. The low-grade fevers kept me drained. I wanted Daddy.

Fantasizing about Momma and Dad getting back together, and remembering the days when life was good before the night monster took control of our lives. It was a way of coping.

One bitter cold evening a week before Thanksgiving, Merl did his dirty business. When he was finished with us for the night, he stole away into Momma's bedroom. Left alone, in our bed, we are silently crying ourselves to sleep.

As I lay there, I remembered: The guardian angel. He saved us from rabid Buddy. I heard Daddy's voice in my mind again, saying Jesus helps those in trouble. Patting Anne's quilt tight around my body and thinking, perhaps she was watching. I trusted she would tell Jesus to help us, again. Figuring, He was a busy fellow. That was the reason for no answer, yet. Never losing Faith, I believed, He would eventually rescue us.

Daddy said that Anne and Jesus were best of friends. I felt the same unexplainable peace that was present the day my Guardian Angel appeared. This was the same peace, I had experienced when falling out of the moving car a few years earlier. I prayed for Jesus to help us get away from Merl.

This time after my prayer, something was different. There was an assurance that welled up inside of me. I just knew that my prayers had reached Heaven. I sensed, God had heard, and He would answer soon. My hope was in Jesus. Despite any doubts I may have had, an unexplainable joy surged through my heart after that prayer and I reached over to comfort Jane.

The next morning, I was standing outside the house by the back porch when I felt that peace again. I became bold as a lion cub. I walked up to Merl and said, "I am gonna tell Momma and Daddy what you are doing to us."

Merl flew into a rage and grabbed my arm. He beat me with his strong, rough hand. Shaking me violently, he barked, "Your dad is crazy! What is he going to do about it? Your mother loves me! She will never believe you. Besides, if you tell, I will kill all of you."

I shouted, "My angel won't let you kill us!"

He laughed hysterically, and I spit in his face. I yelled, "Angel protects us from rabid dogs!"

As the spittle ran off his wrinkled brow and dripped from the end of his nose, he backhanded me across the yard. My nose and mouth were bleeding when Momma came to the back door.

Frowning, timidly, she asked, "What's going on here?"

Venomously, Merl's evil demon eyes stared at me. He ran his forearm over his face and wiped the spit onto his shirtsleeve. His blue eyes were torches of hate as the blood rushed to his face, making red lines in the whites of his eyes. All the while, the veins in his neck pulsated at every beat of his heart.

Puffing from rage and exertion, he vainly ran his fist through his black hair. "Tell her boy," he shouted.

Defeated, on the verge of tears I glanced up at Momma. Shamefully dropping my head, "Nothing," I said.

He mocked, and said, "Damn angel, my ass!"

He proceeded to tell Momma, I back-talked him and he spanked me for the insolence.

Glaring back at him, she opened the screen door. "Saul, come inside. Let me clean your face," she said.

Momma placed a rag, cool and wet on my cheek and wiped away the blood as I sat at the kitchen table. I coughed up a dab of blood as I gasped to catch my breath.

Momma compassionately stroked my hair as she told me to spit it on the rag. I could see the sorrow and fear in her brown eyes as they watered and her hands trembled.

I thought, does she know Merl is hurting our pee-pees? Does she know how mean he really is? Why does she stay with him? Why doesn't she go back to Daddy? Daddy won't be mean to Rambo. Momma, why do you love Merl? I despise him. I will never love him again. I want to tell you Momma, but he will kill us all if I do.

Momma's quiet tears and shaking, shouted volumes of fear. She glanced down, saying nothing that might arouse the wrath of the beast again.

I remained silent. Glancing up, I grinned.

She smiled. "Look there, your front teeth are coming back," she said while placing her hand under my chin. "Son, you shouldn't tell people you saw an angel. They'll say you are as crazy as yah Daddy."

I giggled. Those who do not believe in angels were the crazy ones.

After wiping my face clean, she kissed me on the forehead. "You'll be fine, Saul. Obey Merl and this won't happen again," she said, smiling.

I nodded, forcing a grin as Merl stepped inside. "I'm sorry, Merl. I won't spit on you again. I promise," I said.

I actually felt quite smug but was not about to let him know my true feelings. I think he knew I was not sorry as he rolled his eyes and walked into the adjoining room.

Grimacing, he flopped down on the old car seat in the living room that served as a sofa and reached for the green bottle of cheap wine lying underneath. He turned the bottle up and gulped down several large swallows then he loudly belched.

The same afternoon we had dinner with the neighbors. The Joneses were God-fearing, Baptist people. Merl had helped them kill, and dress-out a hog the week before. They had not given Merl any of the meat. His payment was coming this day, a promised feast. Ham, cracklin' cornbread, sweet potatoes, cathead biscuits, and homemade white gravy were on the menu. Always hungry, Jane and I looked forward to the coming meal with great anticipation. Merl was a little tipsy when we loaded into the car.

Mr. Jones, a short stocky man with orange-red curly hair that he cut close to his head, was about forty-five-years-old. He walked with a slight limp. Mrs. Jones was a foot taller than her husband. She shone strong Native American features, and about the same age. She wore long straight black-hair that hung down past her shoulders. She dressed in men's blue jeans and a plaid flannel shirt. Both of them talked with a funny accent.

When we arrived and went inside, kindhearted Mr. Jones noticed the cut on my lip and the bruises on my face. He smelled the wine on Merl's breath, and shook his head while glancing at his wife.

He stared into my eyes. "What happened to you?" he asked.

I glanced up at Merl. His icy threatening glare said it all, without him speaking. "I was chasing a possum out the backdoor when I tripped over a pile of wadded-up cotton sacks, and fell off the porch," I said.

Mr. Jones nodded.

"Oh really," Mrs. Jones mumbled as she scowled.

Obviously, Mrs. Jones did not buy the story. Mr. Jones looked at me with fixed, sympathetic eyes. He didn't believe me either. They suspiciously watched Jane and me while pulling the chairs back from the dinning room table loaded with the fresh cooked meal.

Mrs. Jones pointed to the restroom. Jane and I took the cue and went into their bathroom to wash our hands. "They don't believe me, Jane," I whispered.

"Merl will whip yah again if they say anything to them," she whispered.

I sighed.

A bit crippled after an accident on his previous job, the Joneses moved to Denton Island from some northeastern part of the United States when Mr. Jones became permanently disabled. The cost of living was cheaper in Arkansas and they were able to survive on his pension, easily and in comfort. All their children grown, and gone from home. They did not have the expense of raising them any longer.

We sat down at the table for dinner. Mr. Jones offered grace before we ate. I bowed my head. Again, prayed silently for God to get Jane and me away from Merl. Nothing was left in me but loathing for him.

Mr. Jones' reverent petition was short, but it felt like eternity. The grub smelled so good, all I wanted was to gorge myself. When he finally finished, I filled my plate and began wolfing down the food like a hungry hound. Momma frowned, and said for me to use my manners. I slowed down a bit.

About midway through the meal, Merl excused himself to take Jane to the restroom. Once they were there, we heard Jane ask him to stop. She was crying and pleading with him not to hurt her again. Her agonizing voice grew muffled. The same characteristic sounds as when he put his hand over her face in our bed at night.

I suspected this would happen. Merl enjoyed taking chances. Perhaps it gave him a greater thrill. Only the mind of a pervert could understand his motivations for the behavior. I did not. He often molested Jane in public restrooms or in the car when he thought no one was watching. Pushing his crimes to the limits of being found out, but never caught in the act.

Mr. Jones ran toward the restroom, and jiggled the knob attempting to get inside. Merl had locked the door. Mr. Jones pounded the facing, and yelled, demanding him to open.

Merl reacted from the other side, as if the lock was stuck. He said, "The latch be jammed."

Mr. Jones kicked it open, and burst into the restroom just as Merl was zipping up his pants. It was obvious what had taken place as Jane wiggled free from Merl's grasp and pulled up her panties.

Furiously, Mr. Jones shouted, "Get out of my house!"

Frightened and sniffling, Jane ran over and held onto my arm. Motioning to her, I put my finger across my lips. I was afraid Merl would kill us, and the Joneses if she said anything about what happened.

Momma stood, fear painted over her expressive face. She was panic stricken for Merl's safety, and ran to his side.

Merl and the Joneses had been friends and neighbors for months. Merl was the ultimate manipulator, but Mr. Jones was no longer deceived. For the first time in my life, I saw terror on Merl's face as the color drained and he began stuttering a whopper in his defense.

Momma tugged at his arm, trying to drag him toward the front door. She flipped her wrist, motioning for Jane and me to run for the car.

The veins in Mr. Jones' neck began to bulge and throb. His face turned flame-red, matching his western shirt. Yelling, shaking, Mr. Jones mustered restraint in his rage by doubling his fist and holding his arms tight against his sides to keep from hitting Merl.

Angry, but cool headed, Mrs. Jones calmly stepped toward the cabinet near the kitchen sink. She opened a drawer and pulled out a handgun. Pointing it directly at Merl's head from across the room, for a moment, Mrs. Jones did not say a word. Her silent disdain spoke volumes.

Seeing the gun, horror wrenched Momma's face as she pulled harder at Merl's arm. Her voice fearfully trembling, she mumbled, "Let's go, Merl."

Smiling sinisterly, Mrs. Jones coldly and contemptuously spoke. "You sack-of-hog-crap, I should blow your sorry ass to kingdom come," she said.

Angry, his voice quavered, Mr. Jones shouted, "You will pay for this evil. God has prepared a lake of hellfire for the wicked like you." He turned to Momma. "How could you allow this beast to do such horrible things to your children?" he asked.

Momma did not answer. Her gaze fell.

"I'm calling the sheriff," Mr. Jones said, "I pray to God; He will deliver these children out of your hands. Get out! I'll kill both of you, if you don't remove yourselves from my sight."

Merl raised his fist and threatened to hit Mr. Jones. He said, "I'll knock your religious head through the floor. No bastard talks to me that way and gets away with it."

Not flinching, Mrs. Jones cocked the pistol.

Momma forcefully pulled at Merl's arm while pleading for him to get into the car. Dragging him out of the house, she scooped up Rambo onto her skinny hip, pausing only to yell at Jane and me one more time to get in the car. I grabbed a cathead biscuit off the table and ran for the door with Jane in tow.

Mrs. Jones cried. "You children do not have to leave," she said.

"Thanks for the supper," I yelled, as I slid onto the backseat of the automobile.

Our only emotional security was Momma. We had become almost numb to Merl's daily abuse. I wanted to stay with the Joneses, but if we did, Merl might kill Momma and Daddy. Then, he will come back to finish us off, making good on his threats. He might even hunt down Bobby in Loafer's Glory. Months earlier, he told me, he would not murder Rambo because Rambo was his son.

He lied to Momma. Love does not beat one's sweetheart, or rape and molest her children. Merl never loved any of us, especially, not Jane or me. Our spirits were near the breaking point. Broken lives because of Merl's brute physical, mental, and sexual abuse. I am seven, but I comprehend, abuse is not love.

Momma was not innocent. Her hands were as bloody. Her passive cruelty and denial were as deadly as Merl's aggressive violations. Their behaviors bled out the joys of childhood for Jane and me.

Standing in their doorway, Mrs. Jones wept. Merl sped the car in reverse out of their driveway. Mr. Jones standing in the front yard was shaking his fist in the air.

I really wanted to thank them for standing up to Merl, but knew I would never get the chance. I questioned if perhaps, they were angels in disguise. Mrs. Jones got it right. How did she know Merl was named Hog Sh**? That is what Daddy called him. She didn't know Daddy.

Momma and Merl stopped at the pickers' shack a half mile down the road. She ran inside and grabbed a few of our clothes. She threw them into paper bags, three sacks in all. She went inside again and carried out Grandma Anne's quilts. She tossed them into the car-trunk.

We made haste and high-tailed-it out of the area. Merl drove the hundred miles to Loafer's Glory. Momma abandoned us at a neighbor's house close to Uncle Chad's place.

The week before, Momma announced, she was pregnant with Merl's second child. We wanted so to see our new sibling. That would not happen.

As for Jane and me, the unseen God, and His Son Jesus, my grandmother Anne's Savior, got the message. We were free of Merl Judas.

Paul E. Treadwell

These Are My Kids

The neighbor's place where Momma abandoned us, was Merl's mother's. She was a cantankerous elderly biddy with mousey-gray stringy-hair. She bragged of herself, claiming to a witch and having supernatural powers.

I thought she was ignorant, domineering, and older than the hills. A selfish woman, and half-cracked in the head. Still, I believed she had cast a spell on me, and maybe Momma too. Needless to say, I did not like her. The feeling was mutual.

Momma said she would be gone in the morning. She was leaving us to our father, and she would go away with Merl and Rambo to start a new life. It would be better for all of us this way.

Holding back her tears, firmly, Momma said, "Son, you must be brave. Be strong, and take care of Jane always."

I whimpered, "But Momma, you can't leave us."

She kissed us goodnight and said, "Hush now, be a man. Be brave. Jane needs you. You have to be strong. I will love you always. This is best for you and Jane. Now, go to sleep."

The next morning when we awakened, Bertha was on the telephone talking with Chad. I heard her say, "Your crazy brother's wife was here with my son and they have run off and left these kids with me. I am too old to raise children that are not mine. You need to come get them."

While leaning off the edge of the bed, I peeked around the corner into the kitchen. I listened as Bertha continued to speak with Chad. There she was as usual, feeding the ends of her hair into her mouth, while nervously gnawing and slicking the gray strands with spit.

An hour later, Chad arrived. He loaded our brown paper grocery bags of clothes into the car-trunk. Bertha handed him a blank envelope.

Every morning before he went to work, Daddy strolled a mile from the old homestead down the road to Cousin Poojam's store, for his morning cup of brew. Eighth of a mile up the road, Daddy watched us crawling into Chad's car. Chad pulled out of the drive onto the main gravel road.

Daddy chased after the automobile, yelling for him to stop. Chad ignored his desperate cries, while chauffeuring us away. Jane and

I watched out the back glass. Daddy was at a full-out-run following behind. We dipped below a hill and could no longer see him racing toward us.

Arriving, we stopped at Poojam's. Across the road we noticed Delena's abandoned restaurant. Delena and Saul divorced. Their May-September marriage went to ruin after the kidnapping. Delena moved to Amarillo where she could be close to Leve. We hoped to see her, but she was gone. The house was empty, the yard grown up with tall grass and weeds. Uncle Chad purchased it from her. Aunt Vanny planned to open the restaurant again within a few weeks.

Inside the store, Chad bought us a bottle of coke to share. Daddy came into sight, trotting and panting across the parking lot. We ran outside and hugged him. He was huffing for every breath, but bright eyed and grinning.

We were elated to be together again. Chad did not share our enthusiasm. The reflection of his scowling face through the windowpanes was fierce.

Daddy was now working for Chad, and living at the old homestead, again. Daddy hoisted us up onto his hips, and carried us inside the store. He put us down in front of the checkout counter. Happily smiling, Daddy said, "I will take my children home with me now. I will raise them without their mother."

Joyfully, we sighed relief, while hugging his legs. Chad's demeanor changed from tight-lipped satisfaction at the sight of our reunion, to rage as he banged his brawny fist against the counter. Breathing heavily he kicked the side of the pop tank, resulting in an unexpected loud bang.

Ten or twelve other customers darted out the doors. They had seen the Hotman' tempers before. Now, both Chad and Daddy were provoked, ready to rumble.

"I don't think so. You can't even take care of yourself. These kids need a home. I'm going to have them placed in an orphanage," Chad shouted.

Daddy had lost a lot of weight. He was skinny and pale. Obviously, he had been recently physically ill. At this point Chad out weighed him and was stout as a bull. Daddy's blue eyes filled with tears and his face became fire red.

"These are my kids! I say what happens to them! I am going to raise my children. You have no say in this matter," Daddy said.

Chad doubled his fist and began to punch Daddy. He was much stronger, but Daddy continued to fight until Chad grabbed his head and beat it against a steel post at the center of the store. The massive steel beam aided roof support. I felt vibrations under my feet at each slam of his skull against the support post.

Tearful, Jane and I screamed for them to stop.

Customers outside were watching through the windowpanes that covered the front wall of the building. We watched the two of them as they toppled a small shelf of bakery goods, sending cakes and pies sliding randomly over the floor. Chad rammed his knee into Daddy's gut, then the groin, and continued to bang his head against a steel post.

"You crazy fool. You haven't got any say," Chad said while smashing Daddy's face against a block wall at the back of the store. "You don't have brains enough to make this decision," he yelled again forcing Daddy's head down and rammed his knee into his nose.

Blood ran down Daddy's cheeks and chin, from a long gash above an eyebrow and out his nose. Chad shoved him against the cash register counter. One more overpowering act of intimidation proclaimed he was still in charge.

"Get your miserable, mindless rump to the mill. There's work to do," Chad shouted.

Great shame surfaced, expressed by Daddy's actions as he bowed his head. His face twisted while trying to hold back his tears. His eyes shamefully flitted toward me.

I knew from the defeated expression, he was embarrassed for what we had witnesses. He sighed and threw his arms in the air. A wild crazy expression of confusion came over him as his eyelids fluttered and his eye balls shifted from side to side, then rolled back inside his head showing only the whites.

Daddy mumbled, "No, no, howdy, howdy. If you don't believe in the American flag, you ain't anything, but a whore!"

He shook his head and was himself again as the wild expression faded. He ran for the back door covering his bloody face with knuckle-skinned hands. Humiliated, he bolted out, leaving a sprinkling of his blood behind on the concrete floor. All the while, Jane and I continued to wail.

Chad's lip was bleeding. Daddy had gotten in one good blow. Glad, as I resentfully watched Chad, dragging his shirtsleeve across his face to wipe away the blood.

I wanted to come to Daddy's defense, holding back the urge to bust Chad over the head with a bottle of coke. That would only make matters worse. The serpent of hate pierced my soul. I never thought that would be possible after having great admiration for Uncle Chad. I had misjudged him too.

We had no contact with Daddy again while we lived with Chad and Vanny through Thanksgiving, Christmas, and until New Years Eve. Chad called Leve on Christmas night. He told her to come get us by the first of the year or we were going into a ragamuffin home. He seemed to take pleasure in speaking the harsh words over the telephone in my presence as he hatefully glared at me.

I searched, but this time, I could not find any kindness behind his scowl. Fear gripped my heart, but I had to be brave. I had to take care of Jane always.

Bossy Stan, Chad's, youngest son's attitude toward Jane and me had not changed since our last visit eighteen months earlier. We were still the unwanted white trash that had invaded his domain and he did not want me sharing his room again. I was ready to leave their house, orphanage, or not.

Intense love and hate mingled in all of our lives. Shame and fear would rule the days to come, as Jane and I continued our struggles for survival.

Alone With Strangers

Leve, tall and pretty, picked us up the last day of 1962; it was New Year's Eve when we boarded a bus in Raccoon Springs. We were heading for our new Texas home. We sat close to her protective presence on the Continental Trailways' passenger coach as we made the trip to Amarillo.

At forty-five-years-old, she was five-nine and had high cheekbones, lean with black-hair having a few signs of graying, a ravishing woman. Her eyes were so deep a blue as to shadow dark violet in color. She reminded me of perhaps an older, larger-framed, darker-complexioned Elizabeth Taylor.

Neither Jane nor I could recall ever seeing her before, but we could sense right off that she was very kind. She made every effort to calm our fears while holding our hands constantly, or placing one of us on her lap. During daylight, we watched out the bus window as the miles swirl bye. She never left our sides, except for restroom breaks.

We changed busses in Joplin, Missouri. The people on the journey from Raccoon Springs to Joplin clearly display the hill culture in their dress, speech colloquialisms, and manner. By the time we arrived in Oklahoma City and changed busses again, the folks seemed a little more sophisticated. At one a.m. the bus rolled into the Amarillo station. People riding from Oklahoma City to Amarillo were polite. They were friendly, smiling and chatting. They did not gossip and scowl, or call me names like on the school bus in Denton Island. No one was mean spirited toward anyone. If everyone in Amarillo was as friendly, I would like this place. I might even enjoy school, and be able to make some friends.

However, there was a language barrier. I only spoke All-American improper Hillbilly-English. The language found in the Ozarks and Appalachian's backwoods country. It would take some time to learn a new tongue, speak with a north Texas accent and dialect.

Chauffeured by taxi, we arrived at their home, 100 North Lamar Street at two a.m. It was New Years Day. The first day of 1963. This day and the coming year held much promise. We would never forget it, our exodus from the turbulent, impoverished, illiterate migrant worker and country existence we had led. This was the beginning of a new start, new home, and with new parents. We were going to be educated city folks now.

The house set on the corner where two paved streets intersected. Two street lamps, one shone in the front yard and the other lit the side and backyard. We never lived under a streetlight before. I could play in the yard after dark and not have to worry about stepping on an unseen copperhead. This would be a great place to ride a bike with paved roads and concrete sidewalks.

The corner lot house was square like all the others rowed on the street. The home appeared dull gray in the dim light. I dreaded walking inside. Who was the man Jake that Leve said was her husband? Would he hurt us like Merl? Was he crazy like Daddy? Was he a drunk like Lou's husband Martin? Did he have girlfriends on the side to make Leve sad and angry, like Martin, and Sonny's husband Dan?

Leve unlocked the front door. I sighed and drew in a deep breath, shuddering at meeting possibly another monster. He was sleeping in the back bedroom.

Leve did not wake him. We would meet him after sunup. I sighed again, relieved. He probably would not like us. He would be like all the rest. We might be, thrown out. Perhaps dumped or kidnapped before six months was up.

She ran a tub of warm water. Jane and I bathed. Then we were off to bed in the other room, all three of us. Jane huddled close to Leve, and I took the outside edge next to Jane.

I awakened the next morning to the aromas of sweet bacon frying and fresh coffee drifting into our bedroom. Leve wasn't there.

The house was warm and comfortable when I crawled out of the bed. I shook Jane to wake her. We quietly toddled into the living room and timidly sat down on the sofa close to each other. We watched a husky bald man wolfing down a large plate of eggs, bacon, and toast in the connecting dinning room. He did not see us as he faced the opposite direction.

Our mouths salivated, while our stomachs burned, churned, and growled for just one taste. We were not about to ask. Momma always insisted we wait for Merl to finish breakfast, and then we got what he left, if anything.

Happily humming, Leve wearing a half-skirt apron tied around her blue silk flowered print dress, her shoulder-length black-hair with tiny streaks of gray pulled back in a ponytail. She stepped out of the kitchen with two plates filled with eggs, bacon, cathead biscuits and gravy. She set them on the table next to Jake. When she saw us, she smiled.

We smiled back. I thought, that man, sure could eat a lot. Maybe, he would share.

"Are you children hungry?" she asked.

We nodded. Jake turned around, smiled and nodded.

"Don't be shy. Come and take a seat. But first wash your hands," she said. We ran for the bathroom and hastily washed. Giggling, Jane said, "Did you see the man? He has no hair on his head. He's a burr head like you, Saul."

I flipped water off my fingers into her face. "I know, he is as ugly as me," I said.

"I wonder if we will get to eat till we're full?" Jane asked.

"I don't know, but if we can't, I'll steal some for later and hide it," I said

We wiped the smiles off our faces, walked back into the dinning room and took our seats as Leve directed. Then she placed a huge plate of food in front of Jane, and the same for me. We could not believe our eyes, and hastily started shoveling down our breakfast before Leve introduced us to Jake. I crammed a huge spoon full into my mouth.

Smiling, as she placed her large but refined hands with long fingers on our heads, "Children, this is your uncle Jake. Jake, this is Saul, and this is Jane," she said.

Smiling, cheeks bulging, and trying to keep lips together so nothing would fall out, I said, "Howdy, Jake."

"Hi," Jane whispered a grunt, through a mouth full of food.

He nodded.

I could not recall meeting a completely bald man before Jake. He was bald as an egg with a paunch of a belly hanging over his belt line. His muscles were firm and his large calloused hands were strong. Something in his big brown eyes spoke that he was a good man. His gaze reminded me of the kindness I saw in Buddy's eyes before he went rabid. His focused intelligent air when he glanced over to read the partially folded newspaper beside his plate, and his sipping on another cup of coffee without making a slurping sound caused me to believe that he was smart too.

Jane and I gobbled down the food he provided for us that first morning, and frequently glanced up at him to see if he was watching us. He was not. Just reading and eating. He was thinking, sizing us up. I could tell from the way the expressions changed on his face unconsciously. His kind face with calm stable demeanor gave me peace. I felt wanted here. I just knew, we were gonna like him. Maybe he would be good to us like Delena's husband Saul.

His voice was bass and kind as he sighed and pushed back his empty plate. He said, "Leve, please bring the coffee pot and set it on the table. Have another cup with me before I leave. Okay?"

Leve sauntered out of the kitchen with a clear glass pot, right off the gas burner filled with hot coffee. It was still gurgling up and perking into the top. She set the pot on the table next to Jake. Pulling a chair out beside me, she took off her half apron draping it over the chair back. She sat down and had breakfast with us.

"This is good." I mumbled, and swallowed.

Jake unfolded the morning newspaper finding more articles to read, glanced at Leve, and smiled.

She smiled back.

Calmly, grinning, he said, "Now you kids eat all you want. There's more in the kitchen."

The next day, Leve enrolled us at Summit Elementary. Jane was in first grade. My second grade teacher Mrs. Jones, Jane's instructor Mrs. Kinder, and the principal Mr. Hardin, received no medical or school records. There were no documents of our births. Leve applied for birth certificates and received them by post within a few weeks. She told school administrators about our backgrounds. Having good reason, there were no great expectations of us academically. They advise Leve not to count on either of us to pass that year.

We could not attend classes until we had immunization shots at the local health office. Jane and I had never received an immunization or booster. Not until Leve and Jake took us in.

Something about this new town gave us a feeling of being safe. Even most of the strangers were nice to us. These were city folks. They used more manners. There were too many people for everyone to be into everybody else's business. No resident in this big city knew everyone. Neighbors who lived next door to one another, residing that close, sometimes did not know one another for years. The other kids at school seemed accepting. They did not know our past, and I wanted to keep it that way.

Reading and writing were skills I had not mastered, although I could print my name with my left hand. The teacher thought I should be right-handed. She said I should always use that one when I did any work for her class. Then she showed me how to hold a pencil properly.

The other children attempted to help me learn and adjust during the first few weeks. Soon the newness of this challenge wore off and classmates got frustrated. I could not comprehend the materials. Most of them ignored me after a while. By the third week, I decided perhaps they too were chicken dookie, like the bullies in Wisconsin. A few make fun of me. One student was an exception. Short and stocky with curly dark hair, Alvin became my first friend.

During the two years prior to December 31, 1962, we had lived with eleven different families. Now twelve, the number was probably more, although the twelve stood-out most vividly. It would take some time for Jane and me to adjust, and be able to trust again.

Daddy's, other sister, Delena, lived up the street from Leve, and was now with yet another husband, Ricky. Her marriage to Saul had only lasted six months. I liked Saul, much better than balding and fat, gruff Ricky. Now, Saul was gone, so I would have to get to know Ricky better.

On Saturday the fourth week after we arrived, Delena walked the eight blocks to Leve's house. I asked her what had happened to Saul.

She explained that Saul took to drinking and gambling. She refused to have the behavior in her home. As she had often raged and got her way as a young girl, she did the same her last evening with Saul. She told us all about that night while we sat on Leve's sofa sipping cokes from six-ounce glass bottles.

My attention bounced back and forth while watching "Felix the Cat," cartoons on an old, tall, black and white, cabinet RCA television set. Jane and I poured a bag of peanuts into our pop as Delena continued to tell her story. She knew we loved Saul.

Folding her arms, she said, "He brought every drunk in the county into my home while I worked in the restaurant. There they sat getting drunk on moonshine, gambling, smoking, and laughing until daybreak. Night after night, he did this after your Momma kidnapped you kids. Before that, he was a wonderful husband. He missed you very badly. He would sleep all day, and stay up all night. Just wouldn't work."

She rolled her eyes and scowled. "Well, I wasn't about to live like that. I came in after closing the restaurant. There they sat every one of them drunk as Cooter Brown. Ol' bald, fat Buck Ives lays passed out on my kitchen floor. He was covered in his own vomit," she says, and takes a deep breath.

She continued, "I was mad as a hornet. My house was a mess and it really ticked me off when Saul asked me to fix sandwiches and coffee for his sloppy guests. I grabbed the heavy ashtray my first husband Shawn used, and commenced cold-cockin'. BAM, BAM, BAM! That was the blunt sound of blows to the backs of their heads. I ran them out of the house. I did. Did indeed," she says.

She laughed. We giggled, and tried to suck the peanuts out of the bottom of our empty bottles.

"Wasn't popular that night. I demanded Saul drag Buck out into the yard. Then I whacked him with the ashtray, and locked them both out. The next morning Buck was gone. Saul was asleep in the lawn chair as I pitched his clothes out the door, and told him to beat it. That was the end of marriage. Terrible drunks, I won't put up with what Ma took off Pa," she seethed.

She had hoped to reform his sinful ways. Her lofty plan backfired when he would not cooperate. She divorced Saul. A month after the divorce was final she sold her home in Loafer's Glory and the restaurant to Chad and Vanny. She used part of the money moving to Amarillo.

Barren, Delena was envious that Leve had two children and she had none. Leve was also unable to conceive. She rejoiced at having us as her own.

Delena was jealous. She determined, at least one of us would be hers. After all, she had been our parent for a few months, almost two years earlier. She considered herself our momma too. By the end of January, Delena convinced Leve, and peace-loving bald Jake to let her raise Jane. Jake gave in, not wanting to deal with Delena's temperamental raging, nagging, and pleading.

His nine-month-old son from a former marriage died twenty-six years before. Four years later, he met and married Leve after his discharge from the Navy at the end of World War II. Jake always wanted a son. Now he had one.

The adults secretly conspired to separate us. Delena and Ricky are married only eight months. Fat Ricky, near fifty, with a large nose, bright blue eyes, bald on top and white short hair bowled around the lower part of his head. He never had children, though he married three times.

Jane and I walked home from school the day they made the decision. We knew nothing about their agreement.

The never-ceasing Texas Plains' winds drove cold February winter air up under our new coats.

Jane played with her red earmuffs, neck scarf, and mittens. She was pulling them off, and sliding them back on again-and-again to admire and savor the moments of having new clothes. Then she shoves her small hands into pockets on her new gray-tweed knee-length winter coat.

I adjusted down the earflaps on my new black-fake-leather cap and snapped the top on the matching pilot jacket. Jake had bought the new coats and winter accessories in anticipation of our arrival, the day after Chad called.

We were proud of our new winter attire, but our street clothes were shabby. Leve promised to take us shopping when the weather warmed up a bit. Since we'd have to ride the city bus while Jake drove to work in their '61 pale-green Chevy Impala. She didn't want us to stand out in the cold waiting for the buses.

The shiny car set on the concrete driveway, right in front of our comfortable, warm home. I was thrilled to see the place every day when I arrived home from school. I was beaming because of the nice surroundings in the community, and the shinny car.

The motorcar looked new. I could hardly wait to take a ride with Jake. He said we would go to the barbershop when my hair grew a bit more. He promised no burrs. I had never been to a barbershop before. I did not know what to expect.

The neighborhood children were older than us. Many of their parents' could not finance a nice set of wheels. They drove beat-up old jalopies. The community thought Jake, Leve, and now Jane and I were rich. They didn't begrudge, and happily looked out for us as Leve requested.

Chasing after monstrous dried tumbleweeds, we were in the center of a group of about eight children as we skipped down the street. When we came to our yard, we told our new companions, good-bye. They strolled on down the sidewalk toward their houses.

Smiling, Delena held the brown paper sack filled with Jane's ragged clothes. She was waiting for us while shivering on the front porch. Something was wrong. Delena was never there when we came home from school. Why was she out in the cold? What was up? Why did she have Jane's clothes sack?

She took Jane by the hand. "Sweetie," she said, "You're going to live with me."

Those were fighting words. I have to protect Jane, always. I promised Momma. Raging, I yelled, "You are not taking Jane anywhere!"

Delena smiled sweetly, while swinging Jane's hands as they stepped off the porch. Jane commenced resisting and moaning while reaching for me as Delena dragged her along. She said, "Now, Son, it's best for all of us."

Wailing, Jane screamed, "I don't want to go. I don't want to leave Saul."

Delena shook Jane, and growled, "Stop it Jane," she said.

Frowning angrily, I said, "I hate you! You will not take Jane from me."

Jane screeched and struggled to break free from Delena's grasp. I threw my books in Delena's face, and grabbed Jane's hand. She managed to jerk away. We ran down the street yelling to the neighbor children to help us. Panic stricken, I hollered to the top of my lungs, "They're kidnapping Jane!"

The children leapt into action. "We'll hide you. Follow us," they said, and came running.

As fast as she could move, closing the space was Delena sluggishly trotting behind, and now she was on our heels. Delena had gotten fat. Fifty years old and quite out of shape, she puffed as she chased after us. She was losing momentum, running out of gas.

We bolted across the street, and turned down an alleyway lined with trashcans. Delena panted, and paused to catch her breath as she called after us, "Honey, come back. It's for the best. I'll give you a good home. I'll be a good mother. You can visit Saul on weekends."

We were not about to stop. We sprinted for our lives as the other children knocked over trashcans in Delena's path when she came after us again. At the end of the alley, Jane and I ran up the street to the next alleyway. Our hands clinched tight together, I dragged her along as she trailed behind.

I was wheezing and coughing. The other children caught up with us a block away. "The old lady gave up. She walked back to the house," they said, panting to catch their breaths too.

Jane sniffled. I grabbed her arm and said, "Stop crying. They might find us. My hacking and your crying will tell them where we are. We have to split up," I whispered. In-between coughs, I softly said, "I'll distract them, lead them off in the opposite direction."

Two of the older boys picked up Jane, and dropped her inside a neighbor's trashcan. I placed the lid on top. Swallowing the lump of grief in my throat and wiping a tear from my eye, I said, "Be brave. Stop crying. I'll come back at dark and we will run away. We'll hitchhike to Indiana, Aunt Lou's house. No one is going to take you from me. No one will separate us. I will look out for you always."

Jane sniffled, "But I'm scared Saul. It stinks down here. I'm cold and I don't like the dark," she whimpered.

"Hush. Do you want them to find you?" I asked.

Jane sobbed, "Be brave! Shh!" she said and was silent.

My coughing eased a bit. I strolled the long way around, back toward the house. I came into the yard opposite the direction from where Jane was hiding. Spying Delena on the porch, I angrily yelled, "You, old fat, hag. You will never take Jane from me!"

Husky Jake ran out the back door, rounded the house, sneaked up from behind and grabbed me. I wasn't expecting him to do that. He caught me off guard. My plan was ruined.

He was crying, as he lifted me off the ground. I squirmed and fought to break free. He dropped me to my feet. His grip was strong holding taut to the waist band of my britches. He dragged me along while I continued to resist, kicking and screaming. Into the house we went. Frowning, he forcefully sat me down in a chair and held on as Delena and Leve walked through the front door.

"Where did you kids hide Jane?" he asked.

I squirmed frantically to get free from his grasp. "You devil. I'll die before I'll tell you," I yelled, and spit in his face.

He wiped the spittle onto his shirt sleeve. Then he asked again. I refused to answer.

Leve calmly sauntered into the room and squatted to my eye level. "Now Saul, calm down. No one is going to hurt you or Jane. Tell us where she is. It's not as if she will live hundreds of miles away. You'll get to see her," she said, as she reached for a napkin on the table and wiped away the lump of dark blood I just coughed up, off my chin.

Continuing to struggle, I yelled, "Get out of my face, you ol' cow. You are like all the others. The whole world is chicken sh**." I bellowed hysterically.

She stood and brushed her shoulder length curled-hair back from her face. Calmly, not even fazed by my name-calling, she glanced at grimacing Jake. Addressing, wild-eyed, frustrated Delena, who was now also standing over me. "She can't be far," Leve said.

Sighing as she and Delena went out the front door. "This child is coughing up blood. Gotta get him to a doctor," Leve said.

"No more doctors." I mumbled.

She and Delena each went down different alleyways. Breaking free from Jake's grasp, I tried escaping out the front door. Not quick enough, Jake removed his belt and swung it at me as I dashed through the threshold. The belt caught my right ankle and I tripped, fell sprawling in the open doorway.

I glanced up and watched Delena dart down the alley where Jane was hiding. Our protectors, the neighborhood children were coming up from behind her.

Jake wept when he cradled me on his lap. With both arms wrapped around me, I fought to break free from his bear hug. It was a hopeless fight and I howled louder. Determined to shake loose from his grip I coughed, and continued to struggle frantically for freedom. My efforts were futile. His strength was greater, than I was.

Silent tears streamed out of his large brown eyes onto my head. He sobbed continually as he held me tight and rocked. Whispering in my ear, he said, "It's okay, Saul. No one is going to hurt you and Jane."

I could hear Delena yelling at the neighborhood kids as they threw dirt clods at her. The children finally gave up and headed toward their own homes. The battle was over. The adults won again when Delena heard Jane sniffling in the empty trash barrel. She removed the lid, and Jane screamed.

When I heard Jane's wails, I knew she would be gone from me forever. I promised to take care of her always. I could not keep the promise. Jane, like everyone and everything I ever loved, stolen, taken away. All went silent.

Delena lifted Jane out of the trash barrel and walked with her to what would now be her new home eight blocks from where I lived.

I could see them through the open front door strolling up the sidewalk a half block away.

Jane continued her screeching after she saw me struggling against Jake's hold. She fought violently, kicking, hitting, clawing and screaming, trying to break free from Delena's grasp. Her fight was useless.

Cold northerly winds whipped into the house through the open door. I wanted to be as swift as the gush of air. I wanted to run after them but exhaustion had set in moments before when Jake lifted me off the floor. My fight was gone. I could not have broken free from Jake no matter how hard I fought. I simply sobbed, defeated, as pretty Leve walked back inside, smiling, and slammed the door shut.

During recess at school on the playground, I could see Jane through the windowpanes of her classroom. We are not, allowed to spend time together. Sometimes she would jump up from her desk and run to the windows waving, but her teacher always dragged her back to her seat.

We were not allowed to speak to, or spend time with one another for almost six months. The adults decided we would adjust to the separation more quickly this way. It was hard at first, a great loss. Jane was my life. She was my only connection to who I am, and where I came from. The last of my family was gone. It was just me now, alone with strangers.

Paul E. Treadwell

Don't Be Rude Today

The week after Jane was taken, Leve decided to buy us new wardrobes. We walked a few blocks to the local city bus stop. Boarding the public transit, she dropped two tokens into the change collector.

Arriving at our destination, we stepped off the bus. Never before had I seen so many strangers marching along the streets. Kept thinking maybe, the next city block might clear the crowd when we turned the corner onto Polk Street. Holding tight to Leve's hand, fearful I would get lost in the sea of pedestrians. I smiled at passers-bye we met. Hoping if any bad bullies were in the bunch, they would go on without conflict.

"Howdy! Hi! Good morning, how is yah?" I say, just as Momma had taught to me. Some of the folks carried solemn ignoring faces set in concrete. Others stared, and some chuckled or cracked a smile while returning my greetings.

Other children with their parents giggled. Some rolled their eyes like those at Rooster Ridge school. One stuck his tongue out at me. That was not nice. What had I done wrong? That was not very friendly.

I tried a little harder at getting them to liking me. Smiling twice as big, inflicted a tinge of pain in my face as muscles stretched their limits. I was determined to make as many friends as possible in this new place.

Leve shook my hand violently. We stopped in the middle of the sidewalk. Other pedestrians walked around us, as she bent down to make eye contact. Placing her hands on my shoulders, she says, "Stop it, Saul. You are drawing attention to us."

I was only trying to be polite. We strolled down half the block and sat on a bus stop bench. "Saul, it's okay to smile and be friendly, but don't you think you're over doing it a bit?" she asked.

I didn't.

She sighed. "Well you are. Try not to draw attention to yourself. Let's play invisible the remainder of our trip. I'd bet you'd make more friends if you didn't try as hard," she said.

I smiled, liking that idea of giving my smile a rest. My jaws were getting sore.

She patted my back. "It may take a little longer for others to warm up to you, but it will be because they want to be with you for who you are. Now, stop the fake smiles," she said.

I nodded.

She chuckled, and said, "Okay."

I happily grinned. Nevertheless, I could not be rude and threw in a happy "Howdy" to the sadder-looking folks. Some gave me weird bewildered stares and went back to their invisible robot mode avoiding making eye contact.

Shopping finished, we headed across the street, and entered an office building. Up the staircase we went. There was a sign on a glass door. The first word started with a "D." I could not read, but I was learning my ABC's.

We walked into the office. People were sitting around reading magazines. Others moaned in pain while holding swollen cheeks. Leve explained she made a dentist appointment for me. Okay, I didn't know what that meant.

She spoke to the receptionist. "We are here to see the doctor," she said.

That was the wrong word. I am anxious.

A few minutes later, guided through a door, down a long hallway, and into a procedure room. The young dentist politely introduced himself and had me to crawl into a seat that resembled a barber chair. Near, the left arm was a fountain with spinning water flowing in a circle round and round, inside a bowl, with a hole in the bottom before it went down the drain.

He explained. He was going to take care of my bad teeth. After examining my mouth, he stepped away, and was doing something at a counter across the room with his back turned toward us. Leve squeezed my arm.

When he turned around, he held a doctor's torture tool. Between an index finger and thumb was a syringe with a long needle on the end. I cringed, wanting to run away.

He says, "Saul, this is only going to sting a little, and then your tongue will feel fat, as your mouth goes numb. We're going to remove your rotten teeth today."

I say, "No. I want to go home," as I glanced up at Leve.

She says, "Saul, the rotten teeth are making you sick. They have to come out. It will only hurt for a little while."

I calmed down, and the dentist gave me the oral shots. Working to hold back the tears, when he was finished, I say, "Ouch that really smarts."

He says, "We'll give it a few minutes to completely take effect. Then we'll remove those nasty cavities."

The worst part was over. I felt no pain as he extracted six of my rotten baby teeth. When he was finished, he handed me a new toothbrush. I had no idea what kind of contraption I held in my hand, until he explained.

My first toothbrush, I'm excited, could not wait to try it out. My speech slurred when I said, "Thank you."

He says, "You're welcome. Just for the record, you have been very brave today." Then he handed me a stick of Dentyne gum. He said I could chew it in a few days after my gums healed.

Leve paid the receptionist. We stroll out of the building and head back to the bus stop for the ride home.

Earlier during the day, several black folks were in town. I said nothing when they passed by. I squeezed her hand a little tighter as we went our way into the clothing stores, where black customers were shopping.

The day's bargain hunting finished, and the dentist appointment over, we took our seats near the back of a bus heading for home. The driver shut the door behind us and started to drive off, when someone yelled from outside.

I glanced out the window. A black woman was running along the side of the moving bus. She shouted again, "Stop, please wait."

The driver braked, and opened the door. Onto the bus bounced a panting heavyset black woman with strong African features. Wide-eyed and trembling, I wanted to speak, but nothing came out as I huddled close to Leve and held tight to her coat sleeve. All I could think of was what Merl had told me in the cotton fields. I suspiciously watched her.

She dropped her token into the change collector, and then strolled toward the back of the bus under heavy labored breathing from her dash.

I thought; black people eat mean white children. They save their heads for trophies. Merl said so.

The closer she got to us, the more she smiled at me and showed her large white teeth. My heart pounded. I struggled to swallow the lump of nothing that cut off my breathing. I could no longer camouflage my fear or pretend to be invisible. Should I smile back or hide? Consumed with terror, I jumped onto Leve's lap, knocking our bags off the seat. The packages slid onto the floor in front of the woman just as she was about to pass us for the bench behind.

Grimacing, Leve asked, "What's wrong with you, Son?"

The black woman bent over and picked up our sacks without saying a word, and set them on the seat next to us. She smiled again and took her place directly behind us.

I thought, I was going to wet my pants, and continued to tremble.

Harshly, Leve asked, "Saul, what is wrong?" She turned to the black woman behind us.

"Hello," she said.

The smiling woman nodded.

"Thank you for picking up the packages," Leve said.

The woman nodded again.

Terrified, wondering why Leve was talking to her? Would she hand me over to her? Was this a set up? Jane? No! Surely, Delena would not be so cruel.

Leve frowned. "What is wrong with you? Stop it now. Sit back on your side of the seat," she said.

I was not about to move one inch. No air would pass over my vocal cords. I simply pointed at the woman behind us and faintly mumbled, "The devil's booger."

Leve scolded me, loud enough for the woman to hear. "Saul, you hush your mouth. I'll paddle you here and now. Don't call her names. You apologize this minute."

Embarrassed, Leve turned and smiled. She said, "This is my nephew, he has never been around people of color. Please forgive his ignorant behavior."

The woman nodded.

Momma told the truth. Humiliated, I wanted to crawl under the seat. Like a mouse, I squeaked, "I'm sorry."

Thank goodness. It was only my imagination causing fear to run away with itself. Jane was okay with Delena. Delena loved her. She wouldn't fatten up Jane to sell as headhunter meat. I sighed, relieved. No, headhunter savages lived in this town.

Now, what was that word, "ignorant?" What was its meaning? Does it imply I am stupid? Stupid is a bad thing to be. I will ask later.

The black woman nodded as she turned from my stares and smirked while gazing out the bus window onto the passing street. I continued to gawk. No longer afraid, I wanted to touch her, wondering if the black would rub off onto my hand.

She turned, smiling, showing all her teeth and winked. Then she went back to gazing out the window. Fascinated by her dark skin and kinky hair, I continued to ogle.

When we got home, Leve asked why I had been so rude. I explained, "Merl says nig*** folks eat bad white children."

Immediately she scolded me, she said, "Don't ever use that derogatory word again! You may use the words blacks, black people, or Negroes, but don't say nig*** ever again!"

I did not know any different, as the only word I had ever heard referring to black people was, nig***. Leve said racism was a bad thing. It was an attitude taught, a learned hate filled behavior found in all cultures. She would not tolerate it her home, as it was a form of hurtful and deadly ignorance.

I understood.

She laughed and told me the truth. She informed me, what Merl had spoken was not so. Then she added, she did not think I was a bad boy, just lacking in social skills.

From that day on my perception of those different from me was that they were not necessarily too be feared. I was instructed to engage with them no differently than the way I would want to be treated. Leve said tolerance was a golden thing, and diversity was good. She said, "I wish every racist would change color to that of those they hate, for just one day. That might change some attitudes if they had to endure what they dished out."

It was a good thing; she addressed my misconceptions and fear of black people. Within a little while, the first children of color arrived at our all-white school. Desegregation laws were being implemented nationwide.

The next morning six one-dollar bills are under my pillow. The tooth fairy had exchanged them for my rotten teeth during the night, while I slept. Leve said so.

Reminding me every morning before I headed out the door for school, she said, "Don't be rude, today."

He Wouldn't Be Back

Mrs. Jones' light brown pageboy hairstyle, streaked with strands of gray. She was stern, getting frustrated as I had a hard time comprehending the simple lessons. She assigned Alvin, the smartest boy in class, as my pal, from the first day of school.

We played together at recess during those first few weeks. He is the greatest support a child could have after separation from a close sibling. While we sat on the teeter-totter one day, right before Easter break, he spoke about God's plan of salvation. He explains in a way I can understand.

On Good Friday, his father came to the classroom, taking him out of school an hour early. Alvin and his family were traveling to Kansas for the holiday to visit relatives. While gone, his father would try out for a pastor' job with a Church of Christ, there. If accepted, Alvin would not be back. The family will move to Kansas if he gets the job.

I returned to school after the break, looking forward to hearing about Alvin's trip. His desk was empty. When classes dismissed that afternoon, I asked Mrs. Jones if Alvin was sick, and if he would be coming to school soon.

She sat me down beside her desk. Somberly, with watering eyes she revealed Alvin was in Heaven. He would not be back. His entire family, killed in a horrible car wreck before they ever got to Kansas. The accident happened the day his dad picked him up from school.

Alvin was with my grandmother Anne, and Buddy. I am sad. Knowing he was with Jesus made the tragic reality a little easier to digest.

Alvin was a Christian, and a friend. He accepted me with all my flaws and shortcomings. The winter and spring of 1963 had filled my heart with great sorrow because of the loss of my sister Jane, and only friend Alvin.

Every evening when I got home from school Leve held me on her lap and read aloud from a book she purchased at a junk sale. I cried a lot those first few months. Eventually, I got interested in the story. The sadness slowly subsided. Leve's reassurance created feelings of safety and love for the first time in a long time.

I experienced these emotions before, when we lived with Delena and Saul. Again, I felt it after the traumatic automobile accident, involving the 57 Bel Air, when Momma held me. I felt most safe when the angel appeared. These were highlights of extreme moments of emotions and incidents burned into my memory. The peace during these events never seemed to last for long. Maybe this time joy would remain.

"Benjamin Bea," a first grade reading book, about a little boy, a dog, and his new friends in a new town. The boy in the story was kind of like me. Leve taught me how to read from the book.

She showered my life with affection. She fed me as though I were a fating hog to try putting some weight on my thirty-five-pound skeleton. The first six months after Jane was gone was a period of mother and son bonding between us. I was learning to trust again because of her kindness and attention. Her unconditional love softened my hardened heart. She helped me to believe that I was not a bad kid. She taught me how to express human kindness and love again. Her love took away part of my fears and insecurities as time went on.

Bonding with Jake would come later. Growing close to him would be more difficult.

Kiss Me

Pretty Barbara Love was a girl in my class. I had a crush from the start, finding my first childhood sweetheart. It was love at first sight. She took a shine to me after the first month when I began sharing graham crackers with her during milk break every morning.

Barb wore her long medium-brown hair in long pigtail braids, just as Vicky had back in Wisconsin. Barb was sweeter, and courteous, unlike Vicky.

We sat beside one another at every opportunity. She helped a lot with my schoolwork, and threatened to sock the other boys who picked on me if they did not shut up. She was the most beautiful girl in class. The other boys were jealous as I had her devoted attentions. They teased me about having a girlfriend. That sort of deviling I didn't mind.

Barb seemed grownup, because she wore makeup and a little lipstick. Other girls' parents did not allow them to wear makeup in public. Barb's peers were a bit jealous because she could put on the big girl stuff; as a result, they refused to play with her.

One religious girl, Sally, wore long blond hair and lengthy dresses. She hurt Barb's feelings during a confrontation at recess. No one wanted to be around Sally either. She was dogmatic, and hateful. A razor had never touched Sally's head.

Scowling, she said, "My momma says any girl who cuts her hair and wears makeup is a Jezebel. Barbara Love, you're goin' to Hell!"

Barb cried.

I whispered to Barb, "Pay her no mind, she is a chicken dookie." Then I stuck my tongue out at Sally, and flapped my hands over my ears, I shout, "Oh, yeah. And your momma is a stupid chicken poop, just like you."

Barb stopped crying, and giggled. Wiping her eyes, she smeared the makeup on her face. We went back to laughing, playing on the merry-go-round.

Sally ran for the teacher. I looked at Barb, frowning. "Sally is a tattletale," I said, pointing at Mrs. Jones stomping toward us.

Punishment came for my words. There would be no recess for me the next day.

I liked her makeup, she reminded me of the ballerina that spun round and round on Leve's music box. Streaked after crying, her beauty aids resembled more, a Halloween mask. I was not about to tell her that. Inside, Barb washes the smeared makeup off her face.

Barb lived only two blocks up the street from my house. We visited frequently. She allowed me to carry her books home every day as we walked. After school on a particular Thursday afternoon in the spring of 1963, we hurried through our studies then ran out to play chase, skip rope, and catch with a soccer ball. When Leve called us in to have dinner, we ate quickly and carried our cookies and milk outside.

A few days earlier, Jake brought home a huge refrigerator box. It was mine to do with as I pleased. He worked at a trucking line, loading freight onto big semi-trucks. That's, where he got the box. It was in the back yard, and I furnished old sofa cushions inside to make seats. I also stole one of Leve's candles for stormy weather, and placed it in a coffee can for light

The sun was just going down as we crawled into the box. We lit the candle, ate our cookies, and drank our milk. Then we held hands. Barb told me she loved me.

No girl had ever told me that before, other than Momma and my aunts. I had a funny feeling inside. A great feeling, I did not fully understand.

"Kiss me." Barb said, closed her eyes, and she pouched out her lips.

I turned ten shades of red and mumbled, "I don't know how to kiss like that, on the lips." That was the way Momma and Daddy, and then Merl and Momma kissed.

She grabbed me, and put her arms around my neck. She kissed me on the cheek. "I'll teach you," she said.

Indeed she did. She kissed me on the lips, again, and again. I really liked that. She giggled and pointed. "Sorry Saul, my lipstick got all over your face," she said, and tried to wipe it off with her bare hands.

Barb's mother was calling from down the street for her to come home. I did not want her to go. I asked her to stay a little longer. I planned to walk her home shortly after dark with Jake's big flashlight. We blew out the candle and crawled out of the box.

Leve and Barb's mom were visiting in the yard. Barb ran and hugged her mother. "Momma, I want to stay the night with Saul."

Her mother and Leve began laughing. Barb's mom, a short skinny, woman with cropped and straight light-brown hair struggled to hold back her laughter as she stared at my face covered in smeared lipstick. "No honey, you have to go to school tomorrow."

Barb said, "Can I stay with him tomorrow night? We have such fun together, and I love Saul."

The two women were smirking. "No honey, not tomorrow! Stop asking," Mrs. Love said.

Barb frowned, almost in tears, she whined and asked, "But why, Mom? You just gotta let us. Can Saul come spend the night with me?"

Barb's mother and Leve began laughing hysterically. Barb took to crying. I was starting to feel quite embarrassed. Why was Barb making such a fuss?

Divorced Mrs. Love already said no. Why was she insisting on staying over? We couldn't play all night. I had spent the night with my cousins but had never had a guest of my own in our house. Why was she so intent on staying with me?

My childhood was not normal. Deprived, of the usual experiences children had with friends. I did not want her to spend the night now. She was acting like a baby.

I say, "Stop crying, Barb. Your momma says, no."

She ignored me.

"Please, Mom, please?" Barb shrieked.

Barb's mother worked hard to muster a straight face as she placed her hands on her hips. "Honey, little girls and little boys don't spend the night together. Only married people do that."

Barb latched hold of my hand. She dragged me ten feet to stand directly in front of Mrs. Love. "Then let's go to the marrying place," she said. Barb was determined to get her way.

Leve and Mrs. Love giggled as Leve strolled over and grasped my hand. She led me toward the front door.

"You have a nice evening, Mrs. Love," she said, as she glanced down at me again and tried to hold back her laughter.

Mrs. Love held Barb's hand in an unbreakable grip while trying to lead the resisting, screaming, and crying Barb. Barb pulled the opposite direction, as Mrs. Love was dragging her homeward. Barb wailed uncontrollably as though some great love had died.

The next morning, Leve sat down beside me at breakfast after Jake was gone to work. She spoke about the-birds-and-the-bees. She informed me of the details concerning the facts of life.

I was appalled. This was disgusting. I did not want to hear all that pee-pee, whoo-whoo stuff. Not any wonder, Barb's mom did not want us to stay the night together.

I had seen Jane raped repeatedly, and I was molested. I didn't understand that was sex when it happened. I had just thought Merl was being mean, and hurting us. The reality of what had happened to Jane and I hit home hard. Wanting to vomit, I pushed my plate back.

I thought Jane was going to have a baby by Merl. I could not tell Leve. Merl would find us and kill us if I told. Jane was too small to have a big belly and give birth to a baby. Would I have a baby? I was too embarrassed to ask, and if I mention the ghost from our past, Merl would kill her, all of us.

Frowning, I asked, "Do they always have a baby?"

"No. Honey, only when the blood is present, is the miracle of life possible. It starts when the girls are teenagers. Boys don't have the blood," she said.

I was relieved to hear the word teenager. Jane wasn't pregnant. I couldn't get pregnant. Yes, I am calming.

Smiling, she said, "It's okay for you to kiss a girl, but don't play with her whoo-whoo."

I felt dirty. I wanted to hide. I felt almost as filthy as after Merl hurt us because of the memories that flooded my young mind. I kept our secrets, and the haunting emotions under control.

Barbara and I had not thought about her whoo-whoo, or my pee-pee. Why did adults have to make everything so complicated and dirty?

Barb's mom told her about the-birds-and-the-bees the same morning, and it was just as disgusting for her. We discussed what we had learned one afternoon when I took fig bars and a bouquet of Iris blooms to her house. I was courting her. I guess, I was in love, but we didn't kiss much after that, and she quit wearing the makeup to school. We certainly had no interest in each other's forbidden zones.

Barb and her mother moved to Colorado the next summer. She liked me when I needed a friend most in my life. She too was there for me when Jane, was taken away.

Paul E. Treadwell

Commit to Memory

By the time school was out for summer break, I had been in numerous fights with peers. Teacher Jones thought I was a troublemaker. As a punishment, she did not allow me out of the classroom during recess the last two weeks of final semester. She did not want to break up any more fights. She was also genuinely concerned for my health, as the respiratory problems worsened. I was sickly and small, but never backed down from a fight, despite the fact I was sure to be whipped. Failing second, held back for the year I would remain to repeat the class again starting in the fall.

When I heard Jane didn't passed first grade, I was elated. Didn't want her in the same class as myself the next school year. I was older and needed to be a grade above her. It was a pride thing.

My health improved during summer. One week after school dismissed, Jake's doctor admitted me into the hospital. Dr. Credit told Leve my lungs scarred badly from all the previous untreated infections, and exposures to Tuberculosis. He said, some how my immune system had encapsulated the virus rendering it inactive, but my tonsils were the most inflamed he had ever seen on any patient. If they did not come out, I would be in a wheelchair by the time I was twenty-one, and probably dead by age thirty. Leve agreed to the surgery.

Dr. Credit, found the enlarged tonsils had displaced other glands in my neck. He did some corrective surgery stitching glands into their proper locations after removing the tonsils. The procedure took much longer than anyone expected. Under anesthesia, I stopped breathing. The operating team worked frantically to energize my lungs in those few critical moments.

Leve immediately fell to her knees, right there in the waiting room. She said she cried out to the Lord to intervene. Later she told me, it was right then I resumed breathing. I remained in the hospital an additional five days.

Though my lungs did not drain properly because of the scar tissue, my health continued to improve during the remainder of the summer. Therapy was for me to run and play, forcing my lungs to work harder. With the added impact of pills to boost my immune system, health wise, I was gaining ground. Following doctors' orders, I slowly regained my health. I grew one full inch and gained fifteen pounds. I was still skinny, but felt better than in the past few years.

Summer brought lessons not related to academics. I learned a myriad of tough survival skills from my rough new childhood friends on our poor side of the tracks in Amarillo. They looked out for me, when around. When they were not there, I had a few encounters with neighborhood bullies on my own, and soon committed to memory--run as hard and as fast as I could from the bigger, stronger ones. The running, helped to clear my lungs of thick mucous. Besides, I grew tired of getting, beaten up.

Leve and Jake were thankful to have me in their lives. They were a great comfort for me as well. Their support and love helped to build self-assurance and confidence. I was grateful to have a good home, plenty of food, and wanted by those around me. Even though I missed Jane, life was good.

Over the next several months, I was slowly making friends and getting along with most of my peers. Realizing by the end of summer, acceptance was a grand thing.

Bonding with Jake, and Leve, could not replace my love for Momma and Daddy. I longed for them occasionally, though the pain of losing my parents was not as severe as it had been when we arrived in Amarillo. The boundaries of my heart grew. There was a fond place for Jake and Leve as well as Momma and Daddy. Still, I had not completely overcome my fear of abandonment, but it was not all consuming any more.

New friends helped to make the adjustment period easier, especially the family living next door. Darla was a year older than me, and a tomboy. Her older brothers, Chester, fourteen, and Harry, sixteen, became my closest companions in the neighborhood as they took me under their wings. They were like older siblings. Without their help and protection, I would never have made the adjustment so quickly.

No Charity for Hobos

Summer break at end, hot, dog days of mid-August were upon us. The neighborhood children and I were exploring the edge of our community at a place called Wild Horse Lake. It was a lake, but it was not at the same time, no more than a low place in the surrounding terrain. This small isolated span of wilderness only held water during the rainy seasons. It was much like a massive pond without water. During late summer, the lake dried up. The bottom was covered in green Johnson grass, and drying tumbleweeds.

Train tracks ran along one side of the lake. Half-a-mile away hobos camped out under Route 66 Bridge that crossed high above, over the tracks. They found shelter there while waiting to catch a free ride on a slowing freight. On occasions the bums wondered into our neighborhood knocking door to door. They begged for food. Sternly instructed, not to give them handouts, as they would tell other homeless vagabonds, and they too would come knocking.

I was not obedient. Remembering the days when I begged, while trying to survive when we worked the Denton Island cotton plantation, I handed a sandwich out the door, now and then. The generosity happened only when Leve and Jake were out of the house. They caught me one day. I was feeding a scruffy, graying, black hobo standing at our back door. They glared at me, but said nothing until the man was gone.

Warned again of the dangers, this time the example stories of folks, being robbed, beaten up, and murdered by wandering fugitives, had a hardening impact. I decided, absolutely no more charity.

Jake did not forbid me from playing around the lakebed. Rather he insisted I use caution, and never speak to the hobos if they happened by. The main restriction, I am not allowed to be there alone. From then on, I am, accompanied by a companion except for one occasion.

Jake said Wild Horse Lake was where the settlers and cowboys established the town of Amarillo. Heavy rains flooded and submerged the buildings. The town folks moved the settlement to surrounding higher ground.

Once she was a great lake that never went dry. Her waters were a major resource for herds of wild horses, and native creatures including buffalo. Indians, settlers, and wild-west wagon trains refreshed themselves in the life-giving waters from the oasis.

The lake was drying up now, because of modern progress. During springtime rains, the small remains of a once large sanctuary filled to the tracks. Eight feet deep in the middle, but the water evaporated during summer. Her wilderness glory was gone, but for a few short weeks, the lake let our community know she had not forgotten her days of untamed splendor.

We fantasized, pretending to be cowboys while riding our stick-horses at the lake's edge. We roped wild mustangs, shooting outlaws, and hunting buffalo as I played with new friends. The older kids laughed at us. We younger ones were having great fun.

September rolled around, and we had a few rain showers, after returning to school for the new semester. One last time on a Saturday afternoon in 1963, we returned to Wild Horse Lake. The neighborhood children gathered there after school. Johnson grass and other weeds had grown way over our heads since the last rain. On the drying lake bottom slithered hundreds of baby snakes.

About fifteen children were with me that day. We ranged in age from eight to fifteen years, and I was the youngest. Running home, we collected one-gallon lard buckets with lids, and dashed back to catch serpents.

Why were we doing this? What was I going to do with a bucket full of snakes? I did not know. Following the lead of the older children seemed like a fun thing to do. They were beside themselves with excitement.

I had to show no fear to fit in with the bigger kids. This was peer pressure. I snatched up six brown wiggling little demons, about as big around as a pencil, and approximately eight inches long. Tossing them into the pail, I ran to collect more.

I spied a grand snake; he was eighteen inches long, and as big around as a quarter for most of its body length. The head was the size of a fifty-cent piece. Without fear, too ignorant to know the possible consequences of what I was handling. I was thinking these were harmless water snakes as the teen boys had said. I believed only poison serpents existed in Arkansas country settings. As far as I knew, no venomous snakes lived in Texas cities. Without reserve of a possible bite, I grabbed it, held the fleeing devil by the tail, and quickly flung it into the bucket, headfirst. Then I slapped the lid on tight.

I was proud; I had caught the largest viper of all. The older kids were going to keep their slithering reptiles and use them in science projects at school that fall. I will keep mine as pets.

Back home, I took Leve's number-two washtub out of the storage shed, and filled it with water. Since my new pets were water snakes, I would give them a place to swim while they were in my care.

Once the tub was full, I opened the lid and dumped them. The largest reptile swam to the edge of the tub. He was striking at the bucket. It slithered out onto the ground and began to chase me around the yard. It was within three feet of my bare feet when I noticed a piece of plank lying under a window on the ground next to the house. I grabbed the board as I ran past and slammed it flat over the snake's back about three inches behind its head.

The wiggling monster fought to free itself, but I held the slat fast. I was safe for the time being, but could not let go. The viper repeatedly shot venom on the surface of the board as its fangs extended, embedding into the wood.

I reasoned this was not a harmless water snake as the boys had said. I didn't know what kind it was, but it definitely was not harmless.

The angry beast struggled violently to break free. Surely, I am going to have a bite wound to contend with, if I release the binding pressure. Just then, dark-haired, pimpled, sixteen-year-old Harry, one of my protectors was walking home after football practice. He sees me in the yard, and asked what I was doing.

"This chicken dookie snake is trying to bite me," I yelled.

He ran to his house next door and brought back a large fruit jar with a lid, a rag, and a small can of Ether.

"Don't let go," he said as he set the jar on the ground, folded the rag, and applied ether onto the cloth.

The smell reminded me of the time I stayed in the hospital. It was not pleasant. I could not walk away, but I wanted to run.

Harry dashed about searching for another smaller slat from behind our storage shed and placed the end of it at the back of the striking serpent's head. Then he laid the rag over the viper's face and sprayed more ether. Soon, the reptile stopped violently thrashing about.

I did not know if it was dead or asleep. I did not care, as long as it could not bite or come after me again. Harry proudly grinned, dropped the limp creature into the fruit jar, and screwed on the lid.

My heart pounding fearfully, I sighed. Relieved that was over, my voice quivering, as I said, "Thanks, Harry."

He had saved my life. He held the glass jar up into the light, and patted me on the back.

"Did it bite you?" he asked.

Still panting from exhaustion, I said, "No, thanks to you," and hugged him.

He winced and stepped way from me.

"Well, I'm glad you're all right. Stop hugging me. What if someone, sees? They'll think we are queers."

I remembered Chad using that word when those two men were kissing in the lunatic asylum. Does that mean crazy? No, it was something else. Kissing and hugging, maybe?

Embarrassed, eyes downcast, as I realized the meaning, I said, "Sorry, I didn't know."

He smiled while admiring the paralyzed snake.

"Well, you do now. Glad you aren't hurt. Can I keep him?" he asked.

I nodded.

He ruffled my hair, turned, and walked across the yard to his house. I decided, right-then-and-there, I did not want any more vipers for pets.

Thinking about what Harry said, I wondered if I was a queer. Merl touched me but I didn't want him to. No, I was not a queer. I did not want to. Chicken thief Merl was a hog sh** queer.

He and Momma were the crazy ones, more so than Daddy. They should have been the nuts locked-up, they were like those I happened to see at the lunatic asylum. Not my daddy! Fanny and Ely needed to be locked-up, too. They were all nuts. Daddy said the whole world was a chicken dookie. I decided he was wrong, not everyone. Though the majority in the world were crazy, especially the adults. Leve was the exception.

Angrily, I shook my head to toss the bad memories out and focused on getting rid of the other serpents. Considering the possibility, maybe these babies would grow up to be mean too.

Cautiously snatching the vipers up, one-by-one by the tail, I flung them, out of the water into the pail. All accounted for, and the lid on tight, I trotted as fast as I could to Wild Horse Lake where I dumped them onto the dry lakebed, a good riddance. They slithered off into the weeds.

Relieved to be free of possible death I strolled up the street. My way home, I crossed paths with a stray. There she was, an adorable little black puppy. She was sitting in a clump of Johnson grass beside the paved road. She appeared lost and frightened.

When I picked her up and cradled her in my arms, she licked my face. With great gusto, her happy tail wagged. She smelled of burning wood smoke. I thought, maybe she had been in a fire and her masters were killed. She needed someone like me to take care of her. She would be a better pet than the serpents. I carried her home, and named her Skipper.

Harry took the sleeping viper out of a shoebox and scared some of the teenage girls during class. Expelled from Tascosa High school that autumn, the principal said Harry jeopardized the safety of the other children.

The science teacher identified the viper as a poisonous Cottonmouth. He killed it, and pickled the serpent in a jar of formaldehyde, placing it on displayed in the science lab. Harry could not return to classes for a week.

When Leve found out about the adventure, cold chills ran down her spine. Quoting a scripture, she said, "Acts 28:5. And he shook off the beast into the fire, and felt no harm."

I had no idea what she was talking about until she said, "God must be looking out for little children."

Enrolled, in Mrs. Black's second grade class, for the 1963-1964 terms, I was ready to get back to school. Kindhearted and stern, Mrs. Black smiled a lot, but swatted us with a ruler when we misbehaved. She was a tiny woman with graying short hair. At first, I was afraid of her.

Soon she realized I needed extra help. She took a special interest while spending extra time with me, so I could understand the work. I was struggling to learn and still behind my new classmates.

I did not know anyone in the group. Last year's classmates had moved on to third grade. Mrs. Black seated us in alphabetical order. Behind me was a husky boy with buckteeth, flat-topped hair, and a cowlick above his left eye at the hairline. Richie eventually became my best friend ever.

Wednesday, five weeks into the term we had a spelling test. I made the lowest grade in the class, spelled only two of the ten words correctly. Barely able to hold back my tears when I saw the score. Mrs. Black sent a note home with me. I gave the scribbling to Leve and began to cry.

She held me in her lap as I told her how stupid I was, and how the other kids made fun of me because I could not learn. She comforted me, and we prayed for God to help me in my schoolwork.

As Mrs. Black requested in the letter, Leve supported my studies and spelling. She willingly gave of her time and patients while I practiced. We were to have a spelling bee the coming Friday. Dreading it, I knew that once again I would be humiliated in front of my peers.

Thursday night, Leve, and I practiced spelling the words covered during the past six weeks. So anxious, I couldn't concentrate enough to spell many of them correctly. I knew how to spell them, but just could not seem to find where my brain had filed that information.

On Friday, Mrs. Black chose two team captains for the spelling bee. The captains picked who would be on their teams until the entire class divided into two groups. I was the last one chosen, as always. Embarrassed, when my turn came to go to the blackboard, I wanted to run out of the room.

My head held down, I misspelled the word. I stepped aside in humiliation to give the other team a chance. Mary, the smartest girl in class, was at the blackboard. If she misspelled it, I could have one more try. As I watched, Mary slowly chalked down the letters; a strange sensation came over me. Something was happening inside my head. My ears buzzed like a swarm of bees. I got dizzy and my vision blurred.

Then, as my sight cleared, the buzzing stopped and I heard a sound like someone quickly turning a channel knob on a radio. There were painful high-pitched squeals inside my head. The sound stopped and my eyes refocused.

The pressure inside my head seemed to have been relieved. Something wonderful had happened. It was as though someone had turned on a bright light in a dimly lit room. I could focus. Retrieving information stored somewhere inside my mind was no longer a labored chore. My nerves were calm for the first time that

I could remember since my parents split up. Peace and warmth surrounded me.

I was no longer afraid of failing, embarrassing myself. Alert and my senses were sharper than ever before. I didn't feel sick or tired anymore. Great joy now filled my heart, and just in time, too. Mary had misspelled the word.

I had another opportunity, and this time I knew the answer. I walked confidently up to the blackboard and spelled the word: "P-R-E-S-I-D-E-N-T." Mrs. Black congratulated me. I could not contain my smile. Smartest girl in our class, she met her match, outdone by the dumbest boy in the spelling bee.

My teammates began to clap along with the teacher. No words can explain the elation when my peers were cheering me on because I did something right. I won the spelling bee for my team.

The following weeks, I excelled in class work, and positively socialized with the other children without fighting. I was having fun in school. I was no longer an outcast. I no longer had the problem of not being able to learn.

God had answered Leve, and my prayers. The secure environment Leve and Jake provided for me along with proper nutrition and medical attention contributed to this miracle. Healed of the learning disability, I knew it was a touch from God.

The leaves had fallen off the trees and the lonesome winds whistled through the cracks around the windows where I sat. The mood was grey for some reason. The atmosphere was gray with heavy overcast cloud cover. There was a sense of melancholy that seemed to fill the day. Winter was on the horizon as autumn slowly was losing her temperance grip to the onslaught of coming winter cold.

My attentions focused on the multiplication test problems before me on the page. Nine times nine is eighty-one, and I wrote the answer down. Principal Hardin's startling, booming voice broke the classroom silence as he made an announcement over the public address box hanging on the wall above the teacher's desk. Speaking with a quaver, I heard him swallow the lump in his throat several times.

I surmised something was terribly wrong, the other students and I laid down our pencils and gave our undivided attention. Mr. Hardin said, "Teachers please come to my office immediately. We will be dismissing school within the next fifteen minutes. Have your students put away what they are working on and get ready to go home. I want all teachers in my office immediately."

Mrs. Black grimaced. The look of worry was on her face as she scowled, and told us to hand in our work. She placed the unfinished test papers on her desk. Smiling, she said, "Gather your things. Shortly, school will be, dismissed. I'm going to the office for a few minutes. You may quietly visit, but whisper. Do not be roaming around the room. Stay in your seats." She raced out.

When she returned, Mrs. Black was crying. She wiped her eyes with a tissue she drew from the box at the edge of her desk and sat. She said, "Quiet down children. I have something very important to tell you."

At first a hush, then a few sniffles as we watched our teacher crying. Stern Mrs. Black's sorrow infected us all. Her tears saddened me as much as, Momma's, and I wept. She got fired? We were too loud? Why is school dismissing this early? What did she have to say? I sighed and waited for her to explain, while choking back my tears.

Making every effort not to breakdown again, grimacing, she said, "The flag in front of school has been lowered to half-mast. Our President, shot in Dallas. It is not known if he will survive."

We heard wailing drifting up the hallway as other teachers told their students. My classmates began with a soft moan, then weeping flooded our presence. Mrs. Black said, "Children let us bow our heads for a moment of prayer."

Great sadness engulfed my entire being. I did not know this man. However, I knew he was the most important person in America, maybe the world. He was kind of like a daddy for the adults, a king of sorts. He was as important to them as Uncle Jake was to me.

In a sense, this President man was like a father in that his decisions influenced us all. Once again, I could not contain my sorrow, and wept.

Mr. Hardin added to our bereavement when he announced that President John F. Kennedy had just died in Dallas. At his grief stricken words the dam burst and unrestrained loud crying, yowls, and howls broke loose. Students and staff at Summit Elementary, along with the nation grieved the loss of our President.

I thought; he was with Alvin. Maybe he was. The bad man who assassinated him will burn for eternity in a lake of fire. Leve said murders go to Hell.

Jake Stay Sober

Soon known, I am the spoiled rich kid on the poor side of town, because I had lots of toys and games. My personality changed from the totally, frightened insecure little boy to bossy and independent. Although, the fear of being cast away again, lingered always in the back of my mind. By the 1964, second semester, I was making the highest grades of all my classmates.

Our first Amarillo summer, Leve and Jake enrolled me in the local community center where I learned to swim and play ball. Delena and Ricky also enrolled Jane in the summer swimming program and we spent Saturdays together. Jane was changing too and I hardly knew her anymore.

The summer of 1963, Ricky and Delena drove to Loafer's Glory and insisted that Daddy sign adoption papers. Reluctantly he signed, but he was adamant about not allowing Bobby or me adopted by anyone. His reasoning being that Jane's name would change someday anyway after she married.

Momma did not show up for court. She had no say. The judge discontinued all of Momma's parental rights to any of us. That did not matter. She never attempted to contact us after she abandoned us. The day she ran off and left us in the care of, the Judas witch, Bertha, burned into my memory as a day of betrayal.

Enthusiastic, Delena and Ricky legally adopted Jane. When they returned, they bought a house five miles across town and moved. We saw less and less of each other. Jane was becoming bossy and independent as well.

She was jealous of the new toys I had, that Delena and Ricky could not afford to buy for her. Ricky was becoming a sloppy lush and spent most of his extra cash on booze. They barely scrimped by.

Jake commenced drinking beer on weekends, and his alcoholism worsened. Jake's addiction had not progressed to the sloppy point of Ricky's daily drunkenness. Nevertheless, dealing with his addiction was no amusement park.

Delena had chosen the wrong man again. After a few more months, I no longer enjoyed our visits because Rick was drunk, and they had so little. I felt guilty because my situation was better.

Taking on Delena's domineering, brazen personality, Jane was like a stranger to me. Eventually, our visits were only on special occasions such as birthday parties and at Christmas. My new friends were becoming more important, and I felt a little guilty that my loyalties toward Jane were slipping away. The fact was at the age of nine, guy-friends were more fun to play with.

Knowing Jane was safe with Delena gave me solace, and I did not have to worry about her welfare anymore, other than when Ricky lost his jobs. Though he was an alcoholic, Jane was the apple of his eye, and she loved him.

Within two years of our arrival in Amarillo, we had accomplished much. I was becoming a normal little boy, and making excellent grades in school. I was well adjusted, and I had many new friends including black schoolmates and playmates. The gains in Jane's life were no less than, mine.

My new personal experiences nullified Merl's past intimidations, and his falsehoods. The implications and lies he used to muster fear within us that he might have total control and domination over our young lives no longer had a hold on me. I found the blacks' color did not rub off. They were neither cannibals, nor the devil's boogers. Some were now my friends. They were no different from me, other than their culture and dark skin. They had the same human feelings and inquisitive fascinations with our differences as I had held. Younger black children at our first meetings checked to see if my lighter skin color would rub off too. Their reactions were just as I discovered when we first met in the 1963-1964 school year.

Life was good with Jake and Leve most of the time. I was happy there, except for weekends after the first year when Jake drank too much beer. He got mean. However, he never hurt me physically.

I was afraid of him, and I abhorred him when he was drunk. During the first few turbulent years of my life, most of the male role models were either, hateful, violent, controlling, perverts, drunkards, wife beaters, crazy, or religious nuts. Now Jake was turning out to be a great disappointment too.

The women in my life up to that point were insecure, domineering, harshly spoken, fearful, undereducated manipulators, conniving, selfish, jealous, self-righteous. Some were greedy man haters in that they wanted a man's support and security, but they also wanted to rule-the-roost. They were bitter. The men in their young lives had hurt them. Momma's betrayal and abandonment of Jane, Bobby, and me had saddened my heart more than all the others put together. I had worshiped Momma. There was no greater loss in this son's life than to lose the love of my mother.

All the women and men had character flaws to the extreme in my eyes, all but kindhearted Leve. In her, I found stability and balance. She was different. She was not emotionally weak. She loved me. She loved Jake, and I believed in her. She had never broken my trust.

Though undereducated, Leve was an intelligent woman with lots of horse sense. She was a strong willed person, but not belligerent or domineering. I loved her. She was my momma now, my strongest source of emotional security. I guess that I was her momma's boy. More than that, she was my most trusted friend. I was grateful that Jake provided for us a comfortable existence most of the time, but I despised his alcoholism.

When Jake got on a ripsnorter, Skipper and I hid under the bed. If his drunken escapades lasted for long, I would get permission from Leve to let me spend the nights with my best friend Richie and his family. They lived up the street, about half-a-block away.

Sometimes Leve and I camped out in the storage shed to get away from Jake's weekend drunken verbal abuse and brawling. Leve created a game. She formulated a psychological positive activity for our hiding out when we ran from him. We called it our camping trips.

Why did she stay with him? Love, she believed God would change him one day. He was a good man, but alcohol was his demon. She did her best to help me feel safe in the midst of his intoxicated confusion. Protecting me was her priority.

Not until the late spring of 1964 did I actually realize how bad the situation was, especially for Leve. The bruising on her arms and legs caused me to resent Jake when he was toasted.

I could not protect her, but I wanted to. I slowly began to lose all respect for him. His drinking escalated. He lost his job the summer of '64 for showing up drunk on a Monday morning. I began to fear for Leve, as the domestic violence became a daily occurrence.

Leve didn't use alcohol and he wanted her to be his drinking buddy. She refused. Instead, she became his unwilling punching bag while he mocked her faith. During his drunken rages, he cursed Grandmother Anne's Christian testimony.

When school was out, Leve was determined to make some changes for us. She knew if she did not, she would succumb. She believed it was the devil using Jake to try to force her into hitting the hooch again. Sober for five years when I came to live with them, she was a licensed Full Gospel minister.

Jake certainly hated her reverse attitude against sin and the booze. After all, he had met her in a bar having a beer nearly twenty years before. He wanted her to drink with him again.

This, Jesus to whom she had rededicated her life was boring for Jake. Leve decided, we could not continue to live this way. For me, other than the alcoholism, this life was heaven compared to the way Jane and I survived when Merl Judas was in the picture.

Despite Jake's intemperance, I was better off. For the first time I had a little self-confidence, and a sense of dignity. I didn't walk in constant fear for my survival. I had meaningful relationships and my own friends. I was able to go to school, enjoyed learning and excelled.

The thought of Leve making changes was okay as long as I did not lose another home, or forced to live with another family. I loved them both deeply. I prayed their problems would be resolved.

Although Jake's intemperance was the big problem, I avoid him when he was drunk. He was a good-guy when sober. I did not want thrown away again. I wanted Jake to be my daddy. If only, he would stay sober.

Portals of Heaven

Grandmother Anne's spiritual guidance and godly testimony had greatly influenced Leve and Delena during their youth. Drawn by the Holy Spirit they accepted Christ as their personal savior in their early teens.

After walking in rebellion and backsliding, drinking and sowing their wild oats for several years as young adults, the sisters had rededicated their lives to the Lord. By 1964, they had thrown out the oppressive clothesline holiness doctrines. They wore pants, makeup, and cropped their hair. They said the Lord was the same for all. It did not matter what style of clothes one wore, as long as it was decent.

In the spring of 1964, they were stylish for the times, as best our incomes provided. Some of the more mainstream holiness religious folks called them backsliding Pentecostal Baptist Jezebels, labeled like Momma, back in Loafer's Glory.

The seeds of faith had fallen on good soil, taking roots inside their hearts. They could not get completely away from Anne's raising. Their experiences of salvation were intact. They were of Pentecostal persuasion in their beliefs.

My uncles were sloppy lushes, sometimes violent. This made for serious marital problems, much as Anne experienced with Grandfather Isaiah. Enduring busted lips and blackened eyes after beatings from their drunkard husbands made their Christian walk a struggle.

Financial stress due to the loss of jobs for both men cursed our lives and cupboards now and then, but it was more of a problem in Jane's home than mine was. Constant turmoil in their relationships eventually would cause both my aunts to backslide in their walk with the Lord again. However, on this day in June of 1964 they were on fire for God, and full of the Holy Ghost.

Ricky and Jake were good to us children when they were not drinking, but they could be quite abusive to all of us when drunk. They never beat Jane or me. However, the verbal, mental and emotional alcohol-induced abuse was horrific at times.

That spring, Jake went on a drinking binge that lasted three months. During one of his drunken stupors, he humiliated us by standing in our yard and screaming obscenities at the neighbors.

Holding a can of beer in one hand, giving the neighbors the BIRD with the other, and wearing only the scowl on his face, he stepped off the front porch. Exposing the pride of his full-blown glory in family jewels and ignorance, he bellowed at the neighborhood.

"I know all you bastard SOBs thinks you're better than me. I have survived more than you can imagine, protecting your sorry ass in the battles at Okinawa and Guadalcanal. The blood of my buddies running under my feet on the ship deck," he shouted.

He continued his drunken sermon. Jake says, "Ugly American Yanks should have let the slant-eyed Jap's keep the damn place."

His violent aggressive shouting went on until late into the night. Leve pleaded with him to hush and not disturb the neighbors as she carried a clean pair of boxer shorts out into the yard and insisted that he put them on. He slapped her, but she wouldn't back down.

She demanded, "Now Jake, the neighbors aren't interested in your feelings or your butt. Stop making a fool of yourself and put these on. Everybody is going to think you're a crazy pervert if you do not stop this yelling and cover yourself," she says.

Hatefully, he snatched the shorts out of her hand, and bent over to put them on just as a carload of teenaged boys drove by honking. Their heads stuck out the windows laughing. Yanking his drawers up, he turned around and gave them the BIRD as they passed the house.

Embarrassed, Leve convinced him to come inside. Once indoors, his anger turned on her and he continued yelling while punching her around in the bedroom.

I stuck my head in the doorway and yelled at him through my tears, "Leave her alone," I screamed.

He staggered after me into the kitchen, pulling a butcher knife off the wall while backing me into a corner where I hunkered down on the floor crying. When he turned on me, Leve pulled herself off the bedroom floor. Leaving a pool of blood behind on the worn linoleum, she leapt to her feet, grabbed a lamp by the bed, and ran shrieking into the kitchen.

Her face wrenched in anger, she whacked Jake good over the back of his bald-noggin'. "You won't hurt my boy," she yelled.

She pounded Jake with one calculated blow after another to the back of his head and shoulders. His scalp bleeding, he dropped the knife to the floor, laughing in his addled state as we escaped out of the house at two a.m.

We locked ourselves inside the storage shed for the remainder of the night. This was the only time he became physically violent toward me. He had not touched me. He just enjoyed the terror on my face.

Inside the shed, Leve prayed, whispering to God all night, while sitting up in a lawn chair and reading her Bible by flashlight. I napped on a tarp in the floor.

Alone, Jake continued his brawling inside the house, until four a.m. Our neighbors were used to his weekend exhibitions and drunken scenes. This one had lasted a little longer. It seemed not to faze them, other than a couple of chuckles and the slamming of doors, closing windows, shades, and then pulling drapes so they could not see or hear him. Jake's antics were no worse than other neighbor's escapades in our rough community on the poor side of the railroad track.

The next morning, out of fear and disgust, Leve decided to leave him for a time. We crept quietly back into the house so not to awaken him. Jake still passed out, naked in the kitchen floor, surrounded by empty beer bottles, blood dried on his hands, and head.

Leve's face is swollen and bruised from the night before. We hurriedly, quietly dressed in clean clothing, and packed a few things. That warm Saturday morning during the first week of summer break, Leve walked with me to the local bus stop, suitcases in our hands.

We boarded the city bus and rode the five miles across town to Delena and Ricky's place. Neither of us spoke. We huddled close together on the bus. The other passengers stared at Leve's bruised arms and legs, swollen busted lips, and blacked eyes. She tried to hide her face behind a newspaper. I glared back at them. They quickly turned away.

Ricky had sobered enough to go to work. He was not there when we arrived midmorning. I had not seen Jane in six weeks. Painfully aware of the growing differences in each other, we went into the backyard to play.

Jane wore blue khaki, baby doll shorts. Delena had made them from the pant leg material of Ricky's worn-out work uniform. She also had on a pale-blue second-hand tee shirt, purchased from the local junk store. Her black-hair cut short again to the base of her head and around her face. Her olive complexion now was deep brown from hours of playing outside in the hot Texas sun.

The neighbor's seventeen-year-old son, Robbie was tall, lanky and pimpled with frogeye thick glasses. He poked fun at Jane's dark complexion. "Nig ***, nig***, nig***," he yells out their back door on may occasions when he sees her playing in the yard.

His younger sister Gina, a year older than me, was sweet. Gina secretly played with Jane when her brother wasn't around. She was too embarrassed to be seen with Jane when Robbie was at home because he called her a nig*** lover.

The strong bond of mutual survival, motivated by fear and instability that had once ripped through our lives and caused us to cling to each other was almost gone. We were not as close anymore, but I loved her.

I told Jane that Gina was not a friend if she was ashamed to be seen with her. Jane sighed. No other children her age lived close enough for playmates every day. Very protective Delena would not allow her to stray from the block.

My medium brown hair greased back like Elvis Presley's and I was proud of the new gray store-bought shorts and Beatle's tee shirt. In her presence, I felt guilty for having new clothes and she wore homemade and junk-store attire.

Inside the older flat-roofed, two-bedroom house, with gray asbestos siding on the outer walls, Leve and Delena began to pray over our home environments and about Ricky and Jake's alcohol addictions. They were also praying God would give Leve direction. She had to make decisions about how to handle our immediate situation.

Jane and I could hear them weeping as they cried out to God in prayer. Sometimes they would speak in the unknown tongues. Horribly embarrassed, I feared the neighbors would hear their wails. For me, the embarrassment of Jake yelling naked in the yard, and their loud babbling of nonsense were no different. I was ashamed of both behaviors. Daddy was right. The whole world is nothing but a bunch of crazy chicken dookies. My attitudes about the tongues were in conflict.

I thought; God, are all adults crazy!

Jane rolled her eyes and nodded. She must have had the same thought. "They're at it again, Saul. Sundee alee ho," she said to mock their loud prayer in the tongues. I didn't mind her laughter over their antics. My fascination of the tongues was no longer intense. I was indifferent, knowing everyone who spoke in tongues was not necessarily a saint to be admired. I didn't fully understand when it was genuine.

We both giggled. I patted her on the head. "You're it," I said, and took off running around the yard with Jane at my heels. It reminded me of the days when we ran naked through the house after Momma would give us our baths at the old homestead.

Passersby, walking on the street in front of the house, would shake their heads and chuckle at my aunts' loud vocalizations drifting from inside. Humiliated, Jane and I ran behind the storage shed and hid.

After about an hour of their caterwauling, Leve came to the back door and called for me to come inside. "The Lord has spoken," she says, boldly proclaiming their prayers have an answer. She smiled and motioned for me to come near.

Apprehensively, I questioned. Is this for real, or is she sick like my daddy and hallucinating?

God had answered her prayers in the past. She could tell me things that would happen months in advance. These insights came when she had been spending hours in travailing prayer at home while Jake was at work. Curious, but a little fearful too, I just did not understand those loud tongues.

She asked me to come inside again so they could pray over me. Reluctantly, I choked back my rebellion and obeyed her. When we stepped through the doorway, I asked if they were going to pray for Jane too, not wanting to face this alone.

She patted the perspiration from her brow with a lace handkerchief, as she looked down smiling. "We will pray for Jane later," she said.

We strolled into the living room. Delena was standing in the corner near a dinning room chair they set there, just for me. Delena was as shabbily dressed as Jane. She too wore blue pants. Handmade peddle pushers made out of material salvaged from Ricky's old work pants and a junk-store flowery blouse with patches sown over the sleeves near the elbows. She seemed exhausted, but sweetness radiated from her as she smiled at me.

"Aunt Delena, may I go next door and play with Gina?" Jane asked.

Delena nodded and smiled, while wiping tears from her eyes with one of Ricky's large white handkerchiefs. "Yes, if that hateful Robbie isn't home," she says.

Smirking, when she darted out the back door, Jane said, "Bye, Saul. Come and play with us when you're through."

Leve held my hand, still silently crying and smiling while leading me to the chair in the corner. The two didn't seem to go together. The tears and smiles at the same moment. I could not understand why they had to cry when they prayed.

Calmly, Leve said, "Son, I feel lead of the Lord to go spend the summer with your aunt Lou in Indiana. I just can't take another beating, or endure another night of brawling out of Jake."

I was elated. "When are we leaving?" I asked.

She raised her chin and with a lilt in her voice, she said, "Probably tomorrow."

I would get to see Alvin, Patsy, and Don, the cousins we had lived with for almost six months. My mind flooded with fond memories of the fun times we had together a few years earlier.

I was glad to be leaving Jake, behind. I had not been looking forward to cleaning up his messes at home when he decided to sober up again. Jake got the squirts when coming off the booze. He would run naked out of his bedroom, vomiting through the dinning room, and losing control of his bowels all at the same time. He left a trail of smelly, nasty stuff on the walls and floor as he rounded the corner into the bathroom.

It was always my job to help scrub the walls before we repainted after Jake's liberal spraying of the house. I did not want to think about carrying out all the rubbish and empty bottles scattered about. The house smelled of a brewery and outhouse toilet.

I was glad to move, instead of having to help Leve clean up after another long alcoholic episode and watch Jake go through the painful withdrawals again. I missed the man who was not there when Jake was drunk. I hated the drunkard. I loved the sober Jake.

Would Leve take me to Lou's house and abandon me as everyone else had? Insecurity gripped my heart. If Leve didn't abandon me in Indiana, perhaps God could fix Jake and answer Leve's prayers. That is what I secretly prayed.

I longed for Jake to stop drinking altogether, so we could be a normal family. I feared they would eventually divorce, leaving me alone again.

Leve said they were going to pray for my protection before making the long trip. Well, I knew about heavenly protection already. I didn't resist too much, but the radical way they prayed really bothered me.

I often wondered if all of these things were contagious and at what age I would begin drinking, beating women, and talking nonsense. I was not looking forward to the possibilities of how I might turn out when I was grown.

If I did, I would never act like any of them. Silent rage and loathing stirred within me as I sat in the chair. The loud praying and all the crying and speaking in tongues were weird, and I truly thought they had lost their minds. However, some reservation tugged at my heart that maybe, just maybe they knew something that I did not.

Anne had prayed in the unknown tongue, on her deathbed. Ol' ugly Fanny babbled nonsense when we lived in Wisconsin. Relatives said Momma even had the Holy Ghost and prayed in tongues at one time before she left Daddy, but I had never heard her do it.

I wanted to believe God was in this, but I had endured abundant pain and suffered many losses. Where was He then? Why did He let that happen if He loved me so much? Iniquity, the sins of our fathers, flowed in my veins. The burden of Loafer's Glory gold in my soul was heavy. My heart still filled with hardness.

I did not have much confidence in adults or their religions. I actually did believe in God at the time, but I also had a bit of doubt that He existed. I had never seen Him. I had not heard His voice. My perceptions of Him were that of an unsaved child.

Perhaps, He was like Santa Claus, for the adults. I did not believe in Santa. Bewildered and confused, I had seen the destruction of double minded "Christians" in my past, including my parent. I did not want that kind of relationship, say one thing and do another. I hoped, He was real, and I wanted to meet Him if he actually did exist.

At the same time, I questioned, how could their God have allowed all of those bad things to happen to me? I remembered many said it was a miracle when God saved me from death after the accident. I remembered how prayers, answered when He healed my mind that day in the classroom, and how He heard my whispering prayer and saved Jane and me from rabid Buddy. These things I considered miracles, and surely, God was in them. Maybe He was only around when people asked for His help. Daddy said He was a help in trouble.

Maybe Jesus did exist, but I didn't know Him. Though I knew, I had a guardian angel. The greatest question I needed an answer for was why. Why, I had lost my family if God loved me so much. If

Jesus was real, I wanted some answers. Maybe, He would speak the truth and give me some form of resolution to the painful past.

If they were nuts--I did not know. Leve had never broken my trust. She couldn't be a lunatic. I didn't know what to expect. Was Jesus real? If He was like some hateful pious folks I knew, I did not want to meet Him.

How do I know the difference between what is real and what is imagination? Tell me not one more Santa Claus story! I do not want to hear the lies, the devil's booger stories. I will not believe them.

As Leve and Delena sat me down in the chair, immediately I wanted to run out of the house as fast as I could, but I didn't. Leve and Delena had treated me better than, anyone else in my life. I decided to bear this, to please them and keep my true feelings to myself. I had experienced worse in my earlier homes, and at least they were praying to the same Jesus. Anyway, I thought they were. The same Jesus, I had prayed the day God sent an angel to protect Jane and me from Buddy's attack. Maybe theirs was the same Jesus as the one who sent the angel.

Was He a pompous God on duty only part-time? Like the part-time Christians, I knew. Would I meet Him?

Okay, I am vacillating. Did I believe or not? I did, and I did not. Religion was confusing.

Leve and Delena lay their hands upon my head and began to pray loudly. They called upon the name of Jesus. Hot tears streamed down their faces as they spoke in an unknown tongue. Their prayer of protection turned into praise and worship unto the Lord as they lifted their hands toward heaven. As they prayed, they got louder.

I began to cry. Fight as I did, I could not hold back my tears. This was not in my plan. This was not supposed to happen. I wanted them to get their filthy hands off me. Now, I was angry. They were lunatics.

I thought about kicking them and running out of the room. I did not think I could subdue my tearful volcanic emotions, my crying, or my anger. My sobbing became uncontrollable. The more I resisted the harder I wept.

Then a sweet presence filled the room. I felt that someone powerful and important had entered the house. I could not see Him, but I knew someone was standing right behind me. Was He my guardian angel?

This was the same presence, I had sensed for a few moments the day Anne prayed for me before she died. That unexplained peace, I experienced during the accident when Momma ran the car over my leg. The same peace, I sensed the day I met my guardian angel. This was a personal, separate kind of peace, so many times in the past when I was in great danger or trouble. Here it was again all around me.

Leve stopped praying and lifted my hands toward heaven. Then she said, "Son, Jesus is here now. He wants to save your soul today. He is waiting for you to invite Him to come live inside your heart. Lift your hands toward heaven, and praise Him. Tell Him that you love Him. Ask Him to forgive all of your sins and come into your heart to be Lord of your life."

I turned to look behind me. No one was there that I could see. How could He get inside my heart? Then I remembered Alvin who was now in heaven and our conversation on the teeter-totter. What I was experiencing at this moment was not like anything I had imagined back then.

Alvin said, "God is a Spirit." I knew someone was in the house. I could feel His presence. Smiling kindly, Leve said, "Son, the Spirit of God is here. He wants you to know how much He loves you."

God is a Spirit! Was that why they called Him, Holy Ghost? I nodded while feeling peace and warmth all around me. This had to be the Spirit of Jesus. With little reservation, I lifted my hands.

I did not fully understand what I was experiencing, but I knew God was in it. When the chains of my pride were broken, I entered into worship with my aunts. Hot tears streamed down my face. It was as though I had begun to cry away all the hurt, hate, rejection, and fear that I had endured in my few, short years. It seemed as though, someone strong and powerful was holding me, comforting me. Wrapped in His embrace, like the father I never had, and He loved away all the pain inside my broken heart.

I spoke, softly, "Jesus. If you are here, come into my heart and save my soul right now." At those words, I traded the family legacy of one-hundred-years, and a mountain of worthless, sad and bitter Loafer's Glory gold, for heavenly treasure.

Instantly, I felt an explosion of the love of God as His living rivers of healing peace burst forth from my belly and surged throughout my entire being. I began to scream for joy, through the flood of tears that gushed out of my eyes when the power of His cleansing Blood washed away the filthiness I had known. These were great tears of joy. God, the Creator, was intimate with me at that moment. He had come into my heart and had become the Lover of my soul.

Jesus set me free that day from all the grief that had gone before. I was free, free indeed. A million pounds slid off my shoulders. I no longer felt dirty and unwanted, fearful and full of loathing. I was clean all over, mind and spirit. The Love of God had lit the darkness in every corner of my broken heart. His Blood scoured away all the past sorrow. I was truly born again. I was a new creation in Christ Jesus.

Now, God was my father. Dread and insecurity no longer gripped my mind and heart. For the first time in my life, I knew what real Love was. The burden of shame was gone. Nothing was the same.

A veil taken off mine mind's eye, I could see clearly by the Spirit of God. I am, consumed in the fire of His Holy Ghost, engulfed within the flames of God's total unconditional Love, and acceptance of His creation. He let me know I was not, just the unwanted result of two angry people having sex.

There was the purpose for my life. His destiny and plan included me and I was able too truly love myself for the first time ever. I was somebody special because He loved me with a whole heart. Now, I could Love others with a perfect Love. That was the purpose for my life, I was to give back to the world, and share what He had given to me. That was His plan for my life. Love never fails.

The people around me looked different. I seemed to be able to discern beyond the outward appearance and sense the content of their hearts. I loved them despite their character flaws. God had not changed the world but he had changed me.

I got up and went into the back yard. Drunk in the Love of God by the presence of Holy Spirit, I could hear a choir singing, somewhere in the distance. I looked up toward the sky as I rejoiced in my salvation.

There, standing on a cloud was a choir of seven angels singing praises unto the Lord. My joy was full. Jane was in the yard next door, playing with Gina. She did not see anything but she yelled at me across the fence, "Saul is the church choir practicing?"

The Methodist church was directly behind her house across the alleyway. Calmly smiling, I responded and pointed toward the sky. I said, "It's the angels."

She and Gina giggled when they could see nothing but fluffy scattered clouds overhead and they went back to playing with

Gina's dog. However, I could see the angels. This was my blessing from God.

The colors of Delena's flower garden appeared more brilliant than any I had ever seen before. The smell of her lilacs perfumed the air with the sweetness of God's glory. Drawn to a fragrant, scarlet peony blossom I knelt down and saw splendid detail I had never imagined, as a fearless monarch butterfly lit on my hand. In awe of God's handy work, I thought, the world truly was a beautiful place.

I looked across the fence again. Godly Love radiated out of my heart for Gina and Jane while watching them playing with the cuddly rag-mop brown puppy. I walked back inside the house and shared with Leve and Delena what I had seen. They explained that the angels in Heaven rejoice when one sinner repents.

This salvation experience was the beginning of a very real, personal relationship with the Lord Jesus Christ. He changed my destiny forever. He gave me a sound mind to know right from wrong and the power to overcome evil sent to destroy my life.

His unconditional Love set me free from the family curses. Jesus crucified, died on that cross some two thousand years ago for the entire world. He knew, then, there would be a very sad, angry, brokenhearted, frightened, bruised, and a lonely nine-year-old boy named Saul living in Amarillo, Texas. He knew this boy from the time of his mother's womb, would accept Him as savior in June of 1964.

I was only an insignificant little child among billions on the planet. On that day in the heart of God, I was most important. He gave me a supernatural explosion of His Love within my being, making up for all I had never known.

His Love healed my broken spirit.

Luke 4:18 "The Spirit of the Lord is upon me, because he hath anointed me to preach the gospel to the poor; he hath sent me to heal the brokenhearted, to preach deliverance to the captives, and recovering of sight to the blind, to set at liberty them that are bruised."

Praying in the Spirit upon her deathbed, Grandmother Anne must have imparted her last blessing. Perhaps she sensed the sometimes, rocky road my young life would often lead. Maybe, her prayer was empowerment for the journey.

Now and then, I imagine Grandmother Anne praying under the shade of the oaks and willows near the old homestead pond. I cannot help but believe from time to time she must look down

Paul E. Treadwell

from the portals of heaven and have to smile, knowing her prayers were never in vain.

THE BEGINNING

Epilogue

Jane's and my young years were not playgrounds of innocence--rather a battlefield. The remainder of our youth was not without problems, though we drew strength from our struggles. Jane never had a spiritual experience such as mine, but she was able to cope. She married, had three sons, and a successful career as a nurse.

Leve and I left Uncle Jake the summer of 1964 when we spent a couple of months in South Bend with Aunt Lou's family. At summer's end, we returned home. Jake was sober but not for long. Eventually, Leve would succumb to his fisting, and submitted to his wishes. She became his drinking partner once again, when I was twelve. That summer, she sent me to live with Delena. It took me many years to get over the pain of losing the one adult in my life that I trusted most. Losing Leve was worse than Momma's abandonment.

Uncle Ricky never wanted me there. When I was fourteen, I am awakened by yelling, "Get rid of the little bastard. I'm too old to raise another child. Besides, I don't like boys," Ricky shouted. After that, I kept my distance when he was home. My teen years were difficult. Not a day passed that he was not drunk, come sunset. By my senior year in high school, Delena was displaying the onset symptoms of Alzheimers.

Worldwide statistics show, approximately one out of a hundred people have some form of schizophrenia. Approximately one percent, 2.2 million American citizens suffer from the condition. The onset of schizophrenia in men is most common between the ages of fifteen to twenty-five-years-old. Women on average display symptoms a little later in life, between the ages of thirty and forty-years-old. Stats vary some but most are close to these figures. It is a disease of the brain, a heartbreaking disability for the patients and their loved ones. If one carries the gene for the genetic type off schizophrenia he can go an entire lifetime and it never kick in. However, one dose of certain street drugs, such as crystal-meth can activate the gene and the person will be insane the remainder of his life. Schizophrenia patients' lives are usually cut shorter than average by about fifteen years. There is a high rate of suicide among suffers of this tragic disease. For more information on this subject, go to: www.schizophrenia.com

Daddy was never able to pastor again. Eventually in 1974, after I was grown and returned to Arkansas, he began proper medication-therapy for the schizophrenia. Ten years later he came to live in our home. We cared for him the last fifteen years of his life. Daddy loved Momma, Jane, Bobby, and me until the day he passed away in June, 2000. I will forever miss him. His love for us was unshakable, even for Momma.

The blank envelope Bertha handed Chad the day he picked us up, it was from Momma. In writing, she told Chad to do with us as he pleased, or put us in an orphanage. She said she would never intrude again. I didn't know for decades the content of the letter. Uncle Chad came to our home in 1992, after Daddy was diagnosed having lung cancer. Chad wept, and asked for our forgiveness. Years before, Daddy and I had already forgiven him. It was then he disclosed the content of Momma's words in the letter written some thirty years earlier. Chad turned ninety-four-years-old in 2014. His mind is intact, and he lives alone in the home where he and his wife Vanny raised their five children. He and Sonny are the only siblings left of the nine in their first family. Chad says his heart yearns to see them again. Though far from perfect, he has a good heart. He was the rock in Daddy's family after Grandma Anne passed away. At thirteen-years-old during the Great Depression, he lied about his age and got a job in the CC camps. He was a water boy for the crews of men building dams and roads in the Ozarks. Always faithful, he sent his earnings home to Anne, providing for his younger siblings. He says he can't die until after his youngest sister Sonny passes away. He has to stick around to make sure she will be taken care of. Sonny is now eighty-six-years-old.

Jake, delivered from demon liquor when he was seventy-two-years-old. That was the day he gave his heart to the Lord. He asked for my forgiveness, and was sober, the remainder of his days. He lived in our home the last four years of his life. In 2001, Jake died peacefully in my arms at age eighty-nine.

Leve quit drinking five years after she sent me away. She regretted the duality of her nature and the pain it caused. The last eight years of her life, she lived in our home. Leve suffered from the same heart condition as her mother Anne. In her old days with humor in her voice, she said, "I was a preacher of the Gospel. Let a-lot-of people down. Now, here I am old and looking back. I should have been stronger. I pooped in my nest and there I sat. What a waste of my young Christian life." Leve was eighty-eight-years-old when she took flight for her heavenly home in 2006.

Delena divorced Ricky in 1974. She returned to the old homestead in Loafer's Glory and lived alone until diagnosed with mid-stage Alzheimer's dementia, at which point Aunt Lou stepped up to the plate and cared for her. After many years of suffering from the ravages of the disease, she had a heart attack and died in the local nursing home. At that point the disease had progressed to the latter stages. She was blind, could no longer communicate, and didn't know anyone.

I know there is a Heaven from my own spiritual experiences. Adding more evidence was the day of Delena's heart attack in 1995. Nursing home personnel jumped on Delena performing CPR. Lucid, she opened her eyes and said, "Why have you brought me back to the horrid place. I was with the Lord in Heaven." After those words she went back to her previous vegetative state, and never spoke again.

Delena had not been able to speak since 1993 when she miraculously made the statement to the medical staff in '95, after they brought her back from death. I call it a miracle. No doubt, there is a Heaven. Perhaps someone needed to hear her testimony that afternoon. After the incident, DNR orders were placed over her bed. Two years later, she died in her sleep.

Ricky joined Alcoholics Anonymous after the divorce. At age seventy, he received salvation and spent the next twelve years helping other drunks get free from the demon liquor addiction. Autumn, 1992, he called my home and asked forgiveness. He said, "I love you, Son." Those were our last words. The next day, at age eighty-three Uncle Ricky died alone in his Amarillo home. His body was not found until a week later.

I believed Momma abandoned us; because, that was the only thing she could do to protect us from Merl Judas, and cover the evil secrets. The responsibility of caring for her many children overwhelmed her. She was not able to provide for us the basic needs of life. Releasing us into the care of Daddy's people was her sacrifice of love, but our blessing. As she said the day she abandoned us, "This is best for us all."

Cancer of the uterus forced an early cesarean delivery. February, 1963, she was near death, weighing only seventy pounds. Six months into her last pregnancy, baby brother Jacob is taken prematurely. Immediately within the same hour, Momma had an emergency hysterectomy. Jacob was her fifth child. She was only twenty-two-years-old at his birth. Over the years Momma, Rambo, and little Jacob suffered much abuse at Merl's hands. Jane and I would not meet our brother Jacob until he was twelve-years-old. Momma has had no contact with Bobby since she abandoned him, when he was nine-months-old.

Bobby married at eighteen. He and his wife have two grown sons and one granddaughter. His life career was in management of produce for grocery stores, and management positions in the Wal-Mart Corporation. Bobby has no desire to meet Momma. We were not raised together. For him, our relationship is more like cousins, and not as siblings. But for me, Bobby will always be my little brother.

Nineteen-sixty-five brought an unexpected opportunity for Momma. She was performing at a Michigan nightclub when the famous Lester Flatt and Earl Scruggs strolled in. They liked her performance, told her she had the right package, with a great voice to be a famous country music star. They nicknamed her Little Loretta, as she resembled the young Loretta Lynn. They gave her an offer to travel with them, and a trip to Nashville for a recording contract. She was elated. When she told Merl, he beat her unmerciful, and forced her not to have any further contact. She remained his submissive slave and punching bag for the next ten years.

We had no contact with Momma until we were grown. Shortly after our first reunion, Merl gave her one last beating during the autumn of 1975. He left her for dead, under a bridge in Springdale, Arkansas. By the Grace of God, she survived one more time. This time, she found the courage to break free. He would never beat her physically again. She refused to press charges, a common behavior for many battered women. In 1976 she finally divorced Daddy and married another man. That marriage lasted only five years. He too was an abuser, and broke her back during one beating. It seemed Momma was only attracted to the bad boys. She divorced him. She vowed to never marry again. To this day, she suffers from Battered Woman Syndrome.

Ora, was the ultimate victim, now her beauty is gone. The hopes and dreams of a beautiful, strong willed young girl that was--once upon a time, now are only memories. Momma withered early, like a plucked blossom. Rebellion, bad choices, lack of education, poverty, shame, fear, alcohol addiction, physical, mental and emotional abuse robbed her of her youthful potential.

Today, at age seventy-five, she makes her home in Arizona. I will love Momma, always, though we have little communication. She says she never had a mother's love inside her heart for her Hotman children. I say she makes that statement out of shame and regret. She was a child raising children. I can hold no grudge. I think perhaps, her Hotman offspring are her haunting ghost from the past. The sight of us may bring back too many sorrow filled memories.

Iris and Daniel had thirteen children. Only seven survived. A few years after the divorce, Grandma Iris had a massive stroke. She died at age forty-five in 1963. Little did we know the last weekend in 1962, the day Vanny drove Jane and me to visit her, would be the last time we would ever see her. That is the only memory of have of Grandma Iris.

Jimmy Driftwood managed to secure an audience with President Lyndon B. Johnson, Congress and the Senate. Daniel and one-hundred members of the Rack 'n Sack Folklore Society drove a caravan of old jalopies, held together with bailing wire and a prayer, all the way to Washington DC, and back. They performed for the President in the Rose Garden. Later the same day, they entertained Congressmen and Senators. On stage, Pops began to jig dance as he played a lively fiddle tune. His shoe flew into the audience and landed in Senator Ted Kennedy's lap. The crowd roared with laughter. Needless-to-say, they got the funding needed to build the Ozark Folk Center in Mountain View, Arkansas. Every spring, thousands of tourist come from all around the world to the Mountain View Folk Festival held during the month of April. Jimmy Driftwood and the Rack 'n Sack Folklore Society put Mountain View, Arkansas on the map. Today it is a thriving little tourist town in the Ozarks.

Daniel and Gert remained together until his death in 1977. Upon his deathbed, Grandpa Daniel insisted Momma vow to him and God; she would never go back to the devil--Merl Judas. She promised. Content, he passed away. Grandma Gert never married again, and at eighty-years-old, she died in my arms. The year was 1996.

Ten years after Merl very nearly murdered Momma, at age fifty he married a fifteen-year-old girl while living in Houston, Texas. They started a new family, and had two sons. When I heard, I could only hope he wouldn't abuse them the way he had all the others in the past.

As children, Jane and I did not know the criminal acts against us were that of rapes, molestations, mental and physical abuse by a demented, perverted, evil sociopath pedophile. We only knew he caused us to feel powerless, and fearful, worthless, and dirty. We were ashamed to speak of the violations, as well as fearful of revealing his crimes. We kept our mouths shut and hid the dirty secret crimes for near four decades. Those were the chapters of our lives from another book, closed for decades, until 1997.

I was a grandfather; in my mid-forties was when we broke our silence. Upon discovering Merl Judas raped and molested yet another seven-year-old little girl in 1997. I reported the crime to the Arkansas State Police. During the investigation, we learned Merl Judas violated dozens of children in numerous states during his life span. He left behind a legacy of sorrow, and broken lives. He betrayed the trust of everyone who loved him.

Only the one police investigation into Merl's crimes against children occurred during his lifetime. Most of the law enforcement officials believed the victims, but too many years had passed for his adult victims of childhood abuse. The statute of limitations run out. However, they could use our testimonies in court to show a history of his illegal behaviors against children. The case of the seven-year-old girl, if convicted, he would have spent a minimum of fifteen-years in prison, probably more without the possibility of parole. He would have been a registered sex offender.

Merl called and threatened Momma to keep her mouth shut when the investigation began. They had been separated twenty-two years but she was still terrified of him. In his defense she told authorities it was all lies, and I had falsely reported him as an act of revenge. She said I did it because I never wanted her to leave my daddy for Merl. After that she refused to have any contact with her Hotman children, until she sent the letter stating she never loved us.

During the heat of the investigation, Merl called my home and threatened to kill us all. His young wife also made several threatening calls. They went on the warpath to discredit me, an attempt at character assassination within numerous state and county government agencies. Government department employees who all knew our work with the disabled, the mentally ill, and foster children were not swayed. Merl and his wife were not successful in the effort. When that didn't work he played the crazy card, pretending he was insane when questioned by authorities. He said the spirits of Crazy Horse, and Sitting Bull would vindicate him, they were his protectors.

The one most important thing in getting a prosecution was missing. Sadly, any physical evidence was gone. There was nothing but the accusations of his numerous victim survivors, against his denial. It was his word against ours. Merl Judas is never prosecuted. In the end, there was no justice in the court-of-law for his decades of numerous criminal behaviors. Silence for months and decades of his intimidated victims had empowered him to violate again and again over the past forty years.

Estranged from siblings, his extended families, including his grandchildren and all of his children, except for the two youngest. Upon his deathbed he was haunted by the ghost of his past. Merl Judas suffered seven massive heart attacks while the police investigation was open. He died an agonizing death, rotting from the inside out with colon cancer at age sixty-four. He died two months after Daddy passed in 2000. Merl's brother Ely said Merl repented at the end. Maybe he did.

The King of Terror, Merl Judas was dead. At hearing of Merl's passing Jane broke down, crying, she said, "We're free. We're finally free."

Our years of silence were to the detriments of many. Silence allows the cycle of abuse to continue for generations. Statistics may vary but on average, before adulthood one in three girls and one in five boys are raped, or molested. Typically, one pedophile ravages one-hundred children during his/her lifetime.

I struggled with health problems for years as a direct result of early childhood neglect. Other than that nuisance, I've had a wonderful adult life. I surrendered to a part-time ministry when I was twenty-four. I worked as a broadcast journalist for decades. Before retirement, I taught independent living skills to mentally ill and developmental disabled adults.

My wife Elisabeth came from a broken home. She was a foster child, raised in nine different foster homes. She understood my passion to help others in need, and being a voice for the many silent victims of abuse.

Returning to Arkansas, we make our home just down the road from Grandma Anne's ol' homestead, the property where Delena built the cafe. It still stands today. We converted the cafe building into a two-bedroom house. Uncle Joe lives there now. Today, Loafer's Glory is a grand space to be--no more monsters found in this place for me.

Elisabeth and I raised our three children, and opened our home to thirty-eight foster kids. There are countless others whose childhood horrors were worse than ours were. Today we are advocates for the rights of children, the disabled, and the mentally ill.

Jane and I are not just survivors, we are thrivers. We were not alone. Just before Merl's death, I pondered what good could come from these tragedies. I realized his type evil when shrouded by secrecy, empowers pedophiles to commit more crimes against the innocent. The new rule is . . . silence needs to be broken. I began sharing our story and started writing this memoir, "Leviathan Kings of Terror." Maybe our experiences described in this book will be a positive influence in the end.

The public scandals of some priest in the Catholic Church today are perfect examples of how decades of silence and covering the shameful crimes perpetuate more evil. Perhaps my words will give others the courage to break the silence, and expose their abusers, violators, pedophiles and rapists. The shame always belongs to the criminals, never a victim. Any adult protecting a pedophile at the expense of a child had may as well be as guilty of the same crime.

There is a price to pay when one speaks up and reports crimes of abuse. Friends and family of the accused will display where their loyalties lie, by defending the perpetrator, and attacking the reporter's moral character and creditability. There can be repercussion for the whistleblowers including threats on their lives, shunning, and ridicule. Some may lose contact and be alienated from family and friends, for doing what is right. On the positive side other unknown previous victims may come forward to help with the case. It takes courage. When the investigation is finished there may not be enough evidence to convict. It is important to report a crime immediately, while physical evidence can be collected. If there is no evidence, it is just one person's and or victim's accusation against the perpetrator's denial. With no evidence there can be no conviction.

The purpose of this book is to encourage all parents to teach their children to always speak up and never be intimidated to keep quiet about a crime that may have been committed against them. Elisabeth and I have seen too many children damaged by abuse. We taught our little ones, beginning as soon as they could speak, to always tell.

With God's help, Jane and I . . . rescued from the clutches of Merl Judas, and the pits of despair. Though not perfect, Leve, Delena, Jake, and Ricky gave us the gift of a better childhood. Because of them, despite their own demons, we had a life.

If it had not been for Faith, Hope found in a higher power, the Lord Jesus Christ, there would have been no healing for my spirit. There would have been no chance of any kind, for a normal existence, if God had not introduced Himself. He became a reality for me on that prayerful day in June of 1964, the day of my Salvation,

Life is a struggle for us all. Finding my religious way through the teen years, and early adulthood had some stumbling. I failed many times, but I knew without a doubt God was real, and He cared about me. My early twenties were marvelous years. With the Lord's help, my path straightened. Found my stride for adulthood and grounded in the Faith, through study of the Word of God. Again, the Lord reassured me that His Love was with a whole heart, unconditional, and everlasting. He truly is a help in times of trouble.

By the power of Holy Spirit, He leads us all into His truth and righteousness, if we seek Him with a whole heart. His Love never fails but strives with fallen men to bring them into the light of His everlasting Word.

The Spirit of God is offended easily. He will not stick around where He is not wanted. Merl Judas fell into the depths of wickedness during his youth. He rejected the Lord completely. I can only take his brother Ely's word for it, that Merl accepted

Christ upon his deathbed. To quote Shakespeare, "The evil that men do lives after them; the good is oft interred with their bones"

Even Christians lose their way sometimes, but their failures do not diminish their first encounter with God the Creator, a true experience of Salvation. That first touch is only the beginning of a personal relationship with the Creator. Babies are not born walking, that is a skill they have to learn.

We live in, and learn to walk out our Christian lives, day by day. Religion is not the power of Salvation. Many in this world are religious, so heavenly minded they are no earthly good. With true Christianity there is power to change lives in a positive and holy way. Without supernatural power given by Holy Spirit we only have a form of godliness, just another religion with rules and precepts to obey in the flesh.

God is a God of many new beginnings, willing to forgive all sin. If we were perfect, we would not need a Savior. The language of the Spirit and communication with the Lord through prayer is the most powerful force on this earth. Prayer to the one true God does change lives, people and circumstances. Prayer is our petition to God for heavenly intervention. Holding bitterness and resentment only severs the lines of communication between man and his Creator. Bitterness is a self-destructive force.

Forgiveness is for our healing, releasing us from the soul ties of our offenders. This is God's plan to set us free that we might get on with our lives, the destiny He has in His plans for us. Forgiveness on our part does not in any way release perpetrators from having to be accountable for their crimes. We are giving those persons to God, because we are powerless to fix them. Forgiveness truly is greater than vengeance. The sons of men are accountable for their deeds to a higher power far greater than you and I, or any court of law. There are no man made laws of justice more powerful than God's laws.

"Hebrews 10:31 It is a fearful thing to fall into the hands of the living God."

We may forget some, forgive, and come to terms with what deeds others may do against us, but we never forget how they made us feel. When spiritual healing takes place, we are set free from the pain, to take back our dignity, and our own personal power. With God's help, survivors are usually strong people when they overcome. Forgiveness is the key to true Salvation and redemption of our lives, which in turn brings healing for a broken spirit.

Paul E. Treadwell

It is not the story of "Leviathan Kings of Terror," that is important. It is the message to never be silent about abuse that is important, and to know spiritual and emotional healing is possible for crime survivors.

"Matthew 6:

11 Give us this day our daily bread.

12 And forgive us our debts, as we forgive our debtors.

13 And lead us not into temptation, but deliver us from evil: For thine is the kingdom, and the power, and the glory, for ever. Amen."

Afterward: by Diana Stevens

I am Diana Stevens (pseudonym) and work as a child-abuse investigator with the Crimes Against Children Division (CACD), formerly the Family Protection Division (FPD), of the Arkansas State Police (ASP). I hold a Bachelor of Arts degree in Social Work from Arkansas State University in Jonesboro, AR. Having been with ASP since April 2000, I was a Family Service Worker (FSW) for Children and Family Services prior to accepting this position. Being an FSW meant that I worked to keep children in their homes, even after the abuse. I worked to reunify children with their parents after placement into foster care.

My role with CACD is one of gathering information, evidence, and proving that a preponderance of evidence exists to support the allegations made to the Child Abuse Hot Line. If this evidence does exist, the offender's name goes on the Central Registry and he/she listed as a Sex Offender or Physical Abuse Offender. If this finding--is not appealed his or her name remains on the Registry for life. In the state of Arkansas, a person can be named as an offender if he is ten years of age or older. After a report is investigated, then determined the allegation are true, everything in our investigation goes to the local Prosecuting Attorney. With our assistance in the court system, charges filed, and a court date is set.

Some of the different forms of child maltreatment that I, along with the approximately ninety other investigators with ASP, investigate are Sexual Abuse, which includes Oral Sex, Sexual Contact, Sexual Exploitation and Sexual Penetration, Suffocation, Immersions, Burns, and any other form of abuse that is considered severe.

With child victims of abuse, in numerous cases a report called in to the Child Abuse Hot Line, years after the abuse has occurred. By this time, any valuable evidence that would be essential in proving and tying the suspect to the victim is gone. That is why; as the author has done his best to point out, no one should ever be silent regarding child sexual abuse. Report it as soon as you are aware of it. Do not wait because someone else says that they are going to report it, because most of the time, they do not!

Many kids feel ashamed and that it must be their fault. That could not be further from the truth. This is what we try to stress in our interviews--the adult was the responsible person, he or she took advantage and did something wrong. It is okay for the victimized child to talk about the abuse and crimes with us, teachers, counselors, the parents of a friend, anyone, as long as they talk to someone they can trust.

This society is too quick to judge the victim. We think there is no way that could have happened in my home, neighborhood, and city, but it does. Day after day, countless children become victims of molestation, and rape. It is not only a problem in lower socioeconomic families, it is just as likely to happen in a $150,000 home, where the father is a Deacon in his local church and the mother a school teacher (these are only examples). It is very uncommon to have a suspect who is a total stranger to the child. We need to spend as much time reassuring our children that no matter who has hurt them, that it is okay to talk, as we do warning them about the danger of strangers.

Following is a list of toll-free phone numbers in which anyone can call at any time of the day or night and report suspected child abuse. If you have ever been a victim, some of these numbers may help you in taking that first step to break the silence.

Since the author of this book is a native of Arkansas and considering my position, I will post phone numbers for Arkansas and then post national numbers.

Remember that anyone can call and report alleged abuse. You do not have to give your name, phone number, or address. These things are helpful to us, but not necessary. Reporters do remain confidential. Following the guidelines of the Arkansas Child Maltreatment Act, we are not allowed to share that information with anyone, unless we are so ordered by a judge in a court of law.

Arkansas-Child-Abuse-Hot-Line-(800)-482-5964
Rape-Abuse-Incest-National-Network-(800)-656-4673-(HOPE)
National-Victim-Center-INFOLINK-(800)-FYI-CALLNINE
For more statistics go to: www.info@childhelp.org

© Copyright 2014
by Paul E. Treadwell/Petmegoose Press

www.ingramcontent.com/pod-product-compliance
Lightning Source LLC
Chambersburg PA
CBHW050127170426
43197CB00011B/1747